Nicaragua:
A Revolution
under Siege

Dedication:

This book is dedicated to the memory of the thousands of Nicaraguans — men, women, and children — who have died as a result of the undeclared war that the United States government is waging against revolutionary Nicaragua. They are the most recent martyrs in the courageous struggle of the Nicaraguan people to become the architects of their own destiny.

Nicaragua:
A Revolution
under Siege

Edited by
Richard L. Harris
and
Carlos M. Vilas

Zed Books Ltd.

Nicaragua: A Revolution under Siege was first published by
Zed Books Ltd., 57 Caledonian Road, London N1 9BU, UK,
and 171 First Avenue, Atlantic Highlands, New Jersey 07716,
USA, in 1985.

Cover designed by Andrew Corbett
Photos courtesy of *Barricada* and Sam Shutman
Maps by Sandra Oakins, Dove Printers, Kirkbymoorside

Printed in Great Britain
at The Bath Press, Avon

1st reprint, 1986

British Library Cataloguing in Publication Data

Nicaragua: a revolution under siege.
   1. Nicaragua — Politics and government — 1979-
   I. Harris, Richard   II. Vilas, Carlos M.
   972.85'053   F1528

   ISBN 0-86232-483-1
   ISBN 0-86232-484-X Pbk

Contents

Tables

Figures

List of Contributors

Richard L. Harris is a specialist in Latin American and African studies. He is one of the coordinating editors of *Latin American Perspectives* and a fellow of the Council of Hemispheric Affairs in Washington D.C.

Carlos M. Vilas is a specialist in Latin American studies and development planning. He is a consultant to the revolutionary government of Nicaragua and the author of numerous works on Latin American political and economic affairs.

Eduardo Baumeister is a sociologist who specializes in subjects related to agricultural development and agrarian reform. At present he is a member of the research staff of the Nicaraguan centre of research and studies on agrarian reform (CIERA).

Gary Ruchwarger is an editor of *Against the Current*, a socialist periodical published in the United States. At present he is living in Nicaragua and writing a book on the Sandinista mass organizations.

Luis Serra is a political scientist involved in popular education and training. He is a member of the faculty of the Central American University in Managua and an organizer for the Nicaraguan national union of farmers and cattleraisers (UNAG).

Gillian Brown is a freelance journalist who has been working in Central America since 1982. While living in Nicaragua, she wrote articles for the London *Sunday Times* and the *Daily Express*.

Manlio Tirado is a Mexican journalist with extensive knowledge of international politics and Central American affairs. He is the correspondent in Nicaragua for the Mexican newspaper *Excelsior*, and is the author of a book on Nicaragua, *La Revolución Sandinista*, published in Mexico.

Regional map of Nicaragua

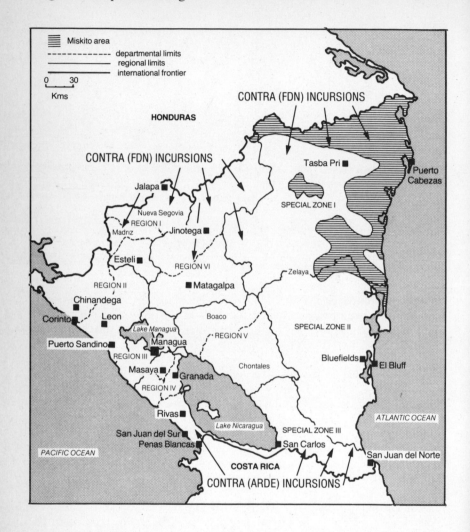

Members of the Sandinista Association of Agricultural Workers (ATC) demonstrating (Banner reads: 'We are not birds who live in the air, or fish who live in the sea. We are men who live on the land.')

Photo: *Barricada*

Comandante Jaime Wheelock distributing land titles as part of the agrarian reform programme's distribution of land to poor peasants.

Photo: *Barricada*

Billboard urging people to vote for the FSLN in the elections of 4 November 1984

Photo: Greg Jacks

Voters waiting in line outside polling station in Estelí during the elections of 4 November 1984.

Photo: Sam Shuman

Demonstration of Christians in support of clergy in the revolutionary government after the Pope had called on these clergy to give up their political posts or the priesthood.

Photo: *Barricada*

An elderly woman militia member receiving weapons training from the regular army.

Photo: *Barricada*

1 Introduction: The Revolutionary Transformation of Nicaragua

Richard L. Harris and Carlos M. Vilas

In the immediate aftermath of the revolutionary triumph on 19 July 1979, most accounts of the Nicaraguan revolution projected a very promising future, with few major problems. The prospects appeared quite favourable for the rapid reconstruction and development of the economy as well as the political democratization of Nicaraguan society. Six years later, this future still seems possible, but the revolution's prospects are now clouded by the increasing complexity of the problems it confronts, and by the undeclared war which the United States is waging against Nicaragua.

In the last six years, important advances have been made in the revolutionary transformation of Nicaraguan society. In every major sphere of social life – the economy, the state, civil society, culture, ideology, etc. – significant changes have been made. The confiscation of the enterprises owned by Somoza and his closest supporters has permitted the creation of a sizeable state sector called the Area of People's Property (the APP); the agrarian reform has turned over land to tens of thousands of poor peasants; unionization of the workers has advanced at a rapid rate and has improved their working conditions; the mass organizations have been strengthened and have promoted popular democracy; the development of a modern democratic state has advanced considerably; and for the first time, the vast majority of the population are enjoying the benefits of public education, health care and a variety of cultural activities. This book analyses these important transformations in Nicaraguan society by focusing on the principal characteristics, dynamics, contradictions, protagonists and problems of the revolutionary process.

Nicaragua's revolutionary leaders characterize their revolution as a popular, democratic and anti-imperialist revolutionary struggle that is based on a political project of national unity and an economic project of a mixed economy.[1] This characterization of the revolution by its leaders raises important questions about the long-term significance and direction of the Nicaraguan revolution. Indeed, every revolution appears to give rise to important questions about its character, significance and final destination. These questions can be articulated at

1

two distinct levels. The first level concerns the more universal aspects of the revolution – those which have to do with our understanding of the laws and nature of revolutionary transformations. The second concerns the particular aspects of the revolution – those which distinguish it from all others. The consideration of both of these levels makes it possible to understand the specificity of revolutionary transformations and at the same time to compare and contrast these transformations with those of other societies in revolution. Although guided by more general questions, this book consists of a series of studies which focus primarily on the second level of questions – those having to do with the specific characteristics of the Nicaraguan revolution.

The essays in this volume reveal the particular character and significance of the Nicaraguan revolution by analysing in depth the major transformations and problems of transformation that characterize this revolution. They draw attention to the particular conditions that appear to set the limits or parameters of the Nicaraguan revolution as well as those which have been responsible for its revolutionary dynamic and potential. In this introductory essay, we will attempt to provide a general overview of the more important characteristics of the revolution. Our intent is to provide a perspective for the essays that follow.

The first characteristic of the Nicaraguan revolution that we believe should be taken into account is the backward and underdeveloped nature of the forces of production in revolutionary Nicaragua, which is a product of its past history of neo-colonial and dependent capitalist development. In many important ways, the revolutionary transformation of Nicaraguan society has been conditioned by its relatively unskilled workforce, its technological backwardness, the lack of spatial integration between the various geographic regions of the country, the disarticulation between the different sectors of production and the external dependency of its export-oriented economy. In this sense, the Nicaraguan revolution approximates the situation confronted by many other struggles for national liberation in the Third World.

Another important characteristic of the Nicaraguan revolution that is related to the country's economic backwardness is the fact that foreign capital, especially North American capital, has not played a major role in the economic development of the country. Nicaragua received very little direct foreign investment and large transnational corporations played a minor role in the country's capitalist development prior to the revolution. Although North American influence over Nicaragua's financial system and foreign trade was important, the country's neo-colonial status was more a result of political and ideological forms of imperialism than it was the result of direct North American control over its means of production. For this reason, the anti-imperialist orientation of the Nicaraguan revolution has from the start been based on predominantly political rather than economic grounds. This helps to explain why there have been no large-scale confiscations of foreign property in Nicaragua – as there have been, for example, in Cuba. In Nicaragua, there are very few foreign firms to confiscate, and those that do exist are not generally viewed as a serious obstacle to the country's national independence. Indeed, it appears that the few foreign firms operating in Nicaragua – most of which are European – have been more willing to co-operate with the new revolutionary regime than most local capitalists.

Also, as a result of the backward and underdeveloped nature of Nicaragua's capitalist economy, small producers exercise an important influence over the productive process – both in agriculture and manufacturing. They also play a major role in commerce and the provision of services. Moreover, their incorporation into the revolutionary struggle has weighed heavily upon the nature of the revolutionary block of forces and the programmes of the revolutionary government. Today, the Sandinista regime is faced with either promoting the development of the small producers or the progressive proletarianization of the population. Because of the political as well as economic importance of the country's small producers, the revolutionary regime has attempted to strengthen small-scale private production, particularly through the agrarian reform programme, while at the same time promoting the modernization of the forces of production under both state control and in the hands of medium and large capital. As a consequence, the 'peasantization' rather than the proletarianization of Nicaragua's large rural population appears to be taking place under the Sandinista regime.

Nicaragua is a society where the processes of economic and social differentiation associated with capitalist development have only partially begun to take effect. For example, the working class is not well differentiated from the self-employed artisans and small producers in the urban areas. Small private enterprise tends to predominate in the commercial and service sectors. The predominance of petty merchants over the distribution of basic consumer products is particularly important. As a result, the revolutionary regime is faced with the choice of completing, stopping or reorienting the processes of capitalist differentiation in Nicaragua. Cuba's largely unsatisfactory experience with the early nationalization of small-scale commercial and service activities appears to have influenced the decision of Nicaragua's revolutionary leaders not to follow this course of action. However, the revolutionary state has been forced to assume an increasing role in the distribution of the imported inputs needed by the small producers, particularly in the manufacturing sector, and this has given the state influence over their activities.

The multi-class content of the revolutionary block of forces is another important characteristic of the Nicaraguan revolution. During the course of the revolutionary struggle against the Somoza dictatorship, a

3

broad multi-class alliance was mobilized by the Sandinistas to overthrow Somoza. Although this alliance has lost certain elements since the establishment of the revolutionary regime in 1979, it still remains a broad block of popular forces and contains elements drawn from all of Nicaragua's classes and social forces. The most important elements within the revolutionary block are peasants, workers, the inhabitants of the poor barrios in Nicaragua's main urban centres, students, radical Christians, small urban producers and retailers and certain so-called 'patriotic' elements of the bourgeoisie.

The revolutionary leadership has sought to maintain this broad multi-class block of forces as the popular base for implementing its political project of national unity and its economic project of a mixed economy. The new regime seeks to maintain what is called 'popular hegemony' over these projects. This means that the capitalist class must be willing to accept a subordinate political position and participate in a process of economic and social development where the interests of the popular majority (the peasantry and the working class) are given priority over, but do not preclude, the pursuit of profit and personal enrichment.

The multi-class and heterogeneous nature of the revolutionary block of forces implies a considerable degree of political pluralism and the acceptance of political opposition on the part of the revolutionary leadership. As a result, the Sandinista regime has committed itself to the institutionalization of a political democracy along Western lines – with regular elections, a parliament, a multi-party system, freedom of the press, separation of governmental powers, etc. Indeed, at present, Nicaragua is experiencing the birth of a new democratic political system – at a stage in the revolutionary process when the basic nature of its future social and economic system has still not been clearly defined. This presents a unique situation without precedent in the history of contemporary social revolutions; it constitutes a very important experiment in revolutionary political change.

The multi-class nature of the revolutionary block of forces in the political domain corresponds to the heterogeneity of forms of property in Nicaragua's mixed economy. Although many other Third World countries possess so-called mixed economies, Nicaragua is one of the few with a mixed economy that is undergoing a social revolution.

Nicaragua's mixed economy combines a relatively broad state sector with a private sector that combines large, medium and small private producers – included in this last category are an increasing number of service and producer co-operatives which are being promoted by the revolutionary government. The private sector controls almost two-thirds of the means of production and generates an equivalent proportion of the gross domestic product. However, the state predominates in certain branches of industry and exercises total control over the financial system and foreign trade.

What is most peculiar about revolutionary Nicaragua's mixed economy is that private capital is subordinated to the priorities of the revolutionary regime, while at the same time capitalist relations of production and forms of accumulation are reproduced within this economy. This has generated contradictions and tensions which the revolutionary regime is hard pressed to resolve.

Another singular aspect of the Nicaraguan revolution, which concerns its international context, is the breadth of international support the revolution has received – both before the overthrow of Somoza and since the formation of the revolutionary regime. The Sandinistas have demonstrated a remarkable ability to maintain a broad international network of alliances with governments and political parties in Western Europe, the socialist countries and governments and political organizations throughout Latin America and the rest of the Third World. This has been of tremendous political importance to the survival of the revolution, and is especially important now that Nicaragua is fighting an increasingly costly and dangerous war against the US-backed counter-revolutionary forces that daily attack the country from bases in neighbouring Honduras and Costa Rica.

The increasing external aggression, the growing possibility of direct US military intervention and the efforts of the United States government to destabilize Nicaragua's economy as well as its revolutionary government, have combined to create a dangerous and threatening international context for the revolution. The effects of the war and Washington's efforts to overturn the revolution have an important impact upon Nicaragua's current economic and political situation, and represent an additional characteristic of considerable importance in understanding the present conjuncture of the Nicaraguan revolution.

The above-mentioned characteristics of the Nicaraguan revolution, as well as others, are analysed in depth in the various essays that form this volume. Combined, they offer a general view of the revolutionary transformation of Nicaraguan society and the conditions which appear to be most important in determining the evolution of the revolutionary process. Individually, they offer insights into the particular advances and problems of the Nicaraguan revolution.

The first essay by Eduardo Baumeister analyses both the structures of production that have dominated the agrarian sector of contemporary Nicaraguan society and the transformations that have taken place in these structures as a result of the revolutionary government's agrarian reform programme. The primary importance of agriculture in Nicaraguan society justifies placing this essay first. Baumeister is one of the leading members of the research staff of Nicaragua's Centro de Investigaciones y Estudios de la Reforma Agraria (Centre for Research and Studies on Agrarian Reform or CIERA), and in his essay on the Sandinista agrarian reform programme, he offers a new perspective not found in the prevailing literature on this theme. He maintains that revolutionary Nicaragua's agrarian reform reflects the structural configuration of agricultural production in the country and combines the demands of small and medium agricultural producers with the revolutionary project of democratizing the society and expanding the forces of production.

Baumeister makes a detailed comparison of the agrarian structures of pre-revolutionary Nicaragua with those in the rest of Central America. He identifies the principal contradictions that have characterized the development of Nicaragua's structures of agrarian production and the manner in which the FSLN was able to assert its political leadership in the countryside. He analyses the most important stages in the implementation of the revolutionary government's agrarian reform programme, the various alternatives that remain open to the revolution and the debates that characterize the present stage of the process.

The second essay, by Richard Harris, provides a general overview of revolutionary Nicaragua's mixed economy and the problems associated with the development of its forces of production. Harris, who is one of the co-ordinating editors of the quarterly review *Latin American Perspectives* and a scholar with broad comparative research experience, concentrates his analysis on the conditions, obstacles and prospects for Nicaragua's industrial development. He argues that significant advances have been made in the transformation of Nicaragua's economic structures during the first six years of the revolution. These transformations are bringing about a reorientation of the economy so that it serves the basic needs of the population, and they have laid the basis for the future development of the country's industrial sector – despite the shortage of foreign exchange, the reluctance of the bourgeoisie to co-operate with the revolutionary regime, and the fact that the country is at war. Harris also argues that the low level of development of the country's productive forces and the existing political context make a generalized socialization of the means of production impractical and highly unlikely in the present conjuncture – although the progressive socialization of the means of production will be necessary in the long run if Nicaragua is to overcome the structural obstacles that block the rapid transformation and integrated industrialization of its economy.

The third essay, by Gary Ruchwarger, on the Sandinista mass organizations, involves an analysis of the relationship between the revolutionary state and civil society in Nicaragua. Ruchwarger, who has conducted extensive research on the subject, analyses the role of these popular organizations in the revolutionary process, especially their relations with the FSLN and the state. He focuses on the extent of internal democracy in these organizations, their political autonomy and their capacity to exercise influence over the content and the implementation of state policies. This essay is one of the few to have been written on the mass organizations in Nicaragua, and represents an important contribution to our understanding of the nature of popular participation in the revolutionary process.

The next essay, by Carlos M. Vilas, on the labour movement and workers' participation, provides information on and insight into a relatively unstudied aspect of the Sandinista revolution. Vilas, an experienced consultant and researcher who has served with the Ministries of Labour and Planning in Nicaragua, provides an analysis of the rapid unionization and the confrontations that took place immediately following the revolutionary triumph. These confrontations arose over the role of the labour movement in the revolutionary process, its relationship to the new state and the FSLN, and the recognition of the workers' demands in the early stage of national reconstruction. Vilas then analyses the development of workers' participation in the management of the industrial enterprises of the APP, the efforts of the unions to gain influence over the reconstruction of the private sector, their mobilization against the decapitalization of enterprises owned by the bourgeoisie unwilling to co-operate with the regime's economic policies, and the dynamic relationship between the unions, the revolutionary government, the bourgeoisie and the working class in Nicaragua.

The ideological struggle in the sphere of religion between the revolutionary and counter-revolutionary forces is the theme of the following essay by Luis Serra, who is a member of the faculty of the Jesuit-run Universidad Centroamericana in Managua and a specialist in popular education and peasant organization. Serra focuses on the participation of Christians in the revolutionary process – both in favour of the revolution as well as against it. He reveals how the class struggle is translated into a religious struggle, and also analyses the relationship that exists between Washington's efforts to overthrow the Sandinista regime and those of certain religious leaders and organizations, most notably the hierarchy of the Catholic Church in Nicaragua, who are also against the revolution. This essay, and the following one by Gillian Brown on the Miskito Indians, clearly demonstrate how imperialism and the counter-revolution take advantage of and utilize those sectors of the population that oppose the revolution more on ideological than material grounds.

The essay by Gillian Brown, who is an experienced international journalist residing in Nicaragua, analyses the case of the Miskito Indians and the efforts of the Sandinista regime to incorporate this ethnic community into the national revolutionary process. She reveals the contradictions and violent results that have been produced by these efforts. The relative isolation of the indigenous population of the Atlantic (Caribbean) Coast from the more developed Pacific Coast of Nicaragua is a product of the country's neo-colonial and unequal development. The errors committed by the revolutionary government in its efforts to extend the revolution to the indigenous communities of the Atlantic Coast reveal how secondary contradictions (for example, conflicts between ethnic, racial and religious groups) are related to the principal contradiction of the Nicaraguan revolution – the struggle for national liberation against US imperialism.

The essay by Manlio Tirado analyses the international context of the Nicaraguan revolution. The author, who is the correspondent in Managua for Mexico's most important daily newspaper – *Excelsior* – and one of the most respected international journalists covering the revolution, examines the relations between Nicaragua and the United States since the revolutionary triumph in 1979. He focuses on the increasingly hostile nature of US policy towards Nicaragua since the start of the Reagan administration, and on the revolutionary regime's strategy of building and maintaining broad international alliances, especially with the countries of Latin America. He also analyses the role of the Contadora Group (Mexico, Venezuela, Panama and Colombia) in seeking a peaceful resolution of the growing regional crisis in Central America.

The final essay by the editors of this volume attempts to draw together the conclusions of the other essays. It also offers a series of reflections on the progress of the Nicaraguan revolution during its first six years as well as its possible course of evolution in the near future. This essay discusses the prevailing tendencies and future prospects of the revolution, and those aspects of the revolution that are of relevance to the theoretical and political debate over the revolutionary transformation of backward and dependent societies.

A brief comment is necessary here about the statistical information used in the different essays of this book. At the present moment, the revolutionary government is engaged in establishing an efficient and reliable system of statistical information. However, until this system is fully operational, it will remain difficult to obtain certain types of information. Some is classified as confidential – including certain conventional economic indicators – because of national security and the ideological struggle that the revolutionary regime is fighting against its opponents, but in other cases it is due to the tendency of some state functionaries to monopolize the information at their disposal. There are also divergencies between different official sources. The various government agencies at present do not use the same estimates or collect their information in the same way. As a result, there are differences between the data used in the various essays in this volume. We want to call the reader's attention to this, even though it does not affect the coherence of this collection or the conclusions of the individual essays.

The authors of the essays in this volume are researchers and experts in their professional fields who have recently worked and lived in Nicaragua. Many have been and are still involved in the revolutionary transformations taking place there. These circumstances have given them an important vantage point from which to observe and critically analyse the nature of these transformations and the problems confronted by the revolution. This also gives their assertions and conclusions a certain degree of authority.

All the authors have based their analyses upon their firm belief in the progressive nature of the Nicaraguan revolution. Nevertheless, they have been equally motivated by their recognition of the need to produce critical analyses which will help others to understand the objective reality of the revolution, particularly the problems that it confronts and the contradictions that underlie its dynamic evolution.

Although the authors of these essays share much in common in terms of their general perspectives, there are differences of approach, interpretation and assessment with regard to specific themes in the various essays that make up this volume. This gives to the collection as a whole a richer quality of analysis and offers the reader a plurality of opinions over quite complex and rapidly changing conditions. Analyses of historic events of such great human importance as social revolutions are inevitably influenced by the values and world view of those engaged in carrying out such analyses. All those who have participated in this volume have been acutely aware of the challenge entailed in this undertaking, and we have consciously sought to provide accurate information and critical perspectives on the nature and prospects of the Nicaraguan revolution. The extent to which this effort has been successful will be revealed by the unfolding of the revolutionary process and the degree to which the analyses provided in this volume withstand the test of time.

Note

1. See, for example, *Habla la Direccion de la Vanguardia* (Managua: Departmento de Propaganda y Educacion Politica del FSLN, 1981).

Author's Note

This introduction differs from that in the Spanish edition of this book. Due to an error, the latter introduction contained, without the authors' permission, parts of the epilogue written by Richard Harris.

2 The Structure of Nicaraguan Agriculture and the Sandinista Agrarian Reform

Eduardo Baumeister*

Introduction

Various aspects of the Sandinista revolution reveal its peculiarity in relation to other processes of profound social transformation in Latin America. The most immediately obvious is the persistence of an important sector of private capitalists alongside political and ideological forces that seek to develop the country in ways that depart radically from its previous course of capitalist development.[1]

In this essay, we provide a perspective for understanding the structural context of the anti-Somocista alliance in the countryside and the agrarian policy of the Sandinista revolution. We will include an assessment of the first stage of the Sandinista agrarian reform and a brief overview of both its second stage and the revolutionary government's current agrarian policy. Our main concern is to demonstrate how certain structural determinants of agriculture in Nicaragua explain the nature of the anti-Somocista alliance and the economic policies of the revolutionary regime. We will also demonstrate that Nicaragua's agrarian structure, particularly the configuration of classes and class fractions in the agricultural sector, singles Nicaragua out from the rest of Central America and Latin America. Thus, we advance the hypothesis that Nicaragua's agrarian reform, at least in the short and medium term, has peculiarities not found in the other significant agrarian transformations that have occurred in Latin America and elsewhere.

We will emphasize the structural peculiarities of Nicaraguan agriculture and the configuration of its agrarian structure. We are aware that the set of public policies developed since 1979 are the result of multiple determinations which cannot be fully understood within a rigid structural analysis. However, we will focus primarily on the structural determinants, instead of the national political situation or the international conjuncture (which are dealt with elsewhere in this volume).

We begin with some comparisons between agriculture in Nicaragua and in the rest of Central America. This is followed by a brief survey of

* *Translated by R.L. Harris.*

the agrarian reform process and of policies towards the agricultural sector. Finally, we will make some observations on the probable course of agrarian transformations in the medium term and in comparison with other cases of agricultural transformation in Latin America.

We start with the following basic propositions: Nicaraguan agriculture differs from the rest of Central America and in general from the typical Latin American case in that its productive base has not been either the large hacienda, the plantation or the mining enclave.[2] This makes the context of the Sandinista revolution structurally different from that of other Latin American revolutionary processes, such as that of Mexico, Cuba and Bolivia. The Nicaraguan case, speaking in terms of the agricultural sector, is characterized by the important role played by the petty and medium bourgeoisie and by wage labour.

Two other basic characteristics of Nicaragua's agrarian structure are: (1) the historical absence of peonage (the use of labourers bound in servitude because of debts owed to the landowner), and (2) a small population and ample uncultivated land. The first of these conditions led to the early introduction of wage labour, while the second has made possible successive expansions of the agricultural frontier, a process that is still taking place.

In more theoretical terms, we can say that capitalism in Nicaraguan agriculture has followed several roads of development, relatively coexistent. Thus, we find the junker road, involving the transition from the pre-capitalist hacienda based on the use of a serf-like labour force to the use of wage labour by the large capitalist landowner engaged in cattle-raising and the cultivation of coffee. At the same time we find the formation of small and medium-sized units of production along the agricultural frontier with the capacity to proletarianize local labour or to attract it from other zones. We also find the classical form of land-leasing in the cotton-producing areas of the Pacific Coast. Finally, we find intensive agriculture in the form of capitalist plantations producing sugar cane, irrigated rice and tobacco.

Another important characteristic of pre-revolutionary agriculture is the expansion in production and the area under cultivation that took place between the end of World War II and the early 1970s. This was the result of the introduction of new products – cotton, irrigated rice, tobacco, etc. – as well as the expanded production of coffee, cattle and sugar. This doubled the area under cultivation and increased the level of proletarianization among the peasantry. Moreover, the expulsion of small peasant producers from the land as a result of the development of cotton and cattle (particularly the latter) led to the deterioration of basic grain production. This dynamic expansion of agriculture during the period following World War II – common to the rest of Central America – differentiates the Nicaraguan situation from the Cuban case, in which a long period of economic stagnation (mainly in the key sector of sugar) preceded the revolution.

Among Nicaragua's agrarian propertied classes prior to the revolution, two well-defined sectors could be distinguished. On the one hand, there was the Somocista sector (comprising properties belonging to Somoza, his family and followers). Although important in the production of sugar, rice and tobacco, it was most important in agro-industry (that is, in coffee mills, rice mills, sugar mills, slaughter houses, cotton mills, etc.), commerce and banking. On the other hand, there existed a sector of entrepreneurs, both medium and large, who were primarily involved in the production of traditional agricultural export commodities (coffee, cattle, cotton) and to a lesser degree in agro-industry, commerce and the financial sphere. In the specific case of cotton, there existed an important sector of producers very similar to the classical capitalist leasehold farmer, increasingly in confrontation, during the second half of the 1970s with a local stratum of rentier landlords. These productive sectors organized into producer associations during the period immediately preceding the revolutionary triumph. In March 1979, they constituted the Union de Productores Agropecuarios de Nicaragua (Union of Agricultural Producers of Nicaragua, UPANIC).

In other words, prior to the formation of the revolutionary government in July 1979, we do not find the classical context for a democratic agrarian revolution, characterized by the predominance of the large semi-feudal haciendas and a mass of peasants subordinated by rents of one kind or another. Nor do we find a well-developed contradiction between productive capital and labour. Rather, we find what is basically a bottom-up revolution, including subordinate sectors of the propertied classes (the small and medium bourgeoisie) within the revolutionary forces. The strictly political confrontation with the Somoza dictatorship was joined with a structural tension in which the latter represented unproductive capital (e.g. financial and commercial capital), which 'unfairly' utilized the state's resources for its own benefit and that of its supporters in the entrepreneurial sector and the National Guard. This structural reality has influenced the orientation of the Sandinista revolution.

Nicaragua and Central America

Nicaragua differs in several important ways from the other Central American countries. In the first place, it does not conform to the stereotype of a 'banana republic' so often used in reference to Central America and the Caribbean. Neither the cultivation of bananas nor the presence of foreign capital in production have been of great significance in terms of the country's economic development.

Unlike Honduras, Guatemala and Costa Rica, Nicaragua has had a relatively unimportant banana enclave. This reflects the fact that

Nicaragua's economy has not been based upon plantation agriculture, as in many Caribbean countries. As a result, it does not have the corresponding propertied or popular classes associated with this form of agriculture. It lacks the type of bourgeoisie associated with plantation economies – small in number, but with a great capacity for economic concentration and closely associated with foreign capital. It also lacks the type of labour force associated with plantation agriculture. Thus, it does not possess a large agricultural workforce similar in character to an industrial proletariat, that is, with an organizational tradition as well as political and trade union experience. In this respect it differs sharply from the Cuban case.

In Nicaragua, we find an important sector of medium-sized agricultural producers alongside the large bourgeoisie. This can be seen both in terms of their numbers and their weight in production. As Table 2.1 indicates, prior to the revolution, Nicaragua accounted for only 11 per cent of the total number of fincas (estates) in Central America, but it contained 40 per cent of the 'medium-sized multi-family fincas' (defined in technical studies as units with between 50 and 500 manzanas – 86 to 860 acres – and administered by their owners).[3]

Table 2.1 Central America: Numerical Weight of Different Types of Fincas

	Central America	Guatemala	El Salvador	Honduras	Nicaragua	Costa Rica
Total	970,980	348,690	226,896	178,361	102,201	114,832
%	100	36	23	28	11	12
Microfincas	233,793	74,270	107,054	—	2,258	50,211
%	100	32	46	—	1	22
Sub-family	532,089	233,800	100,245	120,441	49,678	27,925
%	100	44	19	23	9	5
Family	146,049	33,040	15,235	47,089	27,976	22,709
%	100	23	10	32	19	16
Medium-sized Multi-family	54,325	7,060	3,335	10,164	20,794	12,972
%	100	13	6	19	38	24
Large Multi-family	4,724	520	1,027	667	1,495	1,015
%	100	11	22	14	32	21

Source: Rafael Menjivar, in Torres Rivas, *Centroamérica Hoy* (Mexico City, Siglo XXI), p. 255.

Nicaragua did not have the large haciendas so characteristic of El Salvador and Guatemala, nor, as already mentioned, was its economy dominated by a plantation enclave as in the case of Honduras.[4] Moreover, those with most influence over agricultural production had a weak presence in agro-industry, commerce and finance, while capitalists located in the sectors outside primary production did not own a significant proportion of the fincas involved in agricultural production. However, there was a high degree of concentration of ownership among the capitalists involved in agro-industry, commerce and finance. For example, the owners of the coffee mills (agro-industry) were also important buyers and exporters of coffee, and to a large extent they financed the producers who supplied them with unprocessed coffee. The cattle sector was similar. The owners of the slaughter-houses, most of whom were tied to Somoza, would finance the purchase of cattle by their suppliers, and then process and export the end product.

This situation contrasts with that of El Salvador, where since the 1930s there has been a high degree of integration between agricultural production and the rest of the economic process in terms of overlapping ownership. Both in coffee and cotton, the Salvadoran capitalists involved in production also tend to control the processing, commercialization and financing of these agro-exports. The grand bourgeoisie has a great deal of weight in direct production and a significant presence in the other spheres of agri-business, which gives a considerable degree of cohesion to this class. And one finds a relatively small number of cotton-producers with considerable control over the processing and sale of this crop. In coffee, the large producers tend to be the owners of the coffee mills.

The different forms of cotton production in Central America allow us to illustrate the different ways in which agrarian capitalism has developed in the region as well as the different types of bourgeoisie to be found there. Table 2.2 shows that in the early 1970s, there were 2,671 cotton-producers in Nicaragua, whereas in Guatemala there were only 161 and in El Salvador 1,634. In the Guatemalan case, a small nucleus of large producers controls production and is linked with the financial sector.[5]

In the Salvadoran case, as in Nicaragua, we find a larger number of producers. However, the large producers have greater influence through their control of the Cooperativa Algodonera Salvadorena (Salvadoran Cotton Co-operative), which controls seeds, equipment, credit and foreign sales. In Nicaragua, on the other hand, we find a broader base of producers. Moreover, prior to the revolution, agro-industry, sales and financing were controlled by diverse groups of capitalists who were generally not involved in direct production. Before the revolution, the cotton sector consisted of several thousand producers, 28 agro-industrial processing plants (cotton mills), 11 export firms and 3 banks. Although some producers were involved in all aspects of the process,

Table 2.2   Cotton Areas, Number of Producers and Average Size of Fincas, 1970–71

Countries	Cotton area (in hectares[a])	Number of producers	Hectares per producer
Guatemala	74,565	161	463
El Salvador	63,749	1,634	39
Nicaragua	95,400	2,671	36

[a] 1 hectare = 2.47 acres.

Source: Secretaria para la Integración Económica Centroaméricana (SIECA), 'El Agodón en Centroamérica' (mimeo, 1971).

they were the exception. Moreover, about 50 per cent of production took place on leased land. Somocista capital was behind the banks, the cotton mills and the commercialization of cotton. This is reflected in the present situation, where the revolutionary state controls only about 20 per cent of the total area under cultivation, but about 40 per cent of the processing industry, and has a monopoly over banking and foreign trade.

In the case of Nicaragua, therefore, the basis existed for conflict within the bourgeoisie in both the economic and political spheres. This gave rise to the formation of alliances between certain fractions of the bourgeoisie and other social sectors, motivated by attempts to offset the power of the stronger fractions of capital associated with the Somoza regime. This structural conflict had significant political effects because of the strong influence of the Somoza family and their associates in the intermediary sphere of the economic process. Their control over commerce and banking enabled them to subordinate productive capital. As a result, when the anti-Somocista struggle gathered strength, these productive sectors were disposed to accept an anti-Somocista regime that would be anti-oligarchical and bring about a drastic reduction of land rent in the growing of cotton and basic grains as well as the nationalization of foreign trade and banking. In contrast, the situation in El Salvador and Guatemala seems to indicate that there are fewer structural bases for intra-bourgeois conflict in these countries.

In sum, the confrontations in Nicaragua between capitalists involved in production and those outside of direct production have their genesis in the structural relations between productive and commercial capital as well as between producers and rentier landowners. It is interesting to note that these contradictions arose within the context of the expansion of agro-export production. The growth rate of the agricultural gross domestic product (GDP) between 1950 and 1977 was 4.7 per cent per

15

annum, and the productivity of agricultural labour increased by 4.6 per cent per annum during this same period. These rates were among the highest in Latin America during the years in question.[6] The year 1977–8 saw the largest planting of cotton in Nicaragua's history, good harvests of coffee and sugar cane, as well as high levels of cattle slaughtering for export – all within a context of rising international prices for these exports. The conflicts in the cotton sector originated over the sharp increase in the international price and over the fulfilment or failure to fulfil futures contracts. In the case of beef, they arose around the famous lists of the IFAGAN slaughter-house and their correspondence with the rise in prices in the famous Yellow Sheets of the Chicago stock market. The rise in coffee prices led to similar conflicts, but these received less publicity.[7] In essence, the conflict centred around the failure of the processors/buyers to offer the producers prices which reflected the prices on the international market.

As indicated above, Somocista capital had a significant presence in commercial activities, the coffee mills, the cotton mills, the export slaughter-houses, banking and finance. It was also strong in the agro-industrial sector, primarily in sugar and rice-processing as well as cigar tobacco. As Table 2.3 indicates, these businesses were related to those sectors of agricultural production where large producers predominated. Before the revolution, large-scale sugar production was centred around six sugar mills (four of which belonged to Somocista capital). In rice, Somocista capital accounted for about 73 per cent of production, and in cigar tobacco, Somocista control was total. This explains why today the revolutionary state controls 100 per cent of tobacco production, and is heavily involved in the production of irrigated rice. The Somoza family and their associates also owned extensive cattle haciendas, and this accounts for a large proportion of the area in fincas that is now under the control of the revolutionary state, that is, within the Area of People's Property (APP).

Finally, pre-revolutionary Nicaragua differed from the rest of Central America in terms of the amount of direct foreign investment in its economy. For example, in 1977, total direct foreign investment in Nicaragua amounted to only US $90 million, whereas in Honduras it was $250 million, in Guatemala $270 million, in El Salvador $140 million, and in Costa Rica $270 million.[8] In fact, direct foreign investment accounted for only 4.3 per cent of the GDP in Nicaragua, giving Nicaragua one of the lowest levels of direct foreign investment in all of Latin America, second only to Haiti during this period.[9]

However, it is important to note that Nicaragua was extremely dependent upon external financing. In 1978, the payments on its foreign debt accounted for 23.6 per cent of the country's export earnings, whereas in Guatemala the comparable figure was only 2.9 per cent, in El Salvador 6.2 per cent, in Honduras 9.4 per cent and in Costa Rica 15.8 per cent.[10] Of course, in recent years, the foreign debt of all the countries

Table 2.3   Nicaragua: Weight in Production of Major Strata of Producers[a] before the Revolution (percentages[b])

	Small producers	Medium producers	Large producers	Total
Cotton	6	52	42	100
Coffee	22	58	20	100
Bovine cattle	52	29	19	100
Sugar cane	4	18	78	100
Rice	9	18	73	100
Sorghum	34	28	38	100
Corn	32	57	11	100
Bean	59	38	3	100
Total	25	45	30	100

[a]   Producers in fincas having a total area smaller than 50 manzanas (86 acres) are considered as small producers; those having up to 500 manzanas (864 acres) are considered medium producers; when estates in their total area surpass 500 manzanas they are considered large producers; in the case of cattle-raising, small producers extend up to 200 manzanas (344 acres); medium producers between 200 and 1,000 manzanas (1,720 acres), and large producers above 1,000 manzanas.

[b]   Percentages are approximate and must be interpreted as 'images' of reality rather than statistical data. In the case of coffee, data from the Agricultural Census of 1963 are used. It is very likely that in the years previous to the revolution the weight of large producers had increased in coffee as a result of the important increase in production due to coffee plantation renewal.

Source: E. Valdivia, 'Estructura de la Producción Agropecuario, 1960–1971' (Managua: UNASEC, 1974, mimeo).

in the region has increased dramatically as a result of the worsening economic conditions throughout Central America and the international economic recession.

The Sandinista Agrarian Reform

The structure of agriculture prior to the revolution consisted of a series of well-linked mechanisms. With the revolutionary triumph this structure was broken. As a result, the 'dictatorship of capital' over the labour process was undermined, leading to a decline in labour

17

productivity.[11] The fall of the dictatorship and the disbanding of the National Guard has eliminated the main obstacle to the organization of the workers and land redistribution. The blow dealt to the large landowners by reducing the price of land leases (in the case of cotton, from \$200 per hectare to \$40; and in the case of basic grain production, from \$80 to \$14 per hectare) has created much greater access to land than in the past. The reduction of the area under cotton cultivation to half that during the years prior to the revolution, and the drastic reduction in cattle herds (because of the insurrectionary war and smuggling to neighbouring countries), have increased remarkably the availability of idle or underutilized land, thereby increasing access to land for poor peasants and semi-proletarians. At the same time, the fall in cotton production has reduced the demand for permanent and seasonal labour, thereby diminishing the opportunities for wage labour on the part of the poor peasantry. The increased amount of credit available to the peasantry has broken the back of usurious capital. The statization of foreign trade and the increase in state control over domestic trade have undermined the classical dominance of commercial capital over the small producers. The construction of highways linking the Pacific with the Atlantic Coasts, for the first time in the country's history, has also made it possible to extend the agricultural frontier into the underdeveloped areas of the Atlantic Coast.

These developments have created conditions that would appear to favour the 'peasantization' of important sectors of the semi-proletarianized peasantry (the core element of the popular classes in the countryside). They have also strengthened the middle and rich peasants. If we add to this the democratic framework of the revolution, with its broad social base, the FSLN's historical promise to give land to the peasantry and the pressure of the anti-Somocista bourgeoisie for the creation of a strong 'middle class' through redistribution of the properties confiscated from Somoza and his allies – we have the basis for a classical bourgeois democratic model of agrarian reform.

However, the road followed by the Nicaraguan government has been different, both in order to maintain a broad base of national unity that includes all the propertied sectors and to prevent a process of individual peasantization that would result in a mass of small property-owners.[12] The policy that has been pursued has as its main parameters the following: (1) the formation of a state sector from the fincas confiscated from the Somocistas; (2) the distribution of a part of the confiscated lands to the workers of these fincas or the peasants who fought for the land in these areas so that they can be farmed collectively in what are called Sandinista Agricultural Co-operatives;[13] (3) the reduction of land rents and the harsh terms for leasing land; (4) the extension of credit to all sectors of the agricultural population; and (5) the statization of a portion of domestic trade and all foreign trade.

The First Stage of the Agrarian Reform

All the anti-Somocista forces saw the nationalization of the properties held by the Somocistas as a democratization measure. The programme of the Government of National Reconstruction, itself a product of the convergence of a broad array of social and political sectors, stated:

> An area of state action and social property will be created based upon the recovery of all properties usurped by the Somoza family and its followers. This patrimony of national reconstruction will be destined to solve the problems of backwardness, misery and unemployment suffered by the great majority of the population. This patrimony will be administered by a national trust before being transferred to the *state institutions designated by the government* that will be in charge of incorporating it into the process of national reconstruction, transformation and development. Said administration will take into account the need to foster the constitution of various forms of social property.[14]

At the same time, it was noted that the agrarian reform programme should be advanced fundamentally on the basis of associated forms of production.

In structural terms, the confiscation of the Somocista properties can be considered a severe blow to the grand bourgeoisie, more precisely to its two extremes: (1) the modern sector involved in agro-industry,[15] and (2) the latifundista (large landowner) sector. A clear picture of the structural blow dealt by confiscation is revealed in Table 2.4, which summarizes the characteristics of the confiscated estates.

The average size of the fincas confiscated was 1,364 manzanas (some 2,186 acres). This means that confiscation fell primarily upon the 'large multi-family' estates, that is, units consisting of more than 500 manzanas (864 acres).[16]

In Table 2.5, we offer a general view of the magnitude of confiscation of Somocista properties. These changes in land distribution have affected both direct agricultural production and agro-industry. The figures show the differential impact of nationalization, the strongest effect being in the agro-industrial sector rather than in agricultural production.

The statistics in Table 2.6 indicate the percentages of total production brought under state control as a result of the confiscation of Somocista properties.

In the aggregate, the state controls approximately 20 per cent of the total gross agricultural product.[17] Compared to other agrarian transformations in Latin America, except Cuba, the state sector's contribution to total agricultural production is high. In fact, it is high even in comparison with the socialist countries of Eastern Europe, China and Vietnam.[18]

19

Table 2.4   Average Size of Confiscated Fincas According to Number of Permanent Workers (1980)

Number of permanent workers	Average size of fincas (in manzanas) [a]
4 or less	552
5–12	1,306
13–20	1,372
21–50	1,719
51–100	1,806
100 +	2,532
National average	*1,364*

[a] 1 manzana = 1.72 acres.

Source: CIERA, *Herencia Agraria de la Revolución Popular Sandinista* (1980).

Table 2.5   Magnitude of Confiscation (1980)

	%
Confiscated fincas as a percentage of all fincas in the country	21.5
Percentage of fincas having more than 500 manzanas which were confiscated	42.9
Composition of confiscated properties	
Fincas having more than 500 manzanas	91.0
Fincas having less than 500 manzanas	9.0

Source: CIERA, *Herencia Agraria de la Revolución Popular Sandinista* (1980).

The decision to create a sizeable state sector was determined, on the one hand, by the fact that the modern agro-industrial sector could not feasibly be subdivided. The leadership of the revolution rejected the option of distributing the confiscated agro-industrial complexes and large commercial farms, because it was felt that this would lead to

Table 2.6   Effect of Confiscation upon Different Sectors of Agricultural
Production (percentages of total production by sector)[a]

Cotton	20	Sugar	45
Coffee	17	Tobacco for cigars	100
Sorghum	20	Rice	40
Corn	8	Cotton mills	35
Beans	9	Coffee mills	40
Sesame	3	Cattle slaughtered for export	100

(% = percentage of production produced by confiscated properties)

Source: Statistics from **MIDINRA** (Ministry of Agricultural Development and Agrarian Reform), Agricultural year 1981–82.

considerable differentiation among the rural population. This decision was also influenced undoubtedly by the fact that the privatization of the confiscated properties was advocated by right-wing Social Christian organizations that opposed the Sandinistas. Another influential factor was the perception that extensive production would probably create a shortage of labour for harvesting coffee and cotton, because labour of a semi-proletarian nature (that is, of peasant origin), when it gains access to land, will reproduce itself to a large extent without resorting to wage labour. Empirical validation largely confirms this.

Phase II of the Agrarian Reform

On 19 July 1981, the second anniversary of the revolution, the promulgation of the Agrarian Reform Law was announced. It appears that it was delayed until then because of the revolutionary leadership's objective of maintaining as broad an alliance as possible with the propertied classes. Briefly, the law aimed at those sectors of agrarian capital who were not performing an entrepreneurial role. This included large landowners, who produced very little, and tended to extract ground rent through leasing and sharecropping arrangements. Another target were those landowners who, especially after the revolutionary triumph, decapitalized or abandoned their properties. The remainder of the propertied classes were not affected by the law. Thus, most of the middle bourgeoisie have not been affected, so long as they have less

21

than 500 manzanas (864 acres) of land in the Pacific Coast or less than 1,000 manzanas (1,728 acres) in the interior, or unless they abandon their land.[19]

In other words, the Agrarian Reform Law provides for the expropriation of the following kinds of property: (1) idle or deficiently exploited properties, that is, fincas which remain uncultivated for two consecutive years; (2) properties with less than 75 per cent of their total area in use; (3) cattle-raising properties with a low density of cattle per manzana (less than 0.5 head of cattle per manzana in the Pacific and less than 0.3 head of cattle per manzana in the interior).[20] Also affected are large landowners who lease land. However, small rentier landowners are exempt from expropriation.

The most radical aspect of the law concerns the expropriation of properties in cases where the care of permanent plantings is indispensable to their maintenance and this is not being performed, where the tasks of annual crop preparation are not being performed or, in the case of ranch properties, where there is deterioration because of a lack of maintenance of fences and pasture grounds or an obvious decrease in the cattle herd. Also affected are properties where the agricultural tasks are not being carried out due to lack of repair or replacement of equipment and machinery. The owners of all expropriated properties, with the exception of those that have been abandoned, are compensated through indemnification in long-term government bonds.

By comparing the aims of the Agrarian Reform Law to the existing agrarian structure, it is clear that the criteria of idleness and underutilization are directed at those fincas that have a traditional profile, that is, mainly large cattle estates.[21] The same applies to property-owners who were expropriated because they were engaged primarily in extracting different forms of ground rent. In these cases, we have property-owners who have been guilty of obstructing the development of capitalist agriculture. The criterion of abandonment, on the other hand, is aimed at the more modern entrepreneurs who, because they have stopped working their lands and decapitalized their properties, have abandoned, so to speak, their customary capitalist practices.

Table 2.7 indicates how the two phases of the agrarian reform have affected the two main agricultural regions of the country. The figures show that the Somocista properties were concentrated in the more advanced agro-industry sector and in the backward large landowner sector.

The Agrarian Reform Law has affected the traditional sector more than the more advanced entrepreneurial sector in the Pacific Coast (i.e., the producers of cotton, sugar cane, irrigated rice and the dairy owners). The pace and future application of the law will reflect the extent to which the modern capitalists participate in the mixed economy. Criticism from different quarters has been directed at the nature of the

Table 2.7   Regional Distribution of Agrarian Reform (December 1983)

Regions	% of total agricultural area	Phase I % of total area confiscated	Phase II % of total area affected by reform
Pacific	28	49	36
Interior	72	51	64
Total	*100*	*100*	*100*

Source: MIDINRA and CIERA. Tabulations do not include the Department of Zelaya, since the Agrarian Reform Law does not apply there.

Agrarian Reform Law. From the right wing, it has been criticized for its lack of 'Napoleonic validity' with regard to the distribution of land titles to the co-operatives and individual peasants who have received land under the law. And from the left, the agrarian reform has been branded 'social democratic'.

However, the Agrarian Reform Law must be understood within the wider context of the goal of national unity sought by the Sandinistas, and the type of structural reforms which their revolutionary project calls for in the medium term. The central premise of this project is the idea that in the Nicaraguan case it is possible to bring about structural transformations which strengthen the state and co-operatives in the countryside, while maintaining an important and productive sector of small, medium and even large capitalist producers.

In December 1981, the Minister of Agriculture, Comandante Jaime Wheelock, announced the government's projected profile for the distribution of property in Nicaragua's agricultural sector – some 20 to 25 per cent of the land under state control, 40 to 50 per cent under the control of co-operatives and the rest under the ownership of individual peasant or capitalist producers.[22] In this formulation, the political aspects of a revolution with a broad social base are joined together with the peculiar structural aspects of Nicaraguan agriculture. As a result, we have a model of agricultural development that is quite different from either the model of the plantation enclave or that of the large capitalist enterprise that has evolved out of the traditional hacienda. In the Sandinista model, even if the grand bourgeoisie as a whole are eliminated in the future, the small and middle bourgeoisie will continue to have an important influence.

In another socio-political context, this type of agrarian reform could be considered as 'moderate reformism' since it does not attack the entire fraction of large landowners, nor does it foster land takeovers, invasions or classist confrontations in the countryside. It represents the least violent situation in all of Central America with regard to the agrarian question, even compared to Costa Rica, where violent confrontations occur periodically as a result of peasant invasions of idle land. As in the case of any agrarian reform, the Nicaraguan case must be understood in terms of its structural and political determinants. In this case, these determinants have raised the possibility of articulating a project of profound transformations while maintaining an important sector of agrarian capitalists, the so-called chapiolla or 'countryfied' small and medium bourgeoisie.

The permanence of this chapiolla small and medium bourgeoisie depends, however, on its productive and political behaviour. In the past, the degree of corporative development in this sector was very small. At present, both the grand bourgeoisie, through the UPANIC, and the FSLN, through its affiliated mass organization the National Union of Farmers and Ranchers (UNAG), are contending for the leadership of this sector. Both corporative organizations have the capacity to incorporate the small and medium producers. Even though UNAG has existed for less than five years (it was created in April 1981), it has reached a fairly high level of organizational development and has succeeded in representing a heterogeneous collection of demands concerning prices, roads, credit, land and co-operatives. Its programme includes features of both the government's minimum programme (i.e. credits, price supports, etc.) and its maximum programme (i.e. the co-operativization of the peasantry). This provides it with a great capacity for manoeuvre and for incorporating the interests of the peasantry and the medium-sized producers into its proposals.

However, it is hard to predict what will be the ultimate characteristics of the Sandinista agrarian model. The presence of well-off peasants and medium-sized capitalist producers, the strengthening of the poor and middle peasantry through co-operatives and the general support of agriculture through new investments make possible a broad-based, democratic and non-oligarchical capitalism. In other words, the classical process of *kulakization* – or what, in other cases, has been called the 'farmer road' to capitalist development – is structurally possible in Nicaragua, as is the simple consolidation of the middle peasants.

The consolidation of the Sandinista model will depend mainly upon the state's capacity to organize a vast co-operative movement which at present is only in its incipient stage. Small cotton producers (co-operatives and individual producers) in 1980–1 had only 8,000 manzanas, but by 1983–4 they had 40,000 manzanas under cultivation, largely as a result of the government's agrarian reform programme. UNAG estimates that small and medium-sized producers account for between one-quarter and one-third of total agricultural production. According to an analysis of the agricultural frontier in the departments of Matagalpa and Jinotega, the production of coffee by small producers doubled between 1979 and 1983. Obviously, the strengthening of the sector of small and medium-sized producers creates the possibility for the capitalization of a portion of this stratum and its passing over into the more 'established' and traditional entrepreneurial sector. However, the economic, cultural and political traditions of the typical capitalist in both the oligarchical and urban commercial sectors differ from those of the well-off peasants and small landowners. For this reason, one can assume that the latter will behave quite differently at least in the short and medium term.

During the 1970s in Latin America, modernization did not contribute to democratization as originally assumed by many of the *desarrollista* (developmentalist) theories. In the 1960s, it was assumed that modernization would strengthen the so-called middle sectors of the population as well as the national bourgeoisie, and that this would benefit the development of democracy – both in the economic and the social and political spheres. When we look at the situation of present-day Nicaragua, we can see that the process of modernization being promoted by the government is aimed at strengthening the middle sectors in the countryside, that is, the upper strata of the peasantry and the lower and intermediate strata of the agrarian bourgeoisie. These sectors are now being given access to those resources – land, credit, technical assistance, etc. – which they were previously denied during the Somocista regime.[23]

These processes of modernization and democratization are due basically to the state's increased role in the economy through its control over rents, the nationalization of foreign trade and banking, the provision of services to the producers and the anti-oligarchical agrarian reform. By displacing the fractions that were hegemonic in the past, the state has objectively favoured a process of economic deconcentration that has resulted in the strengthening of the middle sectors in the countryside.[24]

The First Five Years of the Agrarian Reform

Although five years is a relatively short period of time to take as the basis for characterizing a revolutionary process like the one taking place in Nicaragua, it is possible to state that the main characteristic of agrarian policy has been the revolutionary regime's attempt to avoid a 'zero-sum' approach to agricultural development. Having eliminated the Somocista fraction of the bourgeoisie, the Sandinista regime has tried to maintain an alliance with all those productive sectors who abide by the basic rules of entrepreneurship and avoid involvement in counter-revolutionary activities.

On the other hand, another basic element of agrarian policy has been elimination of the rentier landlords through the drastic reduction of ground rents. This has benefited capitalist producers in the cotton-growing sector. For example, in 1977–8, the ground rent was equivalent to the value of 12 quintales (1 quintal = 112 lbs) of raw cotton, and in the 1982–3 cycle it was barely equivalent to the value of one quintal of raw cotton.[25] The reduction in land rents has also benefited the sorghum-producing entrepreneurial sector. Another major blow to the rentier elements has been the elimination of the most exploitative forms of sharecropping and the *colonato* (a practice resembling archaic forms of paying for the use of land through work) that was quite important in the cattle-ranching sector.

Together with the reduction in ground rents, we find an attempt to reduce the price of capital and intermediate goods. This is manifested, on the one hand, by the very favourable exchange rate for dollars that the government gives to producers who wish to purchase productive goods needed for agriculture. It is also manifested in the favourable interest rates charged by the state-run banks to peasants and agricultural capitalists, which are lower than the inflation rate. There is also greater access to capital and intermediate goods through the mechanization services provided by various state enterprises and through the expansion of the number of producers and the area financed by the state banks. According to CIERA's estimates, around 75 per cent of the private producers – peasants, co-operatives and capitalists – have obtained credit from the state banks.[26]

Since the triumph in 1979, the capitalization of the agricultural sector through increased mechanization, irrigation, industrial development projects, storage facilities and new roads has been largely the result of state investment. The state has invested in activities such as the new Tipitapa–Malacatoya sugar mill, numerous irrigation projects, the expansion of tobacco production, intensive cattle-raising projects, the development of African palm oil for export and many other projects. Investments in agriculture increased from slightly over 500 million cordobas in 1981 to about 1 billion in 1983.[27] The tendency has been for the state to concentrate on activities which are highly capital intensive and to maintain a relatively low involvement in direct production. As a result, it appears that the profile of the Nicaraguan state in agriculture will not follow the Cuban pattern, where a few years after the revolutionary triumph, the state controlled about 70 per cent of direct production. In contrast, the intention in Nicaragua is for the state to control around 25 per cent of total production. This resembles the situation in Peru under the reformist military regime of General Velasco or the Mexican pattern of high state participation in the formation of basic social capital (e.g. irrigation works) but a much smaller presence in direct production.

The revolutionary process in Nicaragua upset the balance of forces between capital and labour. This is evidenced by the tremendous increase in unionization since 1979, the government's energetic enforcement of the labour code, wage and salary increases, and the decline in labour productivity. Focusing upon the revolutionary period as a whole, we note that labour costs have tended to increase and productivity has declined as a result of the dismantling of the previous system of super-exploitation of wage labour and the subordination of the poor peasantry through rents that had to be paid in work or in kind. However, the rate of increase in wages has differed considerably between different categories of the workforce.[28] The wages of skilled workers (tractor drivers in the state sector are in first place), administrative workers, young technicians and permanent workers have all increased significantly, while the harvest workers, mainly in cotton and to a lesser extent in coffee, have received much smaller increases. This, plus the effects of giving land to the poor peasantry, have reduced the labour supply available for the harvesting of the country's agricultural export crops.

The shortage of labour for harvesting cotton and coffee has not approached the magnitude of that experienced in Cuba with regard to the harvesting of sugar cane during the first years of the revolution. During the coffee harvest of 1982–3 – the largest in Nicaragua's history – non-traditional labourers (voluntary labour brigades) represented no more than 8 per cent of the total workforce involved. However, during 1983–4, the importance of voluntary labour appears to have increased, due largely to the increase in counter-revolutionary attacks aimed at disrupting the harvests and frightening the rural population. At the same time, the problems of transporting workers were aggravated by the shortage of spare parts and the fact that many vehicles were disabled. It should be noted that the problem of seasonal labour has been a recurrent one in the history of Nicaraguan agriculture. It was solved in part during the 1970s by an influx of Honduran and Salvadoran workers.[29]

The Reactivation and Transformation of Production

Following the revolutionary triumph in 1979, the government's main objective in agriculture was to recover the level of production that had existed prior to the war of liberation. By 1982, there had been a significant advance in the reactivation of the agricultural sector. The main problems were centred in cattle-raising and in cotton. The reactivation of cattle-raising was slow because of the characteristics of this branch of production and because of the widespread slaughter of cattle during the war and the smuggling of whole herds to Honduras and Costa Rica during and after the war. Cotton production did not regain previous levels because of the shift to other agricultural products (basic grains and sorghum), and because of the reluctance of certain producers to plant cotton. The other 'difficult' product was corn, which

Table 2.8   The Reactivation of Agricultural Production

Area	*Amount of land under cultivation (thousands of manzanas)* [a]		
	1970–7	*1980–2*	*1983–4*
Total agricultural area	898	831	932
Area in export crops	408	349	383
Areas in crops for domestic market	490	482	549

[a] 1 manzana = 1.72 acres.

Source: MIDINRA and CIERA.

the peasantry tended to consider as a crop for self-consumption – one which they often abandoned in favour of such 'cash crops' as beans, coffee, sesame and vegetables. However, by 1983-4, we find a marked increase in planting levels for crops sold on the domestic market and for export crops – some reaching levels higher than the historical mean of the 1970s (see Table 2.8). The expansion of production in 1983 was due primarily to the role played by the state as well as the small and medium-sized producers, whereas the large private producers showed a tendency towards stagnation.

Together with the recovery of previous levels of production and their subsequent increase, the problem has been one of transforming the productive structures of the country. The main objectives of the revolutionary regime in terms of the latter have been to increase the level of industrialization in agriculture and strengthen the co-operative sector among the peasantry.

The central aspect of the co-operative movement in Nicaragua is the flexibility of the state's policy for incorporating the peasantry into co-operatives. The majority of producers in the co-operative sector are members of credit and service co-operatives, which group together in a loose association producers who work their land on an individual basis and who have individual title to their land. The basis of their association concerns the obtaining of government credit and services. They account for 65 per cent of all the producers organized into co-operatives.[30] The more socialized production co-operatives (in which the members collectively own and work the land), account for only 12 per cent of the co-operative sector, and are called Sandinista Agricultural Co-operatives or CASs. An intermediary category consists of the owners of individual parcels who gather together to perform some farming tasks in common. These are known locally as *surco muerto* co-operatives and they encompass, according to CIERA's estimates, about 17 per cent of all co-operative members. The remaining 6 per cent of co-operative members are grouped in co-operatives which fall between the credit and service co-operatives and the production co-operatives. This hetero-geneous co-operative sector, according to the Co-operative Census of 1984, cultivates around 40 per cent of the country's agricultural area, with the credit and service co-operatives accounting for most of this figure.

Problems Associated with the Transformation of Agriculture

When analysing the difficulties faced by the revolutionary process in the development of its agrarian project, we have to distinguish between those created by external factors and those which are determined by domestic conditions. Among the former, the general conditions of the world market are outstanding. As is widely known, they have created serious economic difficulties for the Latin American countries, including the fall in prices of primary exports, the protectionism of the central capitalist countries and a general deterioration in the terms of trade. However, the more specific external problem for Nicaragua is, of course, the aggressive hostility of the United States, which has closed off markets, blocked credit, stopped international lending agencies from providing loans to Nicaragua, mined the country's ports and harbours, etc. The Nicaraguan revolution, like the Cuban revolution before it, has been forced to contend with US efforts to destroy it. However, the Cuban revolution took place within a cycle of a long period of international capitalist expansion, which lasted until the early 1970s. In contrast, the Nicaraguan revolution has taken place during a world economic crisis. In some senses, this is unfavourable, but it also has its positive aspects.

The present situation in the rest of Central America is that of a deep economic crisis – much worse than in Nicaragua. This crisis persists, despite the efforts of the US government and the international banking institutions. The socio-political consequences of this are quite signifi-cant. A substantial portion of the bourgeoisie and the middle sectors within Nicaragua are convinced that the 'alternatives' of migrating to the United States or to the neighbouring 'democracies' in Central America are not very attractive.[31]

US economic aggression has been offset in part by the support of Mexico, Venezuela, Colombia, Cuba, Western Europe, the Arab countries and the socialist bloc, which together have provided considerable economic assistance. However, this does not compensate for the negative impact that the shortage of foreign exchange has had on the country's economic development.

In terms of the domestic factors that have conditioned the process of agrarian transformation, one would have to mention the various policies undertaken by the revolutionary government. Perhaps the most important has been the policy of reactivating the economy through relying upon the country's traditional agricultural producers and its historical products. On the other hand, the government has also enacted policies aimed at effecting a transformation in both the means of production as well as in the type of units of production. These policies emphasize agro-industrialization as the basic axis of the country's development, a shift to intensive methods of agriculture and the abandonment of the traditional extensive form of agriculture, the massive development of irrigation, the mechanization of agricultural production, the use of improved seeds, etc. They also are aimed at promoting the co-operativization of the peasantry. Briefly, mixed economy policies, including 'green revolution' type measures, coexist with efforts aimed at the co-operativization of a majority of the agricultural producers. As a consequence, some policies favour reactivation and the mixed economy, whereas others are more interested in technological and social change than in short-term improvements in production.

As occurs in development efforts elsewhere, the different policies are determined to a considerable degree by the state agencies and organizations in civil society from whence they have originated. In general, the ministries which are connected with domestic and foreign trade, as well as banking and public finances, insist on short-term 'pragmatic' results, whereas the Ministry of Agriculture and Agrarian Reform (MIDINRA) emphasizes the need to increase production through the acceleration of technological change. At the same time, outside the sphere of the state apparatus and the FSLN, those who habitually call themselves representatives of the private sector, the producers organized within UPANIC and COSEP (Superior Council of Private Enterprise), favour economic incentives which increase their profits and give them more 'participation' in power. On the other hand, UNAG, which represents a heterogeneous combination of different strata of the peasantry and the lower strata of the rural bourgeoisie allied with the FSLN, have pressured for agrarian reform policies that would give them more favourable prices for their products, credit and commercial services, technical assistance, access to new land, etc.

Looking at the process as a whole, it gives one the impression that what happens between the different social forces is reflected within the state and in state policies. That is to say, there does not appear to be a zero-sum relationship between the different policy initiatives. On the other hand, the success of those policies which are based on the mixed economy model in the area of agro-exports has been far from satisfactory, and is perhaps the most significant agrarian policy problem in the short term. At the same time, we find an emphasis on agro-industrial investments and technological change, mainly in the state sector. The benefits of this approach are expected to come about in the medium run. Doubts about these development efforts have to do with the problems of sustaining this process of accumulation (based on agro-export earnings) through infusions of foreign loans and international co-operation. The advantages of stressing intensive agriculture can also be questioned in a context conditioned by a serious shortage of foreign exchange, the availability of considerable productive land presently being used for extensive cattle-raising or covered by forests, and the difficulties involved in making the transition from traditional technologies to 'intermediate' semi-technical methods of production among the large peasant population in the central part of the country. Nevertheless, the emphasis on investment is in dramatic contrast to the situation found in most underdeveloped countries – a clear indication of the effects of the revolutionary process upon Nicaragua's economic development.

With regard to the process of peasant co-operativization, there has been considerable progress, although very few production co-operatives have been established. However, as international experience has shown, it is not easy to create a new type of social agent that combines the roles of owner, manager and worker – especially in a mercantile economic and private property context. In the last instance, production units which do not have the capitalist entrepreneur at their centre encounter difficulties in replacing the capitalist as the organizer of production and the administrator of the unit's costs and economic profitability. It is a question of endowing a collective with the attributes found in an individual entrepreneur. The Nicaraguan experience shows that the co-operatives which function best, such as the cotton-growing co-operatives in the North Pacific area or those growing vegetables in the Sebaco Valley, are characterized by highly associative conduct among their members and a tendency for a certain division of labour to develop between their leaders and the rest of their members (but with few traits of elitist bossism).

Comparisons with Other Examples of Agrarian Reform

In Latin America there are several cases of agrarian reforms which have developed out of revolutionary processes, e.g. the Mexican, Bolivian, Cuban and now the Nicaraguan case. However, there have been other important experiences in countries such as Chile and Peru where the effects of these agrarian reform efforts have been more limited. The Nicaraguan case reveals a clear tendency towards the prolonged coexistence of various types of production units (e.g. state, capitalist,

31

co-operative and peasant). The reduction of the upper stratum of the agrarian bourgeoisie can be predicted, but the existing profile of Nicaraguan agriculture will probably remain basically the same.

It is important to keep in mind that two of the most important social revolutions in the 20th Century, the Russian and the Mexican revolutions, underwent a prolonged period of social transformation before arriving at their definitive structural expression in the country-side. The Soviet regime did not undertake the massive statization of production and collectivization of the peasantry until 1928–33. In the Mexican case, it was not until 1934–40, that is to say more than 20 years after the end of the revolutionary insurrection, that Mexico's agrarian reform programme based on *ejidos* was consolidated under the administration of Cárdenas. It could even be argued that it was not until after the Cárdenas period that it assumed its final definitive profile – a kind of 'green revolution' based upon intensive capitalist agriculture coexisting uneasily with a very large and poor peasantry.

In contrast with the agrarian structures of other Latin American countries, it can be said that the Nicaraguan case stands out as one in which there is neither the predominance of large capitalist enterprises based upon the wage labour of a sizeable agricultural proletariat nor the predominance of pre-capitalist forms of production based upon an extensive peasant mass which is subordinated to large landowners by exploitative rents. The Nicaraguan case is midway between these two types of agrarian structure. In historical terms, it is different from the classical cases of Czarist Russia and Porfirista Mexico, where rentier schemes prevailed. It also does not conform to the other paradigm of pre-revolutionary Cuba, where there was a considerable degree of capitalist development and a sizeable agricultural proletariat that became an important social and political force.

Moreover, continuing with these kinds of historical and structural analogies, the Nicaraguan revolution does not conform to the classical model of a bourgeois democratic revolution that leads the way to capitalist development by freeing the economy and society from the restraints of semi-feudalism, nor does it resemble the model of a socialist revolution that subordinates a centralized capitalism supported by a mass of wage labourers.

In conclusion, the present structural profile of Nicaraguan agriculture will probably not undergo any significant changes over the short and medium term. However, in contrast to other historical situations, we are far from affirming Nicaragua: *de te fabula narratur*. It is too difficult to predict what course, either in the immediate or more distant future, the Nicaraguan revolution will take. Neither the agrarian reform programme nor the Sandinista revolutionary process as a whole have yet assumed their definitive character.

Notes

1. Today, the state sector controls 21 per cent of agricultural production and 37 per cent of all productive activities (agriculture, industry, mining, etc.). Large private producers account for 25 per cent of production, while small and medium entrepreneurs account for 38 per cent (*Barricada*, 28 November 1983).

2. The mining enclave was more important in the first half of this century. After reaching its most important moment in the early 1940s, it fell into substantial decline thereafter. P. Belli, 'Prolegómenas para una historia económica de Nicaragua', *Revista del Pensamiento Centroamericano*, no. 146 (January–March 1975), p. 270.

3. The lower strata of the rural bourgeoisie and the rich peasantry – which we locate within the category of the medium-sized, multi-family fincas – include, in contrast with El Salvador, those who produce crops for the domestic market as well as for export.

4. In Honduras, 8 per cent of the fincas that produce bananas account for 97 per cent of production, and 25 per cent of the added value of the whole agricultural sector. J. Schatan, 'Situación de la Agroindustria en Centro-américa', a CEPAL internal document (Mexico City, 1983), pp. 44–6.

5. For 1975, it is estimated that production was concentrated in 230 producers (H. Pizarro, 'Los Proyectos Economicos de la Burguesia Guate-malteca', *Revista Centroamericana de Economia*, nos. 5–6 (May–December 1981) and in 1979–80, 142 enterprises having more than 450 hectares produced 76 per cent of the raw cotton in the country. Schatan, 'Situacion de la Agroindustria', p. 76.

6. E. Baumeister, 'Notas para la discusión de la cuestion agraria en Nicaragua', paper presented to the third Congress of the Nicaraguan Association of Social Sciences (Managua, 1982), p. 25.

7. Ibid., pp. 35–40.

8. E. Calcagano, 'Informe sobre las inversiones directas extranjeras en América Latina', *Cuadernos de CEPAL*, no. 33 (Santiago, 1980), p. 31.

9. Ibid.

10. CIERA, *Apuntes sobre Reforma Agraria* (1981).

11. At the beginning of 1981, estimates indicate that the productivity of agricultural labour had declined by 30 per cent in relation to the pre-revolutionary period (CIERA, *Productividad de Trabajo en la Agricultura*, 1981). However, during 1982 and 1983, there was a pronounced increase in labour productivity within the agricultural sector.

12. It is obvious that the leaders of the Sandinista revolution are aware of the history of democratic agrarian reforms in Latin America and the socialist countries, particularly the difficulties involved in making a transition from forms of production based on small parcels (resulting from the subdivision of large estates) to more co-operative forms of production.

13. According to the Co-operative Census of 1982, there are some 8,000 peasants organized into Sandinista Agricultural Co-operatives (CASs), who plant 5.5 per cent of the country's agricultural area. Eighty per cent of their land has come from the state, either as allocations from the agrarian reform programme or land given to them from the APP.

14. Junta de Gobierno de Reconstrucción Nacional (JGRN), 'Programa del Gobierno de Reconstrucción Nacional' (1979, mimeo), p. 8.

15. This was the product of the local version of the 'green revolution', which started in the mid 1960s with the active participation of the Somoza family who were assisted by exiled Cuban technicians. Today, this sector is the most technically advanced sector in Nicaraguan agriculture.

16. Economic Commission for Latin America (CEPAL), *Tenencia de la Terra y Desarrollo Rural en Centro América* (1976), p. 39.

17. Probably an exact calculation which would include a more precise measurement of the value added by agro-industrial processing to the agricultural production of the private producers, plus the importance of mechanization services provided by the state to the private sector (basically the peasants), would increase the state's share of the gross domestic product (GDP). It is also worth remembering that national accounting considers production for self-consumption (important in the peasant sector and also in some activities within the entrepreneurial sector) as being part of the GDP. As a consequence, the weight of the state, seen in relation to the commercial producers, is actually above 20 per cent.

18. Clive Thomas, *Dependence and Transformation: The Economics of the Transition to Socialism* (New York: Monthly Review Press, 1974), p. 162.

19. As of 19 July 1982, the lands expropriated under the Agrarian Reform Law were distributed according to the following reasons for *afectación* (expropriation): 6 per cent because of 'precariousness' (or sharecropping and *colonato*); 7.2 per cent because of 'rentism' (land leasing); 62.5 per cent because of 'idleness'; and 24.3 per cent because of 'abandonment'. (PROCAMPO, MIDINRA). 1983 was a difficult year in the struggle against both the internal and external counter-revolution, but the profile of *afectaciones* continued to be very moderate. Lands expropriated because of abandonment accounted for 12 per cent of the total expropriations; those expropriated because of idleness accounted for 67 per cent and the remainder were expropriated because of rentism and precariousness. CIERA, *Tres Años de Reforma Agraria y la Gestión Económica del Sector Agropecuaria* (1984), p. 14.

20. According to the Agricultural Census of 1971 – the last available – the national average was 0.7 heads per manzana. P. Warken, *The Agricultural Development of Nicaragua* (University of Missouri, 1975), p. 36.

21. According to the opinion of the officials in charge of *afectaciones*, the criterion of deficient exploitation has prevailed over that of idleness, which reinforces the image of expropriation being directed at the least developed estates.

22. J. Wheelock, 'Discurso en el En Cuentro Continental Sobre Reforma Agraria y Movimientos Campesinos' (Managua, December 1981).

23. In 1976, 219 tractors were imported, in 1977 312, 170 in 1978, 142 in 1979, 318 in 1980, and 422 in 1981. With regard to combines, only one was imported in 1976, 12 in 1977, 17 in 1978, 3 in 1979, 151 in 1980 and 128 in 1981 (based on information from MIDINRA). The majority of the recent imports were for state enterprises and co-operatives.

24. In 1977–8, the banking system granted loans to the producers of approximately one third of the agricultural area of the country, the rest financed their activities with their own resources or with loans from intermediaries who imposed upon them usurious conditions. Since the triumph, the percentage of financed area fluctuates between two-thirds and three-quarters of the total agricultural area. Present interest rates are clearly subsidized by the state, the highest rate being 17 per cent annually even though the inflation rate has never

been less than 25 per cent annually and is almost 200 per cent now. CIERA, *Análisis del Censo Cooperativo* (1984).

25. CIERA, *Evolución y Situación de la Producción Algondonera* (1983), p. 73.

26. CIERA, *Análisis del Censo*.

27. CIERA, *Tres Años de Reforma Agraria*, p. 11.

28. E. Baumeister, 'Capitalismo agrario, revolución y reforma agraria en Nicaragua: Un balance provisional', paper presented to the Tenth World Congress of Sociology, Mexico City (1982, mimeo).

29. CIERA, *Mano de Obra Estacional en Cafe y Algodón* (1982).

30. The co-operative sector as a whole encompasses approximately 55 per cent of the producers in Nicaragua (CIERA, *Análisis del Censo*, p. 5).

31. It is worth noting that during the final months of 1983, when the possibilities of a US invasion were real, the cotton-growers of Chinandega and a significant portion of the large coffee-growers from Matagalpa issued statements that they were strongly opposed to a North American invasion (*Barricada*, 23 January 1984).

3 The Economic Transformation and Industrial Development of Nicaragua

Richard L. Harris

Introduction

This essay provides an overview of revolutionary Nicaragua's economy. It seeks to provide a clear picture of the economic transformations that have taken place in Nicaragua as a result of the revolution, as well as the conditions affecting the country's industrial development. Within this focus, the obstacles that limit the country's economic development will be examined, as well as the prospects for the socialist transformation of Nicaraguan society.

Despite the voluminous literature on the underdevelopment and development of Third World countries, there has been surprisingly little attention given to the analysis of the industrial development of small dependent underdeveloped societies such as Nicaragua.[1] This would appear to be the result of certain biases and assumptions underlying current theory and development policy.

The conventional wisdom on development tends to be based upon assumptions (for example, about economies of scale, demand and market size, optimum output, etc.) that preclude the possibility of small underdeveloped economies undergoing a process of self-directed and integrated industrialization.[2] These assumptions are uncritically accepted by many socialist as well as non-socialist economists. However, there are those who reject these assumptions and argue that the autonomous industrial transformation of small underdeveloped societies is indeed possible.[3]

This alternative perspective is based upon the assumption that the population's basic needs for food, clothing, housing, etc., provide sufficient demand to justify the establishment of a wide variety of local industries that produce basic consumer goods. Therefore, the autonomous and integrated industrial development of small dependent underdeveloped countries is feasible and can be achieved, provided that they follow a development strategy based upon the planned convergence of their domestic resource use with their domestic needs, the development of an indigenous industrial technology, the reorientation of agriculture away from agro-exports to the production of basic foods and the primary inputs for domestic industries, the establishment of inter-sectoral linkages between the different sectors of their economies, the introduction of comprehensive economic planning, and the reinsertion of these economies into the international market on the basis of the establishment of complementary economic relations with other Third World countries as well as the socialist economies.

We shall apply this perspective to our analysis of the economic transformations that have taken place in Nicaragua since the revolutionary triumph in July 1979. It will serve as the underlying theoretical framework for our examination of the country's new mixed economy and the prospects for its industrial development.

We begin with a brief examination of Nicaragua's pre-revolutionary economic development. This will be followed by an analysis of the transformations in the economy which have taken place since the revolutionary triumph in 1979. Particular attention will be given to the country's industrial development in these two periods and to the prospects for the accelerated industrialization of the economy in the near future. We will conclude with a discussion of the structural obstacles which presently limit Nicaragua's economic transformation and industrial development.

Nicaragua's Economic Development Prior to the Revolution

Like most small underdeveloped countries, Nicaragua's economic development has been based on agro-exports. As a result, the country's economy has been extremely vulnerable to the price fluctuations of its export products on the world market. This has resulted in trade deficits and balance of payments problems as the prices of Nicaragua's agro-exports have deteriorated and the prices of the manufactured goods it imports have increased. The country's overspecialization in agro-exports has also tended to retard and deform the industrialization of its economy. Instead of experiencing a process of increasing industrial transformation of its basic products, the country has experienced a type of crypto-industrialization based on small light industries that use imported inputs, imported machinery and very few indigenous resources. This type of limited industrialization has served to make Nicaragua quite vulnerable to the vagaries of the international market, contributed to its trade deficits, and left the country with a small and fragile manufacturing sector incapable of promoting the industrial transformation of the rest of the economy.

At the beginning of the 1950s, Nicaragua's economy was based fundamentally on the export of coffee and gold. The development of the country's economic infrastructure of roads, energy, ports, etc. was minimal. The greatest part of the population, more than 75 per cent,

37

lived in the rural areas, and more than 25 per cent of the national income was in the hands of less than 1 per cent of the population.[4]

During the 1950s, the country experienced a relatively high rate of economic growth centred on the boom in world demand for cotton. Nicaragua became a major cotton producer and exporter during this period, and by the mid-1960s, Nicaragua's cotton yields reached the highest in the world – averaging an increase of 33 per cent per annum.[5] During this period the country also began to export sugar, seafood and beef. The diversification and boom of its agro-exports, however, took place at the expense of the reduced production of basic food crops and the displacement of the peasants who produced them. Declining production of the major food crops – corn, rice and beans – led Nicaragua to begin importing food in 1955.[6]

Starting in the 1960s – and largely as a result of the formation of the Central American Common Market – Nicaragua experienced a limited amount of industrial development. But the problem with this industrial growth was that it was based on a model of development which only served to reinforce the imbalanced and externally dependent character of the economy.

The nature of this model is revealed in the report of the mission which the World Bank sent to Nicaragua in 1952 to investigate the country's potential for economic development. First of all, the mission took as an unquestioned premise that Nicaragua would 'continue to be a predominantly agricultural country for the foreseeable future', and that its 'industrial development must necessarily be subordinate to, and dependent on, its agricultural development'.[7] On the basis of this premise, they recommended the growth of small industries centred around the processing of domestic agricultural materials. Among the factors which the World Bank mission felt favoured the industrial development of the country, they gave importance to the concentration of income in the hands of a relatively small portion of the population:

> The concentration of income in the hands of a relatively small part of the population should be a favorable basis for increased industrial production through private capital formation.[8]

In addition, the mission recommended that the government assist the development of industry by enacting laws that would provide for:

1) Free imports of original production machinery and equipment for new industries for a period of five years.
2) Free imports by all industries of raw materials which do not exist in Nicaragua.
3) Tax-free privileges for new industries for a period of up to five years after original construction has been completed.
4) Equal rights for foreign and domestic capital, and a guarantee that profits may be freely transferred into foreign exchange.[9]

These passages and others throughout the mission's report give clear evidence of the World Bank's conception of how industrial development should and can take place in an underdeveloped economy such as Nicaragua. The country's small capitalist class, in association with foreign capital, was expected to invest in the limited industrial development of the country, and the government was expected to provide the proper incentives to encourage this.

This model of industrial development was in fact subsequently incorporated into the plans and programmes of the Central American Common Market, which gave impetus to the type of deformed industrialization experienced by Nicaragua and the rest of the Central American countries during the 1960s and 1970s.

In Nicaragua's case, the larger markets that were expected to result from this effort at regional economic integration induced a limited amount of investment in the establishment of light industries involved in the production of consumer and intermediate products for both the domestic market and for export to other Central American countries. Most of these industries were set up with second-hand machinery imported from the United States, Europe or Japan. In addition to processed foods, leather goods, textiles and furniture – which were already being manufactured largely on an artisan basis in Nicaragua – the main areas of investment were in chemicals, construction materials and metal products. In the case of the latter, most of these industries were set up to assemble or process imported inputs.[10]

Although ostensibly designed to substitute locally manufactured products for imported products, this process of limited industrialization failed to produce an authentic process of import substitution. Nor did it result in any significant development of basic industries such as metallurgy, paper, machine-building, etc., which would have contributed to the integrated industrial development of the economy. It also *increased* Nicaragua's dependence upon imported goods, raw materials and machinery. For example, one study indicates that as of 1974, 96 per cent of the inputs used in the manufacture of rubber products, 95 per cent in electrical appliances, 88 per cent in printing and publishing, 85 per cent in metal products and 65 per cent in chemical products were imported.[11]

The negative effects of this kind of industrialization on Nicaragua and the other Central American countries are recognized in a recent report by the UN's Economic Commission for Latin America, which states that:

> due to the lack of a more vertically integrated industrial development, the changes in the composition of imports involved in actuality a more vulnerable balance of payments due to the concentration on foreign sources of supply in raw materials, parts and components, and in equipment and machinery.[12]

Since the Commission was one of the most important forces behind the formation of the Central American Common Market and the strategy of limited industrialization which was encouraged within the Common Market countries during the 1960s and 1970s, it is all the more significant that the Commission now recognizes that the industrialization which Nicaragua and the other Central American countries experienced during this period not only failed to contribute to the balanced development of their economies, but also served to aggravate their trade imbalance and external indebtedness.

Moreover, Nicaragua's economic growth during the decades preceding the revolution was not accompanied by a comparable degree of social development. Life expectancy during the mid-1970s was one of the lowest in Latin America, nearly two-thirds of the rural population over ten years of age were illiterate, and a 1973 survey found that three-fifths of the rural population had a deficient food intake.[13] And even though the total workforce in manufacturing, construction and services increased significantly between 1960 and 1979, nearly half of the economically active population (EAP) was still engaged in agriculture by the end of the 1970s. Thus, in 1979, the EAP was estimated at approximately 800,000, with some 354,000 persons engaged in agriculture, 83,000 in manufacturing, 34,000 in construction, 95,000 in commerce and 159,000 in services.[14]

By the late 1970s, inflationary pressures from the international market, fluctuations in the prices of Nicaragua's basic agro-exports and the country's growing foreign debt brought its fragile industrial development to a near standstill. Moreover, during the revolutionary insurrection, investments were halted, there was a massive flight of capital from the country, many factories were damaged or destroyed, the flow of imported inputs was disrupted and most of the factories owned by Somoza's supporters were left abandoned and without funds. In the countryside, many fields were left unplanted, herds of cattle were slaughtered and the general disorganization of the agricultural sector left the country with an immediate food shortage. The disruption of agriculture also meant that the country experienced a serious foreign exchange problem, since the level of export earnings was substantially lower than in previous years.[15]

According to United Nations' estimates at the time, direct damage to the economy was in the order of $480 million dollars and at least $1.5 billion dollars in capital fled the country.[16] The financial system was bankrupt and the country faced an enormous foreign debt. The Somoza regime and its supporters had amassed an external debt of $1.65 billion dollars, mostly with US commercial banks in the form of short-term credits. This amount was equivalent to about $4,000 dollars per family and larger than the entire national income.[17]

Revolutionary Nicaragua's Mixed Economy

The new revolutionary government that took power on 19 July 1979 had immediately to face the tasks of reactivating the war-damaged economy and reconstructing the country. One of the new government's first acts was the confiscation of the properties and enterprises that had formerly belonged to Somoza and his closest followers. Most of these had been abandoned, their records destroyed and their funds carried off by their former owners. The new government also took over control of the bankrupt financial system, the insurance companies, foreign trade and the country's run-down mining sector. These confiscated properties and holdings formed the bulk of the new state sector of the economy, called the Area de Propiedad del Pueblo (Area of People's Property or APP). Within this new state sector, the agricultural holdings were placed under the supervision of the new Instituto Nicaragüense de Reforma Agraria (Nicaraguan Institute of Agrarian Reform or INRA), while most of the confiscated enterprises involving some form of manufacturing were by 1980 placed under the new Corporación Industrial del Pueblo (People's Industrial Corporation or COIP).[18]

The revolutionary government made *no* attempt to socialize the entire productive process or eliminate private capital. On the contrary, the government offered guarantees to the private sector that private property would be respected and that private enterprises would be encouraged to play a major role in the reactivation and development of the economy. Since the outset of the revolutionary regime, the political leadership has repeatedly made it clear that the elimination of private enterprise and an extensive socialization of the means of production are not objectives of the Sandinista revolution. This is reflected in the following statement by Comandante Jaime Wheelock, one of the architects of the country's economic strategy:

> It is important to understand that the socialist model is a solution for contradictions that only exist in developed capitalist countries. Now, for a series of reasons, many of them political, and others having to do with hunger and desperation, certain peoples have made a revolution in the worst conditions of social development . . . This is our case. Even though we have socialist principles, we cannot effect the transformation of our society by socializing all the means of production. This would not lead to socialism, rather, on the contrary, it could lead to the destruction and disarticulation of our society.[19]

In other words, the Sandinista model of social transformation and economic development is based on the premise that it is not possible to socialize all the means of production in an underdeveloped country such as Nicaragua. Therefore, it is necessary to enlist the co-operation of private enterprise in the development of a 'mixed economy' in which

Table 3.1   Structure of Property in Nicaragua 1977, 1980, 1982 (as percentage of GDP)

Sector	1977	1980	1982
Agriculture:[a]	22	22	24
APP	(—)	(14)	(21)
Private (large and medium)	(77)	(63)	(54)
Small producers	(23)	(23)	(25)
Manufacturing:	22	25	24
APP	(—)	(25)	(31)
Private (large and medium)	(85)	(60)	(54)
Small proprietors and artisans	(15)	(15)	(15)
Other material production:[b]	9	7	3
APP and state[c]	(10)	(80)	(90)
Private (large and medium)	(75)	(5)	(5)
Small producers	(15)	(15)	(5)
Government:[d]	5	10	9
Commerce and services:[e]	42	36	40
APP and state[f]	(10)	(25)	(38)
Private (large and medium)	(60)	(25)	(12)
Small-scale trade and services	(30)	(50)	(50)
Total of GDP	100	100	100
APP and state	(11)	(34)	(39)
Private (large and medium)	(67)	(38)	(31)
Small-scale prod. and services	(22)	(28)	(30)
Total GDP[g]	*29,353*	*21,892*	*23,420*

[a] Includes sub-sectors, Agriculture, Livestock, Forestry, Hunting and Fishing.

[b] Construction and Mining.

[c] Area of People's Property (APP) did not exist in 1977. Nevertheless, the Somoza Government invested in construction through the state.

[d] By definition, 100 per cent of the property in this sector belongs to the state.

[e] Includes transportation and communications, banks and insurance, electricity and water, real estate, and other services.

[f] In basic services, the type of public enterprises which existed under Somoza were not like those in the APP.

[g] In millions of 1980 cordobas.

Source: Economic Commission for Latin America (ECLA), Centro de Investigaciones y Estudios para la Reforma Agraria (CIERA), Ministry of Planning (MIPLAN).

Compilation: Pensamiento Proprio Collective. (Instituto Nicaragüense de Investigación Económica y Social, Managua).

various forms of property coexist – state, co-operative, small private, medium private and large private.

Table 3.1 reveals the extent to which the structure of property has changed in Nicaragua since the revolution. This chart permits a comparison of the proportion of the gross domestic product (GDP) generated by the following three main categories of property: state property or the APP, large private enterprise (which includes medium as well as large producers) and small private enterprise (which includes co-operatives as well as small individual producers). By comparing the figures for 1977 (the best year economically prior to the revolution) with 1982 (the most recent year for which reliable data are available), it is possible to see how much the different forms of property have changed in terms of their share of the GDP. For example, in 1977 the state sector generated only 11 per cent of the GDP, while large private enterprise produced 67 per cent of the GDP. However, by 1982, and as a consequence of the revolution, the state sector had increased its share of the GDP to 39 per cent while large private enterprise's share of the GDP had declined to 31 per cent. During this same period, small producers, largely as a result of the benefits of the revolutionary government's economic policies, increased their proportion of the GDP from 22 per cent to 30 per cent.

As Table 3.1 indicates, the state sector as of 1982 accounted for 21 per cent of the GDP in agriculture, 31 per cent in manufacturing, 90 per cent in mining and construction and 38 per cent in services and commerce. Large private producers continue to predominate in agriculture and manufacturing, where they account for *over half of the GDP* in both of these sectors. Finally, small private producers generate half of the GDP in commerce and services as well as one-quarter of the GDP in agriculture.

If large, medium and small producers are combined, the private sector today accounts for approximately 60 per cent of the GDP. And in agriculture and manufacturing – the two main productive sectors of the economy – private producers generate 79 per cent and 69 per cent respectively of the GDP. Thus, the importance of private producers in revolutionary Nicaragua's mixed economy is much greater than is generally considered to be the case outside of the country. Actually, the structure of property in Nicaragua is not very different from that in various countries of Latin America (for example, the Dominican Republic). In fact, revolutionary Nicaragua has a smaller state sector than Peru did under the reformist military regime of General Velasco, Argentina under the populist regime of Perón or Chile under Allende.[20]

It is important to note the differences that exist within Nicaragua's private sector. The most important distinction is that between large, medium and small producers. In Nicaragua, the large producer is the cotton-grower who cultivates more than 500 manzanas (1 manzana =

1.72 acres) of land, the coffee-grower with more than 65 manzanas of coffee, the rancher with more than 1,000 manzanas dedicated to livestock and the manufacturer who has more than 100 workers. Medium producers are agriculturists who possess from 50 to 500 manzanas of cotton or food crops, ranchers with 200 to 1,000 manzanas dedicated to livestock, finca (estate) owners with 15 to 65 manzanas of coffee or manufacturers who employ between 30 and 100 workers. Finally, small producers are all those members of the economically active population (EAP) who possess their own means of production but fall below the minimums given above for medium producers.[21]

Large private producers today (see Table 3.2) control 25 per cent of the value of all material production, medium private producers 18 per cent and the small private producers 20 per cent. However, the importance of these three categories of private producers varies considerably between the different sectors of production. For example, the large private producers generate 37.3 per cent of the value of production in export agriculture, *63.9 per cent in agro-industry* and 32.5 per cent in manufacturing. The medium private producers account for 21.7 per cent of the value of production in export agriculture, 30.4 per cent in livestock and 22 per cent in manufacturing. Small private producers predominate in the production of basic food crops for the internal market (61.5 per cent), and are important in livestock (33.9 per cent) as well as fishing (28.1 per cent).

If agro-export production, agro-industry, cattle-ranching and agricultural production for the internal market are combined, the APP or state sector produces only about one-fifth of the value of all agricultural production. Large private capital, the grand bourgeoisie, produces about one-quarter of the value of production, and the medium private producers slightly less than one-fifth. However, small private producers, mainly peasants, produce more than one-third of the total value of production in agriculture.

Within this heterogeneous structure, what is most important in terms of the prospects for industrializing Nicaragua's agricultural production is the fact that most agro-industry is controlled by large private capital. Even though the state sector has increased its influence to the point that it now produces over one-quarter of the value of agro-industrial production, large private producers still control nearly two-thirds of the value of production. In other words, they own most of Nicaragua's coffee mills, cotton mills and slaughter-houses.[22]

The structure of ownership in the manufacturing sector also reflects the importance of private enterprise in revolutionary Nicaragua's mixed economy. The state industries in the APP generate approximately the same total value of production in manufacturing (31.3 per cent) as the large private producers (32.5 per cent). However, medium and small private producers account for another 34.2 per cent of the value of production. In other words, over two-thirds of the value of production in

Table 3.2 Weight of the Different Forms of Property by Economic Sector (Percentage of Total Value of Production) (1982)

Sectors	APP*	Large Private	Medium Private	Small Private	Total
Export Agriculture	24.0	37.3	21.7	17.0	100
Agriculture for Internal Market	15.7	14.7	8.1	61.5	100
Livestock	24.7	11.0	30.4	33.9	100
Agroindustry	28.0	63.9	5.7	2.4	100
Fishing	71.9	—	—	28.1	100
Manufacturing	31.3	32.5	22.0	14.2	100
Mining, energy and water	100.0	—	—	—	100
Total (Productive Sectors)	37	25	18	20	100

Source: MIDINRA, Ministry of Industry, and MIPLAN (*Barricada*, November 28, 1983).

* Area of People's Property

manufacturing is generated by private producers. This means that the development of this sector of the economy, under present circumstances, cannot take place without the co-operation of the private producers.

Nicaragua's large private producers can be divided into three subgroupings.[23] The first group is composed of what are referred to as the 'patriotic bourgeoisie'. They have invested and participated actively in the new mixed economy – either because of personal convictions or because they support the Sandinista regime politically. The second group, which is probably the most numerous, is composed of capitalists who are undecided about whether they should participate actively in the mixed economy. They tend to maintain a minimum level of production. Finally, the third group are opposed to the Sandinista regime and can be considered counter-revolutionary. They are the most politicized and control the Consejo Superior de la Empresa Privada (Supreme Council of Private Enterprise, COSEP). This group has political connections with the Reagan administration and with conservative economic and political forces throughout Central America. As Table 3.3 reveals, the large or grand bourgeoisie in Nicaragua numbers slightly over 2,000 persons, and the middle bourgeoisie around 40,000 persons.

Table 3.3 on the class composition of the labour force, despite its limitations and imprecision, is a useful indicator of the relative importance of the different classes and form of property in revolutionary Nicaragua's mixed economy. Although the data presented in this chart are based on 1980 estimates, they generally represent the current situation, and reveal that nearly half of Nicaragua's economically active population of 908,000 persons in 1980 were involved in agriculture and that almost one-quarter of the EAP possessed their own means of production. In terms of the distribution between state and private sectors, the data for 1980 indicate that somewhat *less than one-quarter of the total* labour force were employed by the state (206,300 persons). Thus, the private sector is clearly the main employer in Nicaragua.

What is perhaps most significant in terms of the class structure of Nicaragua is the fact that nearly 40 per cent of the EAP in agriculture and almost one-quarter of the non-agricultural EAP possess their own means of production. What these statistics reveal is the fact that the country's class structure is characterized by a large number of small producers.

In contrast, Nicaragua's proletariat of permanent wage-earners represents only 20 per cent of the total EAP. The largest sector of this class are the urban wage-earners (153,500), whereas the agricultural proletariat is quite small – about 28,000 in 1980. However, nearly 50 per cent of the EAP fall within either the *semi-proletariat* (25.2 per cent of the EAP) or the *sub-proletariat* (21.2 per cent of the EAP). The first of these two categories, the semi-proletariat, consists of Nicaragua's numerous

Table 3.3   1980 Labour Force According to Social Class and Property Structure in Nicaragua (in thousands of persons and percentages)

	APP	LMP	SPP	Total	%
			EAP in agriculture		
Property-owners[a]	—	40.3	125.9	166.2	39.5
Large bourgeoisie[b]	—	1.9	—	1.9	0.4
Middle bourgeoisie[c]	—	38.4	—	38.4	9.1
Middle peasants[d]	—	—	54.5	54.5	13.0
Propertied petty bourgeoisie[e]	—	—	71.4	71.4	17.0
Non-property owners[f]	78.0	101.0	74.8	253.8	60.5
Salaried petty bourgeoisie[g]	2.0	2.0	—	4.0	1.0
Proletariat[h]	8.0	20.0	—	28.0	6.7
Semi-proletariat[i]	68.0	79.0	2.3	149.3	35.5
Sub-proletariat[j]	—	—	72.5	72.5	17.3
Total EAP[k]	78.0	141.3	200.7	420.0	100.0
Percentages	18.6	33.6	47.8	100.0	—
Total GDP[l]	693	3117	1137	4947	22.6
Percentages[m]	14.0	63.0	23.0	100.0	—
GDP per capita[n]	888	22059	5665	11778	—
Index[o]	3.7	91.5	23.5	48.9	—

[a] Those who possess means of production.

[b] Latifundio owners and the Large Agrarian Bourgeoisie defined as those with more than 500 manzanas dedicated to internal consumption crops, or with more than 65 manzanas of coffee, or more than 200 manzanas of cotton, or more than 1,000 manzanas of cattle pasture, with an average of 912 head of cattle. In non-agricultural sectors, this refers to owners of large industrial, commercial and service enterprises which employ more than 100 workers.

[c] Those who possess between 50 and 500 manzanas of crops for internal consumption, 15 to 65 manzanas of coffee, or 50 to 200 manzanas of cotton, or 200 to 1,000 manzanas dedicated to cattle-ranching, with an average of 311 head of cattle. In non-agricultural sectors, this refers to medium-sized commercial and service enterprises.

[d] Those who possess between 10 and 50 manzanas of crops for internal consumption, or 5 to 15 manzanas of coffee, or 5 to 50 manzanas of cotton, or 20 to 200 manzanas dedicated to cattle-ranching, with an average of 72 head of cattle.

[e] In agriculture, non-remunerated family workers with agricultural property corresponding to category d above. In non-agricultural sectors, this refers to small industry, minor commerce and independent professionals.

[f] Those who do not possess means of production.

Table continues overleaf

47

Table 3.3—*cont.*

| EAP in non-agricultural sectors | | | | | EAP Total | | | | |
APP	LMP	SPP	Total	%	APP	LMP	SPP	Total	%
—	1.7	45.1	46.8	9.6	—	42.0	171.0	213.0	23.5
—	0.3	—	0.3	0.1	—	2.2	—	2.2	0.2
—	1.4	—	1.4	0.3	—	39.8	—	39.8	4.4
—	—	—	—	—	—	—	54.5	54.5	6.1
—	—	45.1	45.1	9.2	—	—	116.5	116.5	12.8
128.3	112.8	200.1	441.2	90.4	206.3	213.8	274.9	695.0	76.5
63.2	24.4	—	87.6	18.0	65.2	26.4	—	91.6	10.1
65.1	88.4	—	153.5	31.4	73.1	108.4	—	181.5	20.0
—	—	79.7	79.7	16.3	68.0	79.0	82.0	229.0	25.2
—	—	120.4	120.4	24.7	—	—	192.9	192.9	21.2
128.3	114.5	245.2	488.0	100.0	206.3	255.8	445.9	908.0	100.0
26.3	23.5	50.2	100.0	—	22.7	28.0	49.3	100.0	—
6750	5202	4993	16945	77.4	7443	8319	6130	21892	100.0
39.0	31.0	30.0	100.0	—	34.0	38.0	28.0	100.0	—
52611	46117	20223	34723	—	36131	32752	13683	24110	—
218.2	191.3	83.9	144.0	—	149.9	135.8	56.8	100.0	—

[g] Administrators and technicians in productive, commercial and service sectors, including state technicians with a monthly income above 1,250 cordobas in 1980.

[h] Agricultural workers with permanent employment, as well as salaried workers in non-agricultural material production, government, commerce and services.

[i] Poor peasants who possess between 0 and 10 manzanas of land dedicated to internal consumption crops, or 0 to 5 manzanas of coffee, or 0 to 5 manzanas of cotton, or 0 to 20 manzanas dedicated to cattle pasture, with an average of 17 head of cattle. In the non-agricultural sectors, this refers to self-employed workers and artisans.

[j] In agriculture, landless seasonal labourers and the unemployed. In non-agricultural sectors, this includes domestic workers and the unemployed.

[k] The economically active population (EAP) refers to those who are either working or actively seeking employment, usually including those between 15 and 64 years of age.

[l] The gross domestic product in millions of cordobas. Information taken from Table 3.2.

[m] The percentage which each form of property contributes to the GDP.

Table 3.3—*cont.*

[n] GDP divided by the number of workers from each form of property, expressed in cordobas.

[o] The index is based on the average per worker in the generation of the GDP.

APP = Area of People's Property.
LMP = Large and medium private producers.
SPP = Small private producers and co-operatives.

Sources: CIERA, MIPLAN, Instituto Nicaragüense de Estadisticas y Censos (INEC) and Programa Regional de Empleo para América Latina y el Caribe (PREALC).

Compilation: *Pensamiento Proprio* Collective. (Instituto Nicaragüense de Investigación Económica y Social, Managua.)

self-employed artisans as well as poor peasants who seek occasional wage-earning employment in order to survive. The second category, the sub-proletariat, consists of the country's large number of landless seasonal workers in agriculture, domestic workers, and the unemployed 'marginal population' in the urban and rural areas.

It is important to note the class composition of the labour force employed by the state sector (the APP). Approximately one-third of the state labour force is composed of petty bourgeois administrators and technicians, another one-third are skilled and unskilled workers, and the final third are semi-proletarianized rural workers. In contrast, the labour force employed by large and medium private producers contains a smaller proportion of petty bourgeois administrators and technicians (about 26,400 persons or 12 per cent of the total workforce in 1980), and a larger proportion of skilled and unskilled workers (108,400 or 51 per cent), and proportionally more semi-proletarianized rural workers (79,000 or 37 per cent). Finally, small private producers employ a large portion of the semi-proletariat and serve as the only source of employment for the country's large sub-proletariat of seasonal rural labourers, urban domestic workers and the unemployed rural and urban population.

Based on this rough sketch of the labour force and its relationship to the class structure of Nicaragua, we can now turn to a more detailed analysis of the mixed economy. We start by comparing the structure of the gross domestic product before and after the establishment of the revolutionary regime. Table 3.4 reveals that the GDP was larger in 1977 than in 1982 (the most recent year for which reliable figures are available). This is because Nicaragua is still suffering the consequences of the revolutionary insurrection as well as the more recent effects of the Reagan administration's undeclared war on the revolutionary regime. The decapitalization of the economy has been a particularly acute

Table 3.4 Composition of GDP – 1972, 1977, 1982 (in percentages)

Sector	1972	1977	1982
Gross domestic product:[a]	100	100	100
Agriculture	24	22	24
Mining and construction	7	9	3
Manufacturing	22	22	24
Basic services[b]	8	7	8
Commerce	22	20	19
Other[c]	17	20	22
Gross domestic product:[d]	100	100	100
Public consumption	7	8	25
Private consumption	74	73	65
Essential[e]	0	35	43
Non-essential	0	38	22
Public investment	6	11	14
Private investment	8	11	2
Change in inventory	– 2	1	2
Exports of goods and services	29	23	22
Imports of goods and services	22	27	30
Trade balance[f]	7	– 4	– 8
Total GDP[g]	*21,211*	*29,353*	*23,420*

[a] GDP by *supply* side.

[b] Includes transportation, communication, electricity and running water.

[c] Includes social services, general government, financial institutions and real estate.

[d] GDP by *demand* side.

[e] Consumption of goods and services considered necessary within the average household.

[f] The difference between exports and imports of *goods and services* during one year.

[g] Total GDP expressed in millions of 1980 cordobas.

Source: Economic Commission for Latin America (ECLA).

Compilation: *Pensamiento Proprio* Collective (INIES).

problem, and recent figures indicate that the flight of private capital out of the country has amounted to almost US $3 billion, an amount larger than the current GDP of the country.[24]

In terms of the composition of the GDP, it appears that on the supply side of the picture, today as ten years ago, approximately one-quarter of the GDP is produced by agriculture, and about the same proportion by manufacturing. Basic services such as transportation and communications have remained about the same, while commerce and mining have declined slightly. However, social services and general government have increased somewhat in importance.

On the demand side, some important changes have been achieved by the revolution in terms of popular consumption. As Table 3.4 indicates, private consumption in general has declined since the revolution, while public consumption (general government, social services, etc.) has increased from 8 per cent of the GDP in 1977 to 25 per cent in 1982. Private basic consumption (food, clothing, basic services, etc.) has also increased considerably, from 35 per cent of the GDP in 1977 to 43 per cent in 1982. Meanwhile, private consumption of non-essential goods (e.g. durable goods such as appliances, automobiles, etc.) has declined from 38 per cent to 22 per cent of the GDP. What this reflects is the revolutionary government's relatively successful efforts to restrict the consumption of non-essential goods and increase popular consumption of basic goods and public services.

The revolutionary regime has pursued a strategy of restricting the importation of non-essential goods (largely consumed by the upper classes) while rationing and subsidizing basic goods in order to increase their consumption by the lower classes. The government has also tried to restrict wage and salary increases. The reasoning behind this strategy is explained by E.V.K. Fitzgerald, one of the economic advisers to the government:

> The lesson of the Chilean experience, and to a certain extent in Cuba as well, was that nominal salary increases only served to increase the prices of food to the disadvantage of the popular classes. Therefore, in Nicaragua it was decided that the only way to produce changes in the economy which would improve the distribution of incomes was through increasing the supply of wage goods.[25]

In other words, instead of redistributing income through increasing the salaries and wages of the popular classes, the revolutionary government has sought to redistribute income through policies that result in the increased consumption of basic goods by these classes.

Table 3.4 also reveals that public investment since the revolution has increased to 14 per cent, while private investment has declined from 11 per cent of the GDP in 1977 to only 2 per cent in 1982. What this indicates is the private sector's reluctance to invest capital in the

51

development of the new mixed economy. According to representatives of the private sector, their reluctance to invest in the economy is due both to the government's failure to give them adequate guarantees (that their property and profits will not be taken away from them) and to government restrictions on foreign exchange, credits and imports.[26] Government officials reply that the reluctance of the private sector to invest in the economy is due largely to political motives and the efforts of the counter-revolutionary elements within this sector to sabotage the economic policies of the revolutionary regime.

The political opposition of a sizeable proportion of the private sector to the Sandinista regime, and to its mixed economy model, has seriously affected the economic recovery of the country. Nowhere has this been more obvious than in the industrial sector. In a confidential discussion paper written in 1982, a World Bank team sent to Nicaragua reported that:

> The recovery of industrial production has been hampered by the reluctance of the private sector to expand production and to invest in the absence of sufficient guarantees. Given its predominant participation in the productive process, the private sector will largely determine the pace and extent of economic recovery through its investment decisions.[27]

As observed by the World Bank team, the weak recovery of industrial production and the economy as a whole is largely due to the private sector's failure to expand production and invest in the development of the country.

The same report blames this situation on the revolutionary government's failure to set 'clear and consistent rules of the game' for the private sector, and its failure to provide 'an effective system of guarantees and long-term incentives'.[28] Because of the government's failure to follow the Bank's recommendations on setting acceptable rules of the game for the private sector, the report concludes that 'the private investment climate has deteriorated to a point that it will be very difficult to improve for some time to come'.[29] The phrase 'clear and consistent rules of the game' is the World Bank's euphemism for stating that the private sector should be given a greater voice in the political process and more autonomy in making investment decisions and disposing of its profits. However, if the revolutionary government followed the World Bank's recommendations in this regard, it would have to renounce its determination to reorient the country's investment priorities and redistribute the national income in favour of the interests of the popular classes. In other words, it would mean renouncing its model of a mixed economy aimed at serving the basic needs of the population and returning to a model of dependent capitalist development based on the interests of foreign and local private capital.

The fact that the revolutionary regime continues to seek the

Table 3.5   Destination of Credit by Economic Sector and by Property
in Nicaragua, 1980-2 (in millions of cordobas)

	Area of People's Property		Private property		Total	
	Millions of cordobas	%	Millions of cordobas	%	Millions of cordobas	%
Agriculture	2,882	32	6,194	68	9,076	45
Livestock	1,293	37	2,163	63	3,456	17
Industry	5,133	66	2,603	34	7,736	38
Total	9,308	46	10,960	54	20,268	100

Source: Corporación Financiera de Nicaragua (CORFIN).

Compilation: Pensamiento Propio Collective (INIES).

co-operation of the private sector in the development of the economy is
evidenced by the amount of credit which the government has made
available to private producers. Table 3.5 reveals that 54 per cent of all
government credit between 1980 and 1982 was given to the private
sector, as opposed to 46 per cent for the state sector. Moreover, in
agriculture and ranching, even larger percentages of credit were made
available to the private sector. The one exception has been the industrial
sector, where between 1980 and 1982 only 34 per cent of all government
credit was directed to private enterprise, as opposed to 66 per cent for the
state industries in the APP. This can be explained in large part by the
reluctance of the large private producers to invest in the development of
the industrial sector.

Due to the lack of investment on the part of the private sector, the
breakdown of the Central American Common Market, the international economic recession and the structural deformations of
Nicaragua's economy that have been inherited from the past – the
reactivation of Nicaragua's economy since 1979 has not reached pre-
revolutionary levels of production. Table 3.6 shows the extent to which
the levels of production in the different sectors of the economy in 1982
compare with the levels of production in 1977 – the economic highpoint
of the pre-revolutionary period. These figures indicate that certain
sectors of the economy, such as agriculture and basic services (water
and electricity), have almost reached the 1977 level of production,
whereas others – such as mining and construction – continue to fall well
below their pre-revolutionary level of activity. As indicated above, the
manufacturing sector has yet to recover its pre-revolutionary level of
production, and in 1982 produced only 79 per cent as much as it
produced in 1977.

Table 3.6   Reactivation of Production, 1977–82 (percentages)

Sectors	1977	1982
Agriculture	100	90
Livestock	100	77
Fishing	100	66
Manufacturing	100	79
Construction	100	32
Mining	100	22
Water and electricity	100	98
Transportation and communications	100	72
Gross domestic product	100	72

Source: Central Bank of Nicaragua (*Barricada*, 18 July 1983, p. 3).

Table 3.7   Reactivation of Certain Basic Products, 1977–82 (percentages)

Products	Index of production	
	1977	1982
Rice	100	202
Beans	100	115
Pasteurized milk	100	170
Cooking oil	100	143
Soap	100	187

Source: MIDINRA and Ministry of Industry (*Barricada*, 18 July 1983, p. 3).

This does not mean, however, that the country's economic performance is in all respects inferior to its performance in the pre-revolutionary period. Mention has already been made of the increased level of
popular consumption of basic goods and services. It is also important to
note that the production of certain basic products has increased
considerably in relation to pre-revolutionary levels. This is the case, for
example, with regard to rice, beans, pasteurized milk, cooking oil and
soap. As Table 3.7 demonstrates, the index of production in these
products is considerably above that of 1977. This is further evidence of
the revolutionary government's efforts to increase the supply of basic
products for popular consumption.

The performance of Nicaragua's mixed economy can also be compared with the pre-revolutionary economy in terms of the level and composition of its foreign trade. In small, underdeveloped economies this is always a critical dimension of economic health, and revolutionary Nicaragua is no different in this respect than any other small Third World country. Most of the country's industry depends upon the importation of essential inputs, its agriculture is centred on the production of agro-exports, and the domestic consumption of certain basic goods is dependent upon the importation of a significant proportion of these goods. As Table 3.8 indicates, the value of Nicaragua's exports have declined since 1977, while the value of its imports have exceeded that of its exports – leaving the country with a negative trade balance. The situation was particularly acute in 1982, due to the fact that the country suffered damaging floods, followed by a severe drought, as well as the economic and military effects of the Reagan administration's undeclared war. Thus, the production and export of agricultural products declined, as did almost all other indicators of economic performance – such as growth in the GDP, in consumption and in fixed investment. Due to the war, export earnings in 1985 are not expected to exceed $450 million.[30]

As a result of the negative trade balance in recent years, Nicaragua has been forced to cover the net loss in payments through incurring short-term loans and credits. In other words, its negative trade balance has increased its external debt, which increased from $1.57 billion in 1980 to $2.4 billion in 1982. By 1985, the country's foreign debt had climbed to $4.5 billion, and interest payments on this debt for 1985 totalled $872 million. Since Nicaragua's annual export earnings have not exceeded $450 million in recent years, it is highly unlikely that the government will be able to make these payments.[31] If one adds to this picture the fact that Nicaragua's annual imports cost more than its export earnings, it is painfully clear that the country does not earn enough foreign exchange from its agro-exports to finance its essential imports and pay its foreign debt.

The country's shortage of foreign exchange has caused a grave crisis in the manufacturing sector, which, as previously mentioned, has a very high import coefficient. Most of this sector is absolutely dependent upon foreign exchange to purchase its basic inputs. Due to this shortage of foreign exchange, the government has been forced to restrict greatly the amount available for the import of industrial inputs. This has caused a decline in total industrial output and severely affected certain industries.

The crisis faced by Nicaragua's manufacturing sector has persuaded the government that this sector of the economy must be reoriented towards the production of basic goods for internal popular consumption. This is justified by the obvious fact that demand for these goods greatly exceeds supply, either through the present level of local

Table 3.8   Nicaragua: Basic Economic Indicators, 1977, 1980, 1982

Indicators	1977	1980	1982
1. Production			
GDP (millions of 1980 cordobas)	29,353	21,892	23,420
Per capita GDP (US$)	1,072	749	767
2. Foreign trade			
Exports (FOB) (US$ millions)	636.2	450.4	414.6
Imports (FOB) (US$ millions)	704.2	802.9	719.6
Trade balance (US$ millions)	− 68.0	− 352.5	− 305.0
External debt (US$ millions)	1,300.0	1,579.0	2,410.0
Servicing of debt as a % of exports	6.9	13.3	47.3
Petroleum imports as a % of export earnings	—	34.9	47.4

Source: *Pensamiento Proprio*, nos. 6–7 (1983), p. 25.

production or through costly imports. The government has also decided that the manufacturing sector should be integrated with the agricultural sector to a much greater extent than has been the case in the past.[32]

In other words, the logic of breaking out of the vicious circle of an economy conditioned by the foreign exchange earnings of its agro-exports has led Nicaragua's revolutionary leadership to initiate an economic strategy aimed at compacting and integrating the country's agricultural and industrial sectors within a transformed economic system that is oriented towards producing basic consumer goods for the domestic market and export products which are processed or manu-factured from local inputs. The following statement by Comandante Jaime Wheelock reveals the essence of this strategy:

> The revolution is beginning to develop a new economic model and this is based on the search for a different role in the international division of labor. We can continue to be producers of the means of consumption, but it is not the same to produce crude means of consumption as to produce means of consumption that have gone through a certain process of transformation. We want to be an industrial country that sells manu-factures: processing our agricultural products, selling our foods packaged, making furniture with our wood . . . This only can be done in a sovereign nation where no one imposes from outside an economic model contrary to our national interests.[33]

Nicaragua's internal economic difficulties, the international recession, the regional political and economic crisis and the effects of Washington's undeclared war on the country, have all contributed to a reformulation of the original model of development elaborated during the first years of the revolutionary regime. The original project sought to achieve the reconstruction of the country in the context of: the redistribution of wealth and income to the popular classes; the diversification of the country's dependence upon foreign markets and financing; the mobilization of the population in the productive process; and the development of a new mixed economy based upon an expanded state sector, a reformed private sector and a new co-operative sector.[34]

The reformulated strategy still incorporates these basic objectives but now has been forced to give priority to defence and to a greatly restricted set of strategic investments and incentives to increase agro-export production, the cultivation of basic foods for the internal market and the manufacture of goods essential to agriculture and the war effort. In other words, the war and the country's acute foreign exchange crisis have forced the government drastically to scale down its investments and place the economy on a wartime footing.

Total losses caused by the war during 1984 were reported to be equivalent to 30 per cent of the nation's export earnings.[35] The escalating Contra attacks have caused a sharp decline in the production of basic grains and export crops. At least one-quarter of the government's budget in 1984 was expended on defence, and this figure is expected to reach 40 per cent during 1985. The financial burden of defence has forced the government to limit funds for education and other social services and postpone most of its previous development plans.

In a public report released by the FSLN on 18 May 1984, the necessity of reorienting the economy primarily towards defence was given special emphasis. Thus, the report states:

> The few resources we have must be divided between the efforts to defend national sovereignty and to satisfy the rest of our basic needs. Economic policies must assure supplies to the war fronts and also give priority to the efforts to improve distribution and maintain consumption of basic foods in order to benefit the poorest sectors of the population.[36]

Among other important changes necessitated by the war and the deteriorating economic situation, the revolutionary government has been forced to discontinue its previous policy of broad subsidies of basic consumer goods and allow their prices to rise on the market. The same report also warns the public that 'food shortages, supply problems, and the lack of certain essential goods, must be understood as part of the difficulties and sacrifices' that will have to be endured as a result of the war and the reorientation of the economy towards defence.

57

A Profile of Revolutionary Nicaragua's Industry

The industrial sector of revolutionary Nicaragua's mixed economy, which produces one-quarter of the country's total value of production, is characterized by a small number of medium and large private industries, a variety of state industries which produce about one-third of the total value of industrial production, and a sizeable number of small private industries which are struggling to survive under difficult economic conditions. Table 3.9, which is based on a survey of the industrial sector by the Nicaraguan Ministry of Industry, reveals the relative distribution of units of production, labour and the value of production between the different areas and branches of industrial activity in Nicaragua. The 188 industrial enterprises represented in this table include all the large and medium industries in the country (that is, all those with over 30 employees).

As Table 3.9 indicates, most of Nicaragua's larger manufacturing industries are engaged in the production of food products, beverages, textiles, clothing, leather goods, wood products and chemical products (which includes pharmaceuticals). Over 70 per cent of the total value of industrial production and employment is generated by these industries. The absence of a genuine basic metals industry as well as a machinery and machine tools branch reflects the underdeveloped and externally dependent nature of Nicaragua's industrial sector. The country's small metal products branch of industrial production produces a very limited range of simple products such as different types of wire, nails, clamps, water tanks, irrigation tubing, wheelbarrows, iron furniture, industrial lamps, aluminium cooking utensils, tin cans, rods, sheet metal and farm implements.

This absence of any significant industrial capacity in the basic metals and machinery and machine tools branches means that Nicaragua's entire industrial sector and the rest of the economy are dependent upon the importation of costly machines, the spare parts for these machines and all basic metals. In view of the country's scarcity of foreign exchange, this is a major limitation upon its ability to maintain and develop its productive base. The development of these basic industries is a structural imperative for the industrialization and economic transformation of all underdeveloped countries, since the historical evidence clearly indicates that such industries have played a crucial role in the industrial and technological transformation of all existing developed societies.[37]

In terms of state versus private enterprise, Table 3.9 reveals that the APP accounts for 45 per cent of the value of production generated by Nicaragua's largest 188 industries, while the private sector generates 55 per cent. However, in terms of employment, Table 3.9 reveals that APP industries employ nearly two-thirds of the total workforce. This table also makes it possible to identify the branches of industry where the

Table 3.9   Industrial Sector: Gross Value of Production and Employment in a Survey of 188 Enterprises

Branches	No. of enterprises			GVP			Employment		
	Total	APP	Private	Total	APP	Private	Total	APP	Private
Food	20	7	13	1,208,206.7	123,501.1	1,084,705.6	2,861	686	2,175
Beverages	8	5	3	1,445,280.3	708,707.9	736,572.4	4,371	3,255	1,116
Tobacco	1	–	1	284,497.6	–	282,497.6	296	–	296
Textiles	15	12	3	748,740.4	686,527.2	62,213.2	4,983	4,746	237
Apparel	6	4	2	222,196.1	196,391.8	25,804.3	1,247	1,074	173
Shoes	4	1	3	307,532.5	24,366.5	283,166.0	963	178	785
Leather	9	1	8	110,065.7	19,488.0	90,577.7	481	76	405
Wood	12	12	–	279,971.3	279,971.3	–	1,949	1,949	–
Furniture	5	4	1	48,305.2	30,684.8	17,620.4	434	325	109
Paper	3	–	3	85,351.7	–	85,351.7	149	–	149
Printing	11	1	10	224,657.3	49,136.4	175,520.9	1,374	348	1,026
Rubber	4	1	3	58,729.4	918.0	57,811.4	159	24	135
Chemicals	43	9	34	1,306,493.4	359,971.5	946,521.9	3,615	1,463	2,152
Non-metallic minerals	12	7	5	438,326.5	376,385.7	61,940.8	1,576	1,408	168
Metallic products	18	9	9	482,091.6	365,821.4	116,270.2	2,066	1,705	361
Machinery and elect. and non-elect. articles	8	4	4	111,997.2	35,468.5	76,528.7	466	273	193
Transportation materials	2	–	2	14,667.6	–	14,667.6	49	–	49
Miscellaneous	7	4	3	259,104.8	190,078.4	69,026.4	1,062	714	348
Total	*188*	*81*	*107*	*7,636,215.3*	*3,447,718.5*	*4,188,796.8*	*28,101*	*18,224*	*9,887*
(% of the total)	*(100)*	*(43)*	*(57)*	*(100)*	*(45)*	*(55)*	*(100)*	*(65)*	*(35)*

Source: Ministry of Industry. Department of Planning. 6 April 1984.

state has the most influence and those where private enterprise predominates. The state sector is clearly predominant in the following branches: textiles, apparel, wood products, non-metallic minerals and metal products; whereas the private sector is most important in the following branches: food products, tobacco products, shoes, paper products, printing, rubber products, chemical products, transport equipment, as well as in the machinery, electrical and non-electrical equipment branches.

In addition to its lack of industrial capacity to produce the basic metals such as iron, steel, tin, copper, etc., Nicaragua also lacks the capacity to produce its own paper, rubber, glass and synthetic fibres – all of which must now be imported at great cost. Standard Oil does operate a refinery in Nicaragua, but all the petroleum it refines must be imported, since Nicaragua has no oil of its own. These basic materials are the essential inputs needed for the manufacture of products currently being produced in the economy. Since they are not produced in Nicaragua, the industrial sector is characterized by an almost total dependence upon the importation at great cost of these basic materials.

Moreover, very few of Nicaragua's industries produce inputs for other domestic industries. Under the conditions of its previous pattern of dependent capitalist development, neither local nor foreign capital had much interest in developing linkages between the different branches of its manufacturing sector. This is particularly evident in the lack of integration between the country's agro-industries and its food and textile industries. For example, even though Nicaragua is a major producer of cotton, its textile industries have traditionally relied upon imported cotton thread and fabrics, because the private entrepreneurs in the cotton sector were oriented towards foreign markets for the sale of their semi-processed agricultural product – cotton – and the textile producers were oriented towards foreign sources of supply for the purchase of their essential inputs such as cotton thread and fabrics. As a result, little was done in the past to link Nicaragua's cotton mills with its small textile industry.

Although several government projects now in the development stage will change the current situation, at present only 5 per cent of the cotton produced in Nicaragua is transformed for use in the domestic textile industries. The country does not have sufficient spinning and weaving facilities to produce the cotton thread and fabrics needed by the textile and clothing factories. A similar situation exists with regard to the food and leather goods industries. Even though there is an adequate potential supply of local cotton seed oil and hides, the food industry now imports cooking oils and the leather goods industry imports hides in order to meet their production needs. Moreover, fruit and vegetable juices (including tomato sauce) are imported despite the fact the country has sufficient raw materials to produce them. And even though Nicaragua has extensive forestry resources and a wood products industry, it does not have the industrial capacity to make paper. Thus, it must import what is in fact a very costly basic material needed by nearly all sectors of the economy. In this case and in many others, key links in the chain of production are missing.

Because of the disarticulated nature of Nicaragua's industrial sector, most of its industries are dependent upon imported inputs and the average import coefficient in production is over 40 per cent.[38] Between 1978 and 1982, industrial inputs (that is, imported raw materials, intermediate products and capital goods) accounted for over 50 per cent of the total value of all imports.[39] However, due to the country's foreign exchange crisis, the government has been forced drastically to reduce the amount of foreign currency allocated to the industrial sector for the purpose of importing inputs. As Table 3.10 indicates, in 1983, only $177 million were allocated to the industrial sector for imported inputs. This contrasts with $443 million in 1982.[40] Naturally, the effects of this drastic reduction in foreign exchange for industrial imports have been severe, particularly in those industries – such as chemicals, food and metal products – that depend on a large volume of imports. As Table 3.10 reveals, this has severely affected private industry since the private sector's share in industrial imports represents close to 60 per cent of the total.

Table 3.11 demonstrates that the revolutionary government has not excluded the private sector from access to the scarce foreign exchange funds at its disposal – for purchasing essential imports and for other necessary purposes. The majority of the foreign exchange made available to the industrial sector in 1983 went to private enterprise (see Table 3.10), and the government also provided the bulk of its short-term financing funds to the private sector rather than the APP (see Table 3.11).

The government continues to give assurances to the private sector regarding the allocation of foreign exchange for the purchase of production materials. In February 1985, President Daniel Ortega and members of the cabinet met with more than 400 small, medium and large producers to discuss government measures aimed at dealing with the country's economic crisis. Among these measures are better prices for the basic goods produced by private industry and the timely provision of credits to guarantee the imported inputs needed by private manufacturers.[41]

Nicaragua's Small Industry Sub-sector

The underdeveloped character of Nicaragua's industrial sector is reflected not only in its dependency upon imported inputs and its lack of integration, but also in the semi-artisan nature of the many small

Table 3.10 Industrial Sector: Imports by Branch and Area of Property, 1983 (thousands of dollars)

Branches	Total	APP	Private
Food	23,157.7	2,506.9	20,650.8
Beverages	12,730.6	7,199.6	5,531.0
Tobacco	1,848.4	—	1,848.4
Textiles	13,907.8	13,307.8	600.0
Apparel	14,992.6	1,832.6	13,160.0
Shoes	10,140.8	580.7	9,560.1
Leather	3,974.2	300.0	3,674.2
Wood	1,919.9	1,919.9	—
Furniture	325.1	255.1	70.0
Paper	4,628.6	—	4,628.6
Printing	7,552.7	3,803.7	3,749.0
Rubber	2,284.3	143.2	2,141.1
Chemicals	39,900.3	12,858.6	27,041.7
Non-metallic minerals	3,453.4	3,053.4	400.0
Metallic products	25,675.1	20,882.6	4,792.5
Machinery and elect. and non-elect. articles	3,038.5	1,285.5	1,753.0
Transportation materials	299.7	—	299.7
Miscellaneous	6,919.1	4,769.1	2,150.0
Total	*176,748.8*	*74,698.7*	*102,050.1*

Source: Ministry of Industry, Department of Planning, 5 April 1984.

enterprises which characterize this sector of the economy. As Table 3.12 indicates, Nicaragua has a very large number of small or 'micro' industries. According to the survey upon which Table 3.12 is based, there were over 9,305 small industries in Nicaragua in 1982, employing some 31,513 workers as compared with 7,993 enterprises employing 27,084 workers in 1980. In other words, under the revolutionary regime there appears to have been a significant increase in the number of small industries producing products for the domestic market. Most of these small units of production are in reality workshops (called *tallers* in Spanish). They are similar in certain respects to the cottage industries and blacksmith shops of the past. They produce food products, items of clothing, leather goods, wood furniture, simple metal products and plastic items. The level of technology tends to be artisan or semi-artisan, with the workers mostly using hand tools, sometimes combined with simple machines (such as sewing machines).

Table 3.11 Industrial Sector: Short- and Long-term Financing, 1984 (millions of cordobas)

Branches	Total			Short-term			Long-term		
	Total	APP	Private	Total	APP	Private	Total	APP	Private
Food	107.8	0.4	107.4	102.3	0.4	101.9	5.5	—	5.5
Beverages	31.0	31.0	—	—	—	—	31.0	31.0	—
Tobacco	—	—	—	—	—	—	—	—	—
Textiles	52.4	33.5	18.9	42.4	23.5	18.9	10.0	10.0	—
Apparel	—	—	—	—	—	—	—	—	—
Shoes	9.0	—	9.0	9.0	—	9.0	—	—	—
Leather	—	—	—	—	—	—	—	—	—
Wood	—	—	—	—	—	—	—	—	—
Furniture	2.0	2.0	—	—	—	—	2.0	2.0	—
Paper	12.0	—	12.0	12.0	—	12.0	—	—	—
Printing	23.8	20.1	3.7	3.0	—	3.0	20.8	20.1	0.7
Rubber	0.1	—	0.1	—	—	—	0.1	—	0.1
Chemicals	103.8	5.2	98.6	91.3	5.2	86.1	12.5	—	12.5
Non-metallic minerals	9.4	8.0	1.4	8.5	8.0	0.5	0.9	—	0.9
Metallic products	13.3	3.5	9.8	13.3	3.5	9.8	—	—	—
Machinery and elect. and non-elect. articles	9.7	7.2	2.5	3.9	1.4	2.5	5.8	5.8	—
Transportation materials	5.0	—	5.0	5.0	—	5.0	—	—	—
Miscellaneous	68.5	36.2	32.3	—	—	—	68.5	36.2	32.3
Total	*447.8*	*147.1*	*300.7*	*290.7*	*42.0*	*248.7*	*157.1*	*105.1*	*52.0*
(% of Total)	*(100)*	*(33)*	*(67)*	*(100)*	*(14)*	*(86)*	*(100)*	*(67)*	*(33)*

Source: Ministry of Industry. Department of Planning, 6 April 1984.

Table 3.12   Small Private Industry (Employment and Enterprises by Industrial Branch)

Branch	To December 1980		To June 1982	
	Employment	*Enterprises*	*Employment*	*Enterprises*
Food and beverages	7,669	2,273	8,515	2,523
Textiles and apparel	5,424	1,598	7,160	2,110
Shoes and leather	6,002	1,786	7,030	2,091
Wood and furniture	3,702	1,089	4,157	1,223
Printing	420	87	420	87
Chemical products	328	98	429	128
Non-metallic minerals	1,341	398	1,430	425
Metallic products	1,560	463	1,629	484
Other manuf.	638	201	743	234
Totals	27,034	7,993	31,513	9,305

Source: Employment and Production Survey, 1982, Extrapolated. Ministry of Industry, Department of Small Industry.

In many ways, these small industries illustrate the basic characteristics and problems of Nicaragua's industrial sector. For example, one of the most important products produced by small industries is bread. This activity requires, like most industrial activity in the country, the importation of basic inputs – wheat flour, yeast and baking powder. The absolute dependence of the bakery industry upon these imports means that this area of industrial activity has been seriously affected by the country's shortage of foreign exchange. In order to guarantee the supply of basic inputs to these industries, the revolutionary government has been forced to take over the distribution of wheat flour and ration its allocation between the numerous small bakeries throughout the country.

Another important area of production where small industries play a major role is in the manufacture of textile products and shoes. Approximately 75 per cent of all items of clothing manufactured in Nicaragua are produced by small industries.[42] Table 3.12 indicates that there are over 2,000 small clothing manufacturers in the country. Like the bakeries, these micro-industries are also dependent upon the importation of basic inputs. They import not only most of the fabrics they use, but also such basic and critical items as thread, zippers and buttons.

Shoes and leather goods are also produced largely by small industries and self-employed persons. More than 7,000 workers employed in over

2,000 small enterprises produce 40 per cent of the national production of shoes, and over 70 per cent of the shoes made from leather.[43] This category of small industry has been seriously affected by the declining supply of hides. As in the case of wheat flour, the state has been forced to take over control of the distribution of hides in order to ration the allocation of this basic input to the numerous small producers of leather goods. This area of production also depends upon the importation of various types of inputs, and as a result, access to foreign exchange has been a critical factor affecting its performance and survival.

Somewhat different conditions affect the over 1,200 small industries producing wood products and furniture. The basic input used in this area of production comes from natural resources controlled by the state through the Corporación Forestal del Pueblo (People's Forestry Corporation, CORFOP). However, the state does not itself distribute the raw materials used by the private wood products industries. In other words, the state controls lumbering but not the marketing of lumber. As a result, the producers must purchase their wood inputs on the open market. This industrial sub-sector is also characterized by a greater degree of mechanization and the quality of their products enables them to compete in the international market for wood products.

The entire small industries sub-sector of the economy is beset by a number of critical problems. For example, the shortage of foreign exchange means that the owners of many of these industries must seek authorization from the government to purchase essential inputs. The government carefully evaluates every request in order to determine if it is justified. This takes time and forces the small producers to submit to a slow and bothersome procedure, while in the meantime their inventories may run out and their production process is paralysed. There are also problems of supply stemming from speculation in and hoarding of scarce inputs. Both professional wholesalers as well as certain producers are involved in the trafficking of these scarce inputs. These problems increase the costs of production and the final price paid by the consumer. They also maintain a thriving black market in the essential materials needed for production. Moreover, the private distribution of certain raw materials such as wood and private control over the distribution of supplementary inputs – such as dyes, yeast, zippers, etc. – prevents the rational distribution of these inputs and obstructs the production of quality products at reasonable prices.

In an effort to address the problems of the small industries and rationalize their participation in the economy, the government has attempted to promote their co-operatization. As of May 1983, some 4,600 small producers had been organized into 77 service co-operatives which pool credit and the purchase of basic inputs.[44] However, the establishment of producer co-operatives has progressed very slowly. The formation of this type of co-operative involves combining several small enterprises into a single new industry in which the means of production and income are socialized. Only 50 such co-operatives now exist.[45] The state has been most successful in promoting the formation of service co-operatives in those branches of industrial activity where it controls the distribution of basic inputs. For this reason, there tends to be a higher incidence of co-operatization in the bakery, leather goods and clothing industries, where the state controls the distribution of basic inputs.

The small industries sub-sector of the economy is an important source of employment within the industrial sector, which the revolutionary government is anxious to preserve for the foreseeable future. It also plays a critical role in the production of goods that satisfy the basic necessities of the population. Thus, this sub-sector of the economy fits into the government's strategy of industrial development as a source of support for the reproduction of the labour force. The government's strategy seeks to encourage the consolidation of these industries, orient their production towards satisfying the basic necessities of the population, and increase their productive output. The government's control over foreign exchange has given it an important means to induce the small producers into co-operating with this strategy.

Nicaragua's Industrial Workforce

We have mentioned that the small industries sub-sector is an important source of employment within the industrial sector. Table 3.13 reveals that in 1984 the total industrial labour force (including persons employed in agro-industries) represented *less than one-tenth of the EAP* and only 11.3 per cent of the total employed population. If we compare the figures in Table 3.12 with those in Table 3.13, we note that in 1982, the total estimated workforce in the small industries sub-sector represented over one-third of the total industrial labour force. Thus, this sub-sector is important within the larger industrial sector. However, industry as a whole is clearly *not* a major source of employment and disposes of a very small proportion of the total labour force. Even in Managua, the most developed city in Nicaragua and the site of most of its industries, the total industrial labour force represents only 12.5 per cent of the employed population of the city.[46]

The occupational structure of Managua reveals that productive wage-earners represent a *declining* proportion of the city's total labour force. In 1963, wage-earners involved in productive economic activity – manufacturing, construction, utilities, etc. – accounted for one-third of the total employed population, whereas by 1982 this sector had declined to less than one-quarter.[47] In other words, the growth of the urban population in Nicaragua's most important cities – now at a rate of 6 per cent per annum – has *not* contributed to the creation of a modern industrial working class, permanently installed in large industrial establishments. The contingents of rural migrants to the cities generally

Table 3.13   Participation of the Industrial Sector in the EAP

Concepts (thousands of persons)	Total population 1	Total EAP 2	Employed population 3	Industrial workforce[a] 4	Rates 5=4+3	6=4+2
					Percentages	
1982	2,961.4	938.8	522.4	85.8	16.4	9.1
1983	3,061.5	973.5	782.8	98.4	11.4	9.2
1984	3,165.0	1,009.6	819.8	92.3	11.3	9.1

[a] Includes agro-industry.

Source: Ministry of Industry, Department of Planning, 6 April 1984.

find employment only in the so-called informal sector. In Managua, this 'informal sector' of self-employed pedlars, handymen and artisans without formal wage-earning employment represents approximately 45 per cent of the economically active population.[48]

In 1982, the estimated total workforce in large and medium industrial enterprises (those with more than 30 employees) was over 37,000 employees or about 43 per cent of the total industrial workforce.[49] It should be noted, however, that not even the largest industrial enterprise in the country has more than 2,000 employees. In the large or medium industrial enterprises, management personnel represent less than 2 per cent of the total workforce, professional and technical employees about 4 per cent, administrative and clerical personnel around 15 per cent, production workers about 60 per cent and general service workers (drivers, janitors, etc.) the remaining 20 per cent.[50] The production workers tend to be unskilled or semi-skilled with a low level of education and technical knowledge. In fact, this low level of technical knowledge is a key feature of the workforce, and stems from the country's past underdevelopment. Moreover, technical training facilities in the country, although they have increased since the revolutionary triumph, are insufficient to meet the existing demand for technically trained workers.

Although it is extremely difficult to obtain reliable data on labour productivity in the industrial sector, all indications are that it is quite low. For example, if one divides the total value of industrial production by the total number of persons employed in the industrial workforce, the total value produced per person employed is less than US $10,000 per annum. Among the causes for this low level of labour productivity are: the scarcity of raw materials and replacement parts which often causes production delays; high absenteeism; labour-management conflicts; the employment of excess personnel; the departure from the country of many technically trained people; the lack of administrative experience and technical knowledge on the part of many of the managerial and technical

67

personnel in the state industries; bureaucratic delays in obtaining foreign exchange and financing; inadequate maintenance of machinery and equipment; and the low level of education and lack of technical training which characterize the general workforce.

Management and Planning in the Industrial Sector

The increasing involvement of the workers in the management of the productive process is an important development which the revolution has stimulated, and as worker participation in planning and administration develops it should contribute to a substantial improvement in labour productivity. However, worker participation in industrial management is largely limited to the industries within the APP. Moreover, it is consultative and is not designed to give the workers control over the production process. Due to the general lack of organizational skills as well as education on the part of the majority of the production workers, there is a definite limit on the degree to which worker participation in planning and decision-making can be achieved under prevailing conditions in Nicaragua. Moreover, the managers and *técnicos* in many of the state enterprises appear to be unprepared to deal with the problems raised by involving the unions and the workers in the management of these enterprises. Many of the managers and technical personnel do not know how to function in a participatory organizational environment. But as time goes by, and more experience is accumulated, this situation should progressively improve.

The organization and direction of the state industrial sector has involved the establishment of a planning and administrative superstructure designed to direct and co-ordinate the diverse industrial enterprises under state control. The central structural mechanism set up to perform these functions is the Corporación Industrial del Pueblo (COIP), under the Ministry of Industry. COIP functions much like a large holding corporation with its own property and financial control over the 81 enterprises under its direction. Apart from a central directive staff it contains a series of operating directorates responsible for what are referred to as industrial complexes – groupings of the various state industries by their branch or type of industrial activity. The administrators of each state enterprise are responsible to the particular COIP directorate that presides over their area of industrial activity. Since 1980, COIP has sought to consolidate a new form of 'Sandinista Administration' in the state enterprises and reorient their production towards satisfying the basic needs of the population.

More recently, the Ministry of Industry and COIP have begun to institutionalize a system of planning at the enterprise, branch and sectorial levels; and long-range planning up to the year 2000 is currently underway. The ministry also seeks to incorporate private industry into the planning process. So far this does not appear to have progressed much beyond consultations and negotiations centred more on matters such as the allocations of foreign exchange and short-term financing than on genuine long-range planning. The opposition to the revolutionary regime by certain large capitalists in the industrial sector represents a major obstacle to the institutionalization of indicative planning in this sector of the economy. Moreover, the general conditions prevailing in Nicaragua and the hostile external environment make it difficult, if not impossible, to design and implement an effective set of plans. This situation has been clearly stated by Comandante Jaime Wheelock:

> Every time that we attempt to implement a plan, we have to make an emergency plan, because, apart from the situation of aggression that we suffer, in a certain sense our variables, because we are such a dependent country, are a function of the international market... It is difficult to plan in a dependent country that has open international relations. And it is even more difficult if in addition to economic reasons, such as the international economic crisis, are added political problems and the military aggression which our country suffers.[51]

In other words, the very external dependency of the economy as well as the hostile international environment tend to undermine all efforts to make and carry out plans.

The major outlines of the Ministry of Industry's strategy for the long-range development of the industrial sector are as follows:

1) the industrial sector will be increasingly oriented toward the task of reproducing the country's labor force through the production of basic consumer goods;
2) since the central axis of accumulation for some time yet will continue to be the agricultural sector, the industrial sector will be increasingly oriented toward both providing the basic inputs for agriculture and processing its basic outputs (i.e., agro-products for the domestic market as well as agro-exports);
3) the industrial sector will also be oriented toward providing the basic inputs for construction, transportation, and national defense; and
4) the integration of the industrial sector will be promoted through the increased production of the intermediary goods needed by local industries.[52]

This strategy is to be implemented through the increased planning and programming of industrial production, with the state industries performing the leading role in the restructuring of the sector. It is important to note that this long-range strategy for industrial development requires significant transformations in the structure and orientation of the industrial sector which go beyond the rationalization and reactivation of industrial production.

The realization of this strategy over the next ten to fifteen years could significantly move Nicaragua in the direction of a planned industrialized economy. However, for this to be a *socialist* planned economy, the present structure of property relations in the industrial sector (as well as in agriculture) will have to be transformed. There is no indication at the present time that the revolutionary regime intends to effect transformations of this sort. The present ratio of approximately 40 per cent to 60 per cent – state versus private property – is considered to be the appropriate mix for the future industrial development of the country. Moreover, government officials believe that they now have sufficient instruments – such as control over the allocation of foreign exchange for the importation of industrial inputs – to control the private sector and preside over the industrial development of the country. It is assumed that the APP will be the main motor of development, and that the APP industries will play the major role in the transformation of the industrial sector. Here it is important to note that co-operation between the government and the few foreign-owned industries in Nicaragua has generally been good. Most of these foreign industries are owned by Europeans and are to be found primarily in the metal and chemical products branches. The government seeks to promote the expansion of production in these industries so long as they continue to co-operate and conform to the government's plans for the industrial development of the country.

As previously mentioned, the integration of the agricultural and manufacturing sectors and the development of agro-industry are key objectives in Nicaragua's global strategy for developing the economy. In this regard, it is important to consider the basic characteristics of Nicaragua's agro-industrial complex. The Ministerio de Desarrollo Agropecuario y Reforma Agraria (Ministry of Agricultural Development and Agrarian Reform, MIDINRA) defines agro-industry as any unit of production which transforms agricultural products and receives a significant amount of its raw materials directly from rural producers.[53] This definition excludes industries which utilize already processed or transformed agricultural products as their raw materials. In other words, agro-industries are conceived as those units of production which are engaged in the *first* transformation or processing of agricultural products. In the case of Nicaragua, these primarily take the form of cotton mills, coffee mills, sugar mills, saw mills and slaughterhouses.

However, it is possible to speak of a considerably larger category which combines these agro-industries with a number of industries that are or should be closely linked with Nicaragua's agricultural production. This grouping of industries or 'agro-industrial complex' (as labelled by MIDINRA) consists of: the agro-industries *per se*; those industries which produce inputs for agriculture (e.g. fertilizer, farm implements and pesticide producers); as well as those industries which use as their raw materials processed agricultural products (e.g. textile industries, food industries, soap manufacturers, wood products producers, etc.). This complex of industries represents as much as 70 per cent of the value-added and over 60 per cent of the total value of production in the industrial sector.[54] Moreover, more than three-quarters of the country's exports and more than 20 per cent of all the raw materials used by the industrial sector are produced in this complex. Thus, it is a critically important element of the economy in terms of both generating foreign exchange and in reducing the expenditure of foreign exchange on expensive imported inputs for the industrial sector.

The food products industry is the central activity in Nicaragua's agro-industrial complex, accounting for approximately 60 per cent of the total workforce and 67 per cent of the total value of production in the complex. Second in importance are the textile and clothing industries which account for about 17 per cent of the workforce and 10 per cent of the value of production. The main site of both of these components of the agro-industrial complex is Managua, where most of their plants are located and 60 per cent of the total value of production is generated. This reflects the urban and concentrated nature of much of the complex. As previously mentioned, most of the productive units and the total value of production in Nicaragua's agro-industry are privately owned.[55] This poses serious obstacles to the comprehensive planning and the integrated development of this important sector of the economy, and it raises the important question of whether or not the state has the capacity to effect the necessary transformations in this sector without further socialization of the productive process.

A more detailed examination of the products in the agro-industrial complex reveals the following hierarchy in terms of their relative importance:[56]

1) meats
2) sugar
3) milk products
4) organic oils and soap
5) textiles
6) coffee
7) animal feeds

This hierarchy is based on their relative importance in terms of their total value of production, generation of foreign exchange and consumption of local raw materials. What is most significant about this hierarchy is that most of them are essential to the reproduction of the country's labour force, since they tend to be the main consumer goods that satisfy the basic needs of the population. Obviously, the expanded production of most of these products would represent a significant improvement in Nicaragua's capability to feed and clothe its population through the use of its own natural resources.

Symptomatic of the deficiencies in Nicaragua's industrial sector is the lack of linkages between the various industries in the agro-industrial complex and the fact that most are not operating at full capacity due to inadequate supplies of raw materials. The best example of this is the lack of integration between Nicaragua's cotton-producers, cotton mills and textile industries. The integrated development of this component of the agro-industrial complex is essential since it will not only reduce the dependence of the textile industry on costly foreign imports and thus save valuable foreign exchange, but will also permit Nicaragua eventually to export a finished product rather than a semi-processed raw material and in so doing increase its export earnings. Finally, the same positive results can be achieved in the case of linking the cotton sector with the cooking oil and animal feed industries, which can substitute the derivatives from cotton-processing for the imported raw materials upon which they presently depend. In view of the country's critical shortage of foreign exchange and debilitating dependence upon the importation of costly raw materials for its industries, the integrated development of its agro-industrial complex is obviously of primary importance. Moreover, the important multiplier effects of increased employment, full utilization of existing facilities and the achievement of self-sufficiency in the production of basic consumer goods are further reasons for giving priority to this type of industrial development.

In sum, the present state of Nicaragua's agro-industrial complex reveals that insufficient supplies of agricultural raw materials are responsible for the underutilization of the installed capacity of the industries in this complex and for the country's costly dependence upon imported raw materials as well as imported food and textile products that could and should be produced locally.

The Prospects for Nicaragua's Industrial Development

Industrial development is clearly a critical requirement for the structural transformation of Nicaraguan society. It is necessary in order to overcome the backwardness, unequal development, external dependency and inefficient nature of Nicaragua's productive base and to develop the productive forces capable of producing an adequate standard of living for its population. Industrial development is also an indispensable requirement for a future transition to socialism, if the Nicaraguan people choose to take this course of development. Clive Thomas forcefully argues this in reference to all small, underdeveloped societies:

Structural transformation, disengagement from capitalism, socialist development – all these imply industrialization in the basic sense of the progressive spread of industrial techniques of organization and resource use into all branches of economic activity, as part of the struggle to make the material environment serve the community's needs. This relationship between industrialization and the degree of development of the productive forces is readily perceived when one looks at the global distribution of industry and the marked concentration of industrial production among those countries which have solved the problem of mass poverty and have achieved self-sustaining increases in the level of material production.[57]

Since we are in basic agreement with this perspective, the premise of this essay is that Nicaragua can achieve the integrated industrialization of its economy. As previously indicated, in order to achieve this structural transformation, the country must follow a strategy of development based on the vertical integration of its demand structure with its domestic resource endowment.[58] It must utilize intensively its domestic resources to satisfy the basic needs of the population. It must also produce the primary inputs required by the manufacturing and agro-industrial sectors. In addition, it must develop an indigenous technology centred on its own basic metals and machine-building industries, establish adequate facilities for the technical training of its labour force, develop a small capital goods industry, introduce democratic planning, promote collective over individual consumption and establish complementary trading relationships with other Third World and socialist countries in place of its present unequal trading relations with the major capitalist centres. With this in mind, we now turn to an assessment of Nicaragua's prospects for industrial development.

First, it is clear that in the short space of six years, the new revolutionary government of Nicaragua has launched the country on a course of development which seeks to achieve most, if not all, of the conditions required. Significantly, the industrial development of the country is viewed as not only desirable but attainable. Thus, what Thomas (pages 45–50) refers to as a particular 'combination of prejudice and pragmatism' that presumes the 'eternal backwardness' of small underdeveloped countries is not reflected in the policy statements or plans of the revolutionary government. The government's long-term development efforts are directed at restructuring domestic demand in relation to the country's resources, and increasing the utilization of domestic resources to the point of achieving self-sufficiency in industrial production of most of the basic goods needed by the population.

In terms of its present domestic resource base, Nicaragua has the resource capacity to provide the basic raw materials for the following industries:

1. food products (including animal feeds)
2. textiles
3. shoes and leather goods
4. wood and paper products
5. soap
6. organic oils (cottonseed, coconut, african palm, etc.)
7. rubber products
8. certain chemical products (e.g. salts, fertilizers, etc.)
9. construction materials (e.g. cement, clay bricks, etc.)
10. gold and silver mining
11. fishing
12. hydroelectric and geothermal power

As this list indicates, Nicaragua has a diversified resource base capable of providing the raw materials for the industrial production of a wide range of products, including most of the goods (food, clothing, housing, etc.) required to satisfy the basic needs of the population. However, it does *not* presently have the resource base for petroleum products, basic metals (iron and steel), metal products, machinery, electronics, motorized transportation equipment, etc., even though it does have industries producing some of these products with imported raw materials.

The government's plans and projects for the development of both agro-industry and the manufacturing sector are geared to using domestic resources to produce basic goods and to increase the value added to its agricultural exports by processing them before export. An examination of the present array of development projects either in the execution stage or in the preliminary stages prior to execution reveals the extent to which the revolutionary government seeks to restructure and expand the industrial base of the economy. Table 3.14 reveals the main areas of investment represented by these projects. In essence, they reflect a model of agro-industrial development based on the twin objectives of generating foreign exchange and producing basic foods for the population. The amount of investments in projects which are fundamentally aimed at increasing agro-export production is roughly equivalent to the amount of investments aimed at increasing the production of basic foods (about 3.8 billion cordobas or about US $135 million at the rate of 28 cordobas to 1 dollar).[59]

The main emphasis in terms of sub-sectors is on sugar production, cattle-raising, integrated rural development (projects aimed at establishing co-operatives, basic infrastructure and services in the underdeveloped regions of the north), tobacco, oils and basic grains. What is significant about these sub-sectors is the fact that they contain a relatively high component of agro-industry – sugar mills, slaughterhouses, tobacco processing plants, etc. Moreover, many of the projects, such as those involving the production of vegetables, are aimed not only

Table 3.14 Nicaragua's Principal Areas of Investment in Agriculture, 1982–7 (millions of cordobas)

Area of investment	Amount	% of total
1. Sugar	2,380.0	26.1
2. Cattle	1,927.7	21.1
3. Integrated rural development	1,317.6	14.5
4. Tobacco	823.8	9.0
5. Oils (palm, coconut)	661.1	7.3
6. Grains	446.2	4.9
7. Various	434.7	4.8
8. Vegetables	393.0	4.3
9. Frijol negro	297.6	3.3
10. Cacao	309.0	3.4
11. Poultry	119.0	1.3
Total investment	9,109.7	100

Source: MIDINRA, *Plan Anual de Trabajo* (1983) as reported in *Barricada*, 5 December 1983.

at providing the population with an adequate supply of fresh vegetables, but also with canned, frozen and dehydrated products made from these vegetables.

However, Nicaragua's emphasis on agro-exports raises questions about the advisability of this aspect of the country's development strategy, particularly in view of the instability of the international market for such products. As Thomas notes:

> the sale of primary products overseas, which often dominates domestic resource use, has been characterized by low prices and income elasticities of demand ... as well as a considerable instability in the value of export earnings. This in turn not only has expected harmful consequences on rural incomes, employment and investments, but has also reinforced the dynamic tendencies toward divergence between agricultural resource use and domestic consumption of agricultural products.[60]

Thomas further argues that the most important objective of a successful strategy of development for small agro-export economies is: 'to find a dynamic basis for planning agricultural output in such a way as to orient the economy *away* from its present export specialization in tropical staples'.[61] He further suggests that the most obvious alternative is to reorient production towards the agricultural commodities that have historically displayed the highest income elasticities of demand: milk, eggs, cheese, butter, meats, vegetables and fruits.[62]

In all fairness to Nicaragua's strategy of agricultural development, it should be noted that an important effort is being made to increase the production of basic foodstuffs. Moreover, many of the new investment projects in sugar and tobacco will create new jobs and promote the modernization of agriculture. For example, Nicaragua's biggest new agro-industrial project – the large sugar complex at Tipitapa/Malacatoya – will produce badly needed energy from sugar *bagazo* or waste pulp and employ 3,000 persons in what will be Central America's largest and most mechanized sugar production and processing operation. Finally, it is important to take into consideration the fact that Nicaragua has at present very few alternatives in terms of generating the foreign exchange it needs for the purchase of essential imports. Sugar and meat are the agro-exports which produce the highest net return in foreign exchange, and they also happen to be important foods in the diet of Nicaraguans.[63] Nevertheless, the experience of many small under-developed societies in recent decades clearly indicates that 'whatever may be the need for foreign exchange, and whatever are the short-run pressures on employment and income, *primary export production in this historical era does not contain enough dynamic potential to transform agriculture*'.[64] Nicaragua's own experience tends to confirm this. The annual earnings from its agro-exports are not sufficient to cover its essential imports, let alone finance developments in other sectors of the economy.

Turning to the manufacturing sector, here we find evidence that Nicaragua is attempting to make a radical departure from its previous pattern of industrial development. The current long-term strategy emphasizes investment projects which will be intensive in the use of local raw materials and which will produce basic goods for local consumption. The 1984 industrial investment programme totalled 1.45 billion cordobas (about US $58 million at 28 cordobas to $1). The vast majority (1.35 billion cordobas) of this amount was for projects in the state sector, involving almost every branch of industry in Nicaragua. Most were based on the intensive use of domestic resources and the production of basic consumer goods. A few key projects were aimed at supplying Nicaragua with basic metals and a local machine-building industry which will enable the country to produce badly needed replacement parts for its existing stock of machinery. This type of industry is a necessary prerequisite for the industrial transformation of small underdeveloped societies like Nicaragua.[65]

Certain features of the machine-building industry make it quite feasible to establish in countries like Nicaragua once the initiative for development no longer depends upon the profit-making interests of local private and/or transnational capital. For example, this kind of industry is *not* significantly capital intensive and it mostly satisfies a demand for made-to-order products rather than standardized mass-produced products. Thus, the scale of production is quite small. This kind of industry can respond creatively to specific orders and function as a dynamic component of technological change.[66]

Nicaragua's industrial planners are clearly aware of the importance of establishing a machine-building industry in Nicaragua. They have initiated a major first step in this direction by locating in León what they call a *Taller Central de Mantenimiento* or Central Maintenance Workshop – a facility which will be capable of making replacement parts for all types of machinery. Finance and the initial machine tools are being provided by Bulgaria. Related to this project is one that involves the establishment of a small steel foundry in León. This foundry, which is funded by Cuba, will enable Nicaragua to cast steel parts from scrap metal, which can then be used in the central workshop. The Ministry of Industry also has plans to establish a mini-steel mill, which will make steel from scrap iron and imported iron pellets. It is estimated that this project will cost over $20 million; as yet, the finance for this important project has not been obtained. Another important project in this same sector is already producing an array of metal farm implements as basic inputs for the agricultural sector. The combination of these projects will give the country a minimum basic metals and machine-building sector, upon which further industrial development can be based. In the case of the Central Maintenance Workshop, for example, one can expect that the skilled workers in this shop will first develop the capacity to duplicate machine parts, then begin modifying the machines that are sent to them for repair, and at some later point build new machines better suited to local needs.

The importance of developing a local basic metals complex cannot be overemphasized. The material content of most products depends upon a relatively reduced number of basic materials. Three of these – iron, steel and textiles – have been the mainstay of industrial production. Nicaragua has textiles, but it does not have a local capacity to produce iron and steel. The development of an indigenous industry capable of producing these materials is essential to the integrated industrialization of the country. It is possible for small underdeveloped countries to develop a basic metals industry – even if they do not have local deposits of iron and coal. Charcoal can replace coal in iron metallurgy and pre-reduced iron ore can be imported at reasonable cost. These factors make it possible for iron and steel to be manufactured in small countries where coal and iron are not available locally.[67] It should be noted here that there is a possibility that substantial iron-ore deposits exist in the Monte Carmelo region of Nicaragua.[68] If further study proves this to be the case, then the possibility exists for Nicaragua to develop an integrated metallurgy industry.

Several other important projects illustrate the importance Nicaragua's industrial planners are attaching to vertical integration, the increased use of domestic raw materials and the substitution of domestically produced basic goods for costly imports. A glass factory is being established in the north at Ocotal. Several plastic products factories are being established in Managua, which will use locally produced PVC. With financing and machinery from the Soviet Union, a $20 million spinning mill is being built which will give the country the capacity to produce enough yarn from local cotton to satisfy the needs of the textile industry up to the year 2000. A related project which is still in the preliminary stage will establish an integrated textile complex in Esteli, to produce from domestic cotton enough fabrics to supply the domestic demand for cotton pants and towels by 1990. Another project, with funding from Cuba, is in progress which will produce industrial salts. This project is located in León, and will primarily use local raw materials. It should be noted that industrial salts are one of the basic materials used in a variety of industries, including the paper industry. The production from this plant will not only satisfy domestic demand but also provide a source of industrial export earnings. Finally, over $20 million in credits and loans have been negotiated for the construction in stages of a large complex of forestry and wood products industries, including a wood pulp and paper factory. However, the implementation of this important project (and others) is obstructed by the fact that it is located inside the northern war zone.

Nicaragua has the potential to produce most of the basic materials needed for its industrial development. However, the planned industrialization of the country requires two further conditions:

> a strategy of comprehensive planning for structural transformation requires the domestic production of those basic materials which are required as primary inputs for the manufacture of the basic goods of the community ... It also follows logically from this that a comprehensive and rational planning of industrialization must be preceded by two necessary conditions: an up-to-date and reliable inventory of the country's natural resources and the establishment of facilities for rapid and effective technological training.[69]

In this regard, it should be noted that the Instituto Nicaragüense de Recursos Naturales y del Ambiente (Nicaraguan Institute of Natural Resources and the Environment, IRENA) is involved in producing an inventory of Nicaragua's natural resources, since little is known about the resource potential of vast areas of the country. As for the establishment of technical training facilities, a combination of short-term training programmes, technical institutes and engineering schools is presently operating in Nicaragua. However, much more needs to be done in order to co-ordinate and plan the technical training of the workforce. This is especially important in view of the low level of technical knowledge and skills which characterizes the majority of the industrial labour force.

The additional energy needed to develop new industries will have to be produced locally, since the cost of importing the added amounts of petroleum would exceed the country's capacity to pay. Therefore the government has undertaken a series of key energy development projects, including the construction of two new geothermal plants. The first of these plants, located at the foot of the volcano Momotombo, is already in operation and can generate 35 megawatts of electricity. For 1984, it is expected that this plant alone will generate 21 per cent of the country's electricity needs and save between $15 million and $16 million annually in petroleum imports.[70] Nicaragua's hydroelectric potential is tremendous: and it is estimated that only 1.8 per cent of its total potential is presently being utilized.[71] Several important hydroelectric projects are presently underway in various parts of the country which will significantly increase the electrical power generated by local resources. The development of these local sources of energy is essential to the industrial development of the country.

The development of new sources of local energy, machine-building and basic metals industries, adequate technical training facilities for raising the technical level of the workforce, and new intermediate and consumer goods industries based on the intensive use of domestic resources are necessary steps for the industrial transformation of Nicaraguan society. Along with the emphasis on the development of agro-industry, they constitute an important basis for the expanded industrial development of the country and the convergence of domestic resources with domestic needs. However, without a structure of planning capable of effectively directing and co-ordinating the industrial development of the country, the integrated industrialization of Nicaraguan society will not be possible. Although the potential for such a structure exists in Nicaragua, at present it is not fully developed or operational.

All the state enterprises under COIP (and within the APP) are required to prepare annual operational and investment plans, with special emphasis placed on output targets, employment, imports, exports and financing. Planning targets are set by the complex co-ordinators in consultation with their subordinate plant managers. These are presented to the Ministry of Industry, and are then submitted to a joint inter-ministerial co-ordinating commission. The adjusted targets are then channelled back to COIP and then to the enterprise level. Alongside the process that establishes global and enterprise targets is a process for co-ordinating future investment projects. The staff of COIP assist the individual enterprises in preparing investment project proposals which are reviewed in the Ministry of Industry and prioritized. They are then sent to an inter-ministerial co-ordinating body where sectoral priorities, financing and development objectives are considered by the representatives of the various ministries and government agencies involved in the national investment process. This process appears to have a number of organizational problems which debilitate the approval, financing and execution of investment projects. Moreover, a clearly defined long-range national investment strategy does not yet exist. However, it appears that a conscious effort is being made to solve these problems and develop an effective system for investment planning and implementation.

Democratization of the planning process appears to be an open question. Worker participation in enterprise planning is in its infancy. A bottom-up, decentralized development planning process does not exist nor does it appear feasible under present conditions in Nicaragua. A discussion of the prospects for state-planned industrial development in Nicaragua must confront the question of whether or not it is possible to include the private sector in the planning process. In theory this should be possible, but in fact the experience of many countries indicates that private enterprise is not interested in any form of planning that does not give them control over the income which they generate. Moreover, as long as an important fraction of private capital in Nicaragua believes that the United States will succeed in over-throwing the Sandinista regime in the near future, it will not be willing to co-operate with the regime in any kind of planned development of the country. Thus, control of a sizeable proportion of the means of production by large and medium private capital presents a major obstacle to the planned industrial development of the country, and is a major contradiction within Nicaragua's mixed economy. Planning is really only possible in the state sector: this means leaving a sizeable proportion of the economy outside of the planning framework. Thus, planning does not extend to the entire economy and cannot prevent anomalies from occurring between the state and private sectors. It is not yet clear how this contradiction will be resolved in Nicaragua. However, for the planned development of the economy to take place, it is obvious that further socialization of the means of production in both the manufacturing and agricultural sectors is required. It should be noted here that socialization does not have to take the form of centralized state ownership, since it can also involve other forms of ownership such as co-operativization, worker self-management, municipalization, etc.[72]

Economic Assistance from the Socialist Countries

This brings us to another important factor bearing upon the prospects for Nicaragua's industrial development, namely, the country's association with the socialist countries. As previously mentioned, a number of very important investment projects are currently underway in

Nicaragua as a result of financial and technical assistance provided by one or more of the socialist countries.

Nicaragua does not have the foreign exchange it needs to purchase the new equipment, machinery, raw materials and technical skills it must initially import in order to develop its productive base. Therefore, it must obtain grants or loans from foreign sources to import these necessary items. Generally speaking, financial and technical assistance can be obtained from the socialist countries on far more favourable terms than from multilateral lending agencies such as the World Bank and the IMF, private banks or the governments of most other countries. Nicaragua has sought to take advantage of the financial and technical assistance that the socialist countries provide, particularly in view of the fact that the Reagan administration has succeeded in blocking off most of Nicaragua's past sources of financial assistance. However, Nicaragua has not fallen into the kind of dependent relationship that can result from too close an association with the larger and more technologically advanced socialist societies.

Nicaragua seems to have been successful so far in maintaining a balanced relationship with the socialist countries. Table 3.15 reveals that loans and grants from the socialist countries are an important source of financial assistance, but that they are balanced by a diversity of other sources, including substantial assistance from other Latin American countries – Mexico being the most important. Moreover, the socialist countries which have provided the most assistance to Nicaragua are Cuba and Bulgaria, two of the most appropriate in terms of their size, technology and past development experiences.

The continued financial and technical assistance of the socialist countries, as well as recently industrialized countries such as Mexico, Brazil, Argentina and Venezuela, is of critical importance to Nicaragua's industrial development. Nicaragua cannot transform its economic structures alone without substantial assistance from other countries whose interests coincide with its own. Increased trade and other forms of association with other Third World nations as well as the socalist countries are viewed by Nicaragua's revolutionary leadership as an important means of breaking the country's past ties of economic dependence upon the United States and a few other major capitalist countries.

Conclusion

As the preceding sections of this essay have indicated, it is clear that the revolutionary regime has made significant progress in transforming Nicaragua's economy during the last six years. Before the revolutionary triumph in 1979, the country had little prospect of undergoing any significant degree of industrial development. It was one of the most

Table 3.15 Loans and Grants to Nicaragua from 19 July 1979 to 28 February 1983 (in US$ millions)

Origin	1979	1980	1981	1982	1983	Total	%
Multilateral organs:	213.0	170.9	86.2	93.6	2.8	566.5	26.3
BCIE[a]	–	36.3	44.5	9.2	2.8	92.8	4.3
World Bank	–	57.0	33.7	16.0	–	106.7	5.0
IDB[b]	113.5	67.6	8.0	34.4	–	223.5	10.4
Others[c]	99.5	10.0	–	34.0	–	143.5	5.6
Bilateral sources:	84.9	301.8	426.9	460.2	8.8	1282.6	59.6
United States	–	72.6	–	–	–	72.6	3.4
Western Europe	14.6	38.7	60.2	38.7	8.8	161.0	7.5
Latin America	70.3	87.5	153.5	170.6	–	481.9	22.4
Socialist countries	–	103.0	110.2	247.9	–	461.1	21.4
Others[d]	–	–	103.0	3.0	–	106.0	4.9
Other sources	–	24.6	–	–	–	24.6	1.1
Sub-total loans[e]	297.9	497.3	513.1	553.8	11.6	1873.7	87.0
Sub-total grants[f]	83.5	121.8	55.1	18.6	–	279.0	13.0
Total	381.4	619.1	568.2	572.4	11.6	2152.7	100.0

[a] Central American Bank for Economic Integration.

[b] Inter-American Development Bank.

[c] International Agricultural Development Fund (IADF), Organization of Petroleum Exporting Countries (OPEC), Fondo de Estabilización del Mercado Común Centroamericano (FOCEM) and Associated Banks.

[d] Libya and Taiwan.

[e] Data up to 28 February 1983.

[f] Data up to 31 August 1982.

Source: International Reconstruction Fund (FIR).

Compilation: *Pensamiento Proprio* Collective (INIES).

economically backward countries in Latin America, with a fragile and import-dependent sector of light industry. The economic transformations that have been set in motion by the revolution entail a reorientation of the economy to serve the basic needs of the population and this in turn requires the rapid development of both its agricultural and manufacturing sectors. Significant steps have already been taken to develop the industrial sector, in spite of the shortage of foreign exchange, the reluctance of large private enterprise to co-operate with the revolutionary regime, and the fact that the country is at war.

However, in order to achieve the industrial transformation of the economy and progressively raise the standard of living of the majority of the population, Nicaragua's revolutionary regime must overcome the following structural obstacles:

(1) The economy continues to be overspecialized in the production of a narrow range of agro-exports that have unstable market conditions. This situation is reinforced by the existence of an agrarian bourgeoisie and petty bourgeoisie that depend upon these agro-exports for their income.

(2) The production process is extremely dependent upon costly imported inputs; the country does not have sufficient foreign exchange earnings to purchase these inputs.

(3) The economy is dependent upon foreign technology – equipment, machines, techniques of production and technical knowledge.

(4) The various sectors of the economy are disarticulated from one another. This is particularly true of the various branches of industry.

(5) The country's human resources are underdeveloped. In particular, the industrial workforce is characterized by a low level of education and technical skills.

(6) The state apparatus and the private units of production are characterized by a low level of organization and planning.

To these structural obstacles must be added the war that the US government is waging against Nicaragua.

In a very real sense, the same structural conditions that were responsible for Nicaragua's economic underdevelopment and neo-colonial dependence in the past continue to obstruct its development today. The revolutionary process in Nicaragua confronts these obstacles at every turn. The advance of the revolution and the realization of the Sandinistas' revolutionary project are contingent upon eliminating these obstacles. New structures must be established that will facilitate the rapid, balanced development of the society's productive forces as well as its reinsertion into the international economy on more favourable terms.

The low level of development of the productive forces and the general political context, both national and international, make an immediate and sweeping socialization of the means of production impractical and unwise. Thus, a transition to socialism in the immediate future does not appear probable. Yet the logic and impetus for moving in this direction over the long run will probably be generated by the necessity of resorting to socialist means to overcome the structural obstacles that now block the country's autonomous and integrated development.

In the long term, it seems clear that the only way these structural obstacles can be overcome is through the state's increased intervention in the economy and the progressive socialization of the means of production (through state ownership, co-operative ownership, mixed state/private ownership and other forms of collective ownership and management). This will require an herculean effort to increase many times over the state's present capacity to plan and manage production. At present, the state's capacity in this regard is extended to its fullest in order to maintain the operation of the productive enterprises within the APP. As more experience is gained in the administration of APP enterprises, and as the state's human resources develop, the state's capacity to plan and manage production will increase. At the same time, one can expect a comparable increase in both the organizational capabilities and the political consciousness of the popular sectors (the working class, the peasantry, the semi-proletariat and the sub-proletariat). These developments should greatly enhance the prospects for a future transition to socialism.

However, in the meantime, it appears that the economic development of the country will largely depend upon: the revolutionary government's ability to make limited investments in the state sector; the effects of the war upon the economy; and the performance of Nicaragua's private producers. The war has set back the economic recovery of the country and diverted scarce resources away from development into defence. In a very direct sense, the government of the United States is responsible for creating the present precarious state of Nicaragua's economy and for blocking the revolutionary regime's efforts to bring about a rapid and balanced development of the country's productive forces.

Notes

1. The concept of 'dependency' is widely recognized as central to an understanding of the economic structures of the Third World societies. There is, however, considerable disagreement over what factors are most responsible for the external dependency of these societies. Nevertheless, there does appear to be agreement that external dependency takes the form, on the one hand, of a lack of internal linkages between the different sectors of the economy of these societies; and, on the other hand, of strong external linkages to the international capitalist system. For a discussion of this question, see: Morten Ougaard, 'Some Remarks

Concerning Peripheral Capitalism and the Peripheral State', *Science and Society*, XLVI, no. 4 (Winter 1982-3), pp. 385-404.

2. For an excellent critique, see Clive Thomas, *Dependence and Transformation: The Economics of the Transition to Socialism* (New York and London: Monthly Review Press, 1974), pp. 13-20.

3. This is the position taken by Thomas, ibid., and Samir Amin, *Class and Nations, Historically and in the Current Crisis* (New York: Monthly Review Press, 1980).

4. International Bank for Reconstruction and Development (IBRD), *The Economic Development of Nicaragua* (Baltimore: Johns Hopkins University Press, 1983).

5. Jaime Biderman, 'The Development of Capitalism in Nicaragua: Economic Growth, Class Relations and Uneven Development', *Latin American Perspectives*, vol. X (Winter 1983), p. 14.

6. Ibid., pp. 16-17.

7. IBRD, *Economic Development of Nicaragua*, p. 109.

8. Ibid., p. 116.

9. Ibid., p. 125.

10. Biderman, 'Development of Capitalism in Nicaragua', p. 25.

11. John Weeks, *Análisis Preliminiar del Desarrollo Manufacturero 1960-1979* (Managua, 1981), p. 19.

12. CEPAL, *Caracteristicas Principales del Proceso y de la Política de Industrialización de Centroamérica, 1960-80* (Mexico: E/CEPAL/MEX 1982), p. 21.

13. IBRD, *Nicaragua: The Challenge of Reconstruction*, Report no. 3524-NI (Washington DC, 1981), p. 32.

14. Ibid., p. 67.

15. George Black, *Triumph of the People: The Sandinista Revolution in Nicaragua* (London: Zed Press, 1981), p. 201.

16. CEPAL, *Nicaragua: El Impacto de la Mutación Politica* (Mexico: E/CEPAL/G. 1147, 1981), p. 35.

17. E.V.K. Fitzgerald, *Acumulación Planificada y Distribución del Ingreso en Pequeñas Economiás Socialistas Periférices* (Managua: Instituto de Investigaciones Economicas y Sociales, 1982), p. 202.

18. Black, *Triumph of the People*, pp. 207-10.

19. Jaime Wheelock, *El Gran Desafio* (Managua: Editorial Nueva Nicaragua, 1983), p. 101.

20. 'La Economia Mixta en la Tierro de Sandino', *Pensamiento Proprio*, nos 6-7 (July-August 1983), p. 25.

21. Ibid., p. 27.

22. 'El Peso de los Distintos Sectores Socioeconómicos en la Producción del Pais', *Barricada*, 28 November 1983, p. 3.

23. 'Nicarague en la Encruci jada', *Envio*, no. 9 (July 1983), pp. 20-1.

24. Ibid., p. 18.

25. E.V.K. Fitzgerald, 'The Economics of the Revolution' in *Nicaragua in Revolution*, ed. John W. Walker (New York: Praeger, 1982), p. 14.

26. See Cámara de Industrias de Nicaragua, *Informe Anual*, 1983 (Managua, 1983).

27. IBRD, *Country Program Paper, Nicaragua* (Discussion Draft) (Washington DC, 1982), p. 16.

28. Ibid.

29. Ibid., p. 12.
30. 'Distribuyendo las cargas', *Barricada Internacional*, 14 February 1985, pp. 6–7.
31. Ibid.
32. *Envio*, p. 19.
33. Wheelock, *El Gran Desafio*, p. 110.
34. *Envio*, pp. 22–3.
35. 'Economic Policy Reoriented', *Barricada Internacional*, 28 May 1984, p. 3.
36. Ibid.
37. Thomas, *Dependence and Transformation*, pp. 212–15.
38. *Envio*, p. 19.
39. INEC, *Anuario Estadistico de Nicaragua* (Managua, 1983), p. 84.
40. Cámara de Industrias de Nicaragua, *Boletin*, no. 1 (February 1984), p. 3.
41. 'Producers Air Opinions', *Barricada Internacional*, 28 February 1985.
42. 'La Pequeña Industria en Nicaragua', *Barricada*, 17 October 1983, p. 3.
43. Ibid.
44. Ibid.
45. Ibid.
46. 'La Estructura Ocupacional de la Ciudad de Managua', *Barricada*, 2 January 1984, p. 3.
47. Ibid.
48. Ibid.
49. INEC, *Anuario Estadistico*, p. 141.
50. Ibid., p. 42.
51. Wheelock, *El Gran Desafio*, pp. 117–18.
52. Most of the information presented in this section was carefully compiled specifically for inclusion in this essay by the staff of the Nicaraguan Ministry of Industry. In particular, Reynaldo Bermudez, the Ministry's Director of Planning, was an invaluable source of assistance, information and support. The information on the textile industry, specifically, was obtained from James Zablah, Director-General of the Textile Branch of Nicaragua's Ministry of Industry.
53. MIDINRA, *Estructuro y Organización de la Agro-Industria Nicaragüense* (Managua, 1982), p. 1.
54. Ibid.
55. Ibid.
56. Ibid.
57. Thomas, *Dependence and Transformation*, p. 177.
58. See Amin and Thomas, passim.
59. *Barricada*, 5 December 1983, p. 3.
60. Thomas, *Dependence and Transformation*, p. 144.
61. Ibid.
62. Ibid., pp. 145–6.
63. MIDINRA, *Estructura y Organización*, p. 29.
64. Thomas, *Dependence and Transformation*, p. 167.
65. Ibid., p. 212.
66. Ibid., pp. 213–15.
67. Ibid., pp. 202–4.

68. Valeria de Ahlers and Max Nolff, 'Algunos Lineamientos para el Desarrollo del Sector de las Industrias Metalmecánicas de Nicaragua', mimeo (Managua, 1981), p. 49.

69. Thomas, *Dependence and Transformation*, pp. 201–2.

70. 'Situacion Energética Nacional y sus Perspectivas (primera parte)', *Nuevo Diario*, 8 March 1984, p. 5.

71. Ibid.

72. Charles Bettelheim, *The Transition to Socialist Economy* (Sussex: Harvester Press, 1978), pp. 31–110.

4 The Sandinista Mass Organizations and the Revolutionary Process

Gary Ruchwarger

Introduction

This essay attempts to assess the role of the Sandinista mass organizations in the Nicaraguan revolutionary process. After discussing their pre-triumph origins, it examines the popular associations'[1] relationship to both the Frente Sandinista de Liberacion Nacional (Sandinista National Liberation Front – FSLN) and the revolutionary state. The essay also explores the development of democratic practices within the popular associations and the power they wield in the revolution.

What exactly are mass organizations and what role do they play in a revolutionary society? A mass organization is a collective association that represents the fundamental interests of a particular social or demographic sector of society. There are five principal Sandinista mass organizations: the Sandinista Defence Committees, the National Union of Farmers and Cattle-raisers, the Sandinista Workers' Federation, the Rural Workers' Association and the Luisa Amanda Espinosa Association of Nicaraguan Women.[2] These organizations are called Sandinista because they recognize Nicaragua's ruling party, the Sandinista National Liberation Front, as the guiding political force in the country.

Three of the five mass organizations are class-based, that is, they represent specific socio-economic groups in Nicaraguan society. The Union of Farmers and Cattle-raisers represents a large proportion of the country's peasants, the Rural Workers' Association represents most of the agricultural workers on both private and state farms, and the Sandinista Workers' Federation represents the overwhelming majority of Nicaragua's industrial workers. The Nicaraguan Women's Association, on the other hand, is open to all women regardless of socio-economic status. Finally, the Sandinista Defence Committees are made up of people who live in the same neighbourhood. Although neither the women's organization nor the neighbourhood associations are class-based institutions, the overwhelming majority of activists in these two mass organizations are peasants, workers, artisans and poor merchants. Consequently, they share many concerns with the strictly class-based popular associations.

The Sandinistas call the mass organizations 'schools of democracy'. But what do they mean by 'democracy'? Most political theorists associate democracy with a system in which potential decision-makers compete for the people's vote. This view of democracy – what might be called the orthodox position – is the dominant conception of democracy in advanced capitalist countries. To the Sandinistas, however, democracy is associated with a system in which citizens participate in political, social and economic decision-making. In the tradition of such theorists of democracy as Jean-Jacques Rousseau, John Stuart Mill and G.D.H. Cole, the Sandinistas believe that participation is crucial to the creation and maintenance of a democratic society.[3] In a speech delivered in July 1983, Sergio Ramirez, the current Vice-President of Nicaragua, offered the FSLN's view of democracy:

> For us, the efficiency of a political model depends on its capacity to resolve the problems of democracy and justice. Effective democracy, like we intend to practice in Nicaragua, consists of ample popular participation; a permanent dynamic of the people's participation in a variety of political and social tasks; the people who give their opinions and are listened to; the people who suggest, construct and direct, organize themselves, who attend to community, neighborhood and national problems; a people who are active in the sovereignty and the defense of that sovereignty and also teach and give vaccinations; a daily democracy and not one that takes place every four years, when at that, or every four, five or six years when formal elections take place; the people don't go as a minority but in their totality, and they consciously elect the best candidate and not one chosen like a soap or deodorant, a vote freely made and not manipulated by an advertising agency, a vote for change to improve the nation and not in favor of a transnational finance company or an industrial military trust ... for us democracy is not merely a formal model, but a continual process capable of giving the people that elect and participate in it the real possibility of transforming their living conditions, a democracy which establishes justice and ends exploitation.[4]

The Nicaraguan people are 'transforming their living conditions' mainly through their activity in the mass organizations. Approximately two-thirds of the country's adult population are involved in these collective associations. In fact, many Nicaraguans are simultaneously active in at least two grassroots organizations. Through a painstaking process of trial and error, popular association members are learning how to participate in a revolution that is increasingly becoming a transformation of their own making.

The Origins of the Sandinista Mass Organizations

Although each of the mass organizations had distinct origins and tasks before the revolution, all of them shared certain fundamental characteristics: they created an opening for the development of political consciousness, contributed to the physical defence of communities and defended particular group interests. More importantly, however, all of them acted as 'intermediate organizations', consolidating the FSLN's relationship to different sectors of the anti-Somoza mass movement.

Following a series of military defeats suffered shortly after its formation in 1961, the FSLN recognized that it had to develop strong links with the oppressed majority of the population. Furthermore, the Sandinistas were convinced that certain social sectors were ready to be organized; for by the end of the 1950s the first workers' and students' cells had appeared in Managua and León, and rural workers were organizing in the sugar and cotton mills of Chinandega and in the coffee plantations of Matagalpa, Estelí Somoto and Ocotal.[5] The FSLN began to build ties with these sectors by creating a clandestine and semi-legal network designed to furnish logistical and political support for the armed struggle.

During its pre-triumph history, the Sandinistas' strength could be measured by gauging its relationship to the mass movement via the mass organizations. When the FSLN was forced underground after the National Guard attack on a Managua safe house in 1969, the need to assert its presence through the popular associations became more crucial than ever. In the early 1970s, the Sandinistas carried out intensive organizing efforts in the factories and working-class barrios and laid the foundations for their subsequent gains in trade union organization. During this period the FSLN also penetrated the universities and revived the student organization, the Frente Estudiantil Revolucionario (Revolutionary Student Front – FER).[6]

To create these mass organizations, their founders and early activists had to overcome tremendous obstacles. Both FSLN cadres and non-FSLN organizers were operating in a society with no history of mass organization and amid a climate of intense National Guard repression. They were also working with a population characterized by a low educational level[7] and very little political consciousness.

The Sandinistas encountered great difficulties in organizing women.[8] Isolated from one another, Nicaraguan women – with few exceptions – were unable to develop a feminist and revolutionary consciousness before the late 1970s. This common legacy of isolation stemmed from circumstances which varied with, but also cut across, class differences. For peasant and working-class women, the burdens of subsistence and illiteracy reinforced their marginalization. The physical isolation of peasant women in remote regions and the effects of seasonal migration compounded the organizing difficulties. For most urban women who worked outside their homes, especially those employed as street and market vendors, work experiences strengthened a competitive and individualistic worldview; only a tiny fraction of working-class women were organized in trade unions. While middle- and upper-class women did not share the same problems of basic physical survival with women of other classes, the ideology of the nuclear family and domesticity simultaneously exalted and marginalized them, turning their homes into isolated cells.

Despite these obstacles, a series of developments between 1972 and 1977 helped break down the barriers to women's participation in the struggle against the dictatorship. The aftermath of the 1972 earthquake, the increasing strength and visibility of the movement against Somoza, and the deepening economic crisis and political repression stimulated the development of the Nicaraguan women's movement. As Somoza's regime became more and more brutal and the economy worsened, women of all classes began to unite. Finally, in September 1977, a small group of women established the Asociacion de Mujeres Ante la Problematica Nacional (Association of Nicaraguan Women Confronting the National Problem – AMPRONAC).

Winning the support of the rural population in the early years of the FSLN was no easy matter. Deprivation and isolation had made the Nicaraguan peasant withdrawn and taciturn, wary of strangers. Despite a lingering sympathy for Sandino, many peasants were loyal Somocistas, while others were at least to some degree influenced by the dictatorship's ideological hegemony. For the Sandinistas, the problem was to distinguish between these two types of peasants in order to avoid the constant danger of being uncovered and reported. Because family relationships are the essence of Nicaraguan peasant communities, FSLN cadres were fully accepted only after they had completely integrated themselves into the family life of the peasants.[9]

For many years National Guard repression thwarted FSLN efforts to organize in the countryside. For example, the attempt to form a union in the cotton-growing region of Chinandega led to the slaughter of some 300 peasants and rural workers by the National Guard.[10] As the Epica Task Force notes:

> In contrast to most of Central and South American countries with long histories of rural movements, the National Guard's political repression and Somoza's private agro-business expansion effectively thwarted any efforts to organize campesinos until the 1970s.[11]

Progressive church groups, working closely with FSLN members, succeeded in mobilizing many rural peasants and workers during the 1970s. The Catholic Church had traditionally fostered passivity and resignation among the population in the countryside. But when Christian activists devoted themselves to enabling peasants to improve their lives, Sandinista militants were forced to acknowledge that religion could play a dynamic role in the struggle against Somoza. The combination of the Jesuit-inspired training/reflection seminars, the social work practised by the 'Delegates of the Word' and FSLN organizing efforts led to the official establishment of the Asociacion de Trabajadores del Campo (Rural Workers' Association – ATC) in March 1978.[12]

As its first public act, the Association organized a march and hunger strike in Diriamba on 9 April 1978, to protest the debilitating conditions of the peasant population. Despite the National Guard's efforts to prevent the demonstration, the ATC mobilized 1,200 members and supporters.

Although the Guard managed to break up the protest march, a tremendous feeling of solidarity developed among other anti-Somoza forces. Women from AMPRONAC, high school students and university opposition groups initiated hunger strikes throughout the country to show their support for the militants in the ATC.[13] The hunger march and the subsequent hunger strike propelled the Rural Workers' Association into political alignment with the FSLN:

> The grassroots committees of the ATC thus became committees in support of all-out war [against the dictatorship] and carried out their political line in conjunction with the FSLN. During May, June, July, and August, hundreds from the ATC armed and organized themselves in popular militias, while others continued their work on plantations and farms. Their homes became virtual Sandinista strongholds and their goal was one and the same with the FSLN: 'Death to the dictatorship; Death to Somocismo.'[14]

In June 1978, the Movimiento Pueblo Unido (United People's Movement – MPU) was formed. Within the framework of the MPU, the Sandinistas joined 23 political, student, labour, women's and civic organizations to develop a concrete plan for mass activity, and to build unity in the revolutionary movement. The MPU was the fruit of long years of work by the pro-Sandinista mass organizations, and played a crucial role in the last year of the insurrectionary struggle against the dictatorship.

In August 1978, the MPU established a network of underground neighbourhood cells, called Comites de Defensa Civil (Civil Defence Committees – CDCs). During the last year of the war against Somoza, these cells provided urban residents with an autonomous power structure. Activists in the CDCs (which subsequently became the Comites de Defensa Sandinista – CDSs) carried out many tasks: they organized the stockpiling of food, medicine and weapons; built air-raid shelters; and trained people in first aid, military strategy, barricade-building and the use of weapons. After FSLN military forces had liberated a city, the CDCs met the emergency needs of the population.

All the mass organizations participated in the final drive to oust Somoza. The ATC, for example, took up an active combat role against the National Guard in the September 1978 insurrection. Armed with outdated weapons, Association combatants provided cover for the Front's withdrawal from the cities of Chinandega and Carazo. And throughout the 1979 fighting, the ATC carried out a series of harassment operations against Somoza's troops.[15]

AMPRONAC members played a key role within the CDCs during the final insurrection, contributing to every aspect of the war effort: they constructed barricades; hid combatants, weapons and medicine; administered first aid and delivered messages; prepared food and fabricated bombs; and engaged in vigilance and combat.[16]

The originality of the Sandinista strategy lay in the relationship they had fostered between the vanguard and the mass organizations. This dynamic unity provided the necessary counterweight to the highly-trained, better-equipped National Guard, which outnumbered the Sandinistas ten to one. The FSLN realized that victory depended not on its own members but on the popular forces that rose up against Somoza. Sandinista Defence Minister Humberto Ortega emphasizes the centrality of the mass movement:

> It is very difficult to take power without a creative combination of all forms of struggle wherever they can take place: countryside, city, town, neighborhood, mountain, etc., but always based on the idea that the mass movement is the focal point of the struggle and not the vanguard with the masses limited to merely supporting it.[17]

The massive participation in the overthrow of Somoza provided the FSLN with the basis of its post-triumph legitimacy. The close working relationship that FSLN cadres and mass organization activists had developed during the anti-Somoza struggle served as a foundation for the subsequent ties between the party and the grassroots organizations. Because the organized masses toppled the dictatorship, the embryonic popular associations were prepared to assume a central role in the post-victory revolutionary process.

The Mass Organizations vis-á-vis the FSLN and the State

The relationship between the mass organizations and the two other power centres of the revolution – the party and the state – raises a number of fundamental questions. Does the FSLN encourage the mass organizations to function as a parallel source of power in the revolution? Or do the Sandinistas manipulate the mass organizations from above and deny these organizations an independent role in the new regime? Do the constituencies of the popular associations regard the FSLN as their vanguard, and if so, what action do the grassroots organizations take when they oppose party positions? Does the state permit popular participation in the formation of government policy? Or does it employ the mass organizations merely as instruments to implement executive decisions? Do the mass organizations carry out their tasks in close collaboration with the government, and if so, how does such collaboration affect their ability to act as a watchdog of the state?

The Mass Organizations and the FSLN

The relationship between the mass organizations and the FSLN is complex. While the popular associations receive political and ideological guidance from the party,[18] they have maintained organizational and financial independence.[19] Although the grassroots organizations often serve as a rearguard and support system for FSLN projects and activities, they have had significant conflicts with the party, and are independent actors in their own right. The following discussion outlines both the co-operative and conflictual aspects of the mass organization/ party relationship, focusing on the extent to which the popular associations exercise autonomy vis-à-vis the Frente.

The FSLN did not have a coherent plan for the direction of the mass organizations in the early period of the revolutionary process. In fact, a number of Sandinista leaders took the position that the mass organizations ought to evolve independently, without the FSLN imposing a blueprint on their development. For example, in early 1980 Comandante Monica Baltodano, head of the FSLN's Secretariat for Mass Organizations, commented: 'We were working to give answers to problems as they presented themselves, but we didn't have lines laid out.'[20] Even if they had wanted to exert their influence, the Sandinistas at that stage lacked politically experienced cadres capable of guiding the transformation of semi-autonomous, embryonic committees into independent, mature national organizations.

The Sandinistas did not view the popular organizations as agitational agents, nor as vehicles to communicate policy to various sectors of the population. Although the mass organizations partially served these functions, FSLN leaders insisted that the grassroots organizations act independently on behalf of their members. In a speech delivered on 20 April 1980, Carlos Nunez defined the party's position on mass organization autonomy:

> We would like to generate the consciousness within the mass organizations that they should work to preserve the revolutionary political project and that they also should be instruments capable of autonomously expressing the demands of the sectors that they represent. And they have to express these demands employing methods ranging from the most usual to the most unusual.[21]

In addition to supporting the independence of the popular associations, the FSLN views the organized masses as the 'architects of history' in the new Nicaragua. Agustin Lara, a Sandinista regional political secretary, underscores this idea:

> The FSLN has the conception that the role of the masses in the revolutionary process is something fundamental; it is not an accessory nor something secondary. The masses themselves have demonstrated that they themselves are the principal agent in revolutionary transformations; they are the active and conscious agents of the revolution. As a political organization we relate ourselves to them.[22]

The FSLN relates to the mass organizations in terms of its self-conception of vanguard. But this conception relies intrinsically upon the Sandinistas' relationship to the people. 'The FSLN', says Comandante Nunez,

> came to be and is the vanguard of the Nicaraguan people not only for having defined the correct way of struggle, but also for having clearly defined that the masses were the forces capable of moving the wheel of history. If yesterday, oriented and directed by their vanguard, they were the motor of the overthrow of the dictatorship, then today, directed by that vanguard, they are the motor of the revolution.[23]

While the vanguard role entails carrying out a leadership function for the masses, this does not mean that the Sandinistas regard the relationship as a static one. Ricardo Wheelock of the FSLN has described the relationship as follows:

> In Nicaragua the people aren't isolated from the vanguard or vice versa. There's intercommunication between the two of them. That's an important dynamic. Neither is our vanguard thinking in terms of utopias, nor are our people making revolution independently of the vanguard.[24]

The Sandinistas and the mass organizations have formalized their means of communication. Zonal and regional officials of the grassroots organizations regularly send written reports to the zonal and regional offices of the FSLN, detailing both the achievements and problems of the popular associations. In turn, the FSLN sends *orientaciones* – orientations – to the mass organizations' leadership bodies. Orientations either set broad policy lines for pro-Sandinista organizations to follow, or call on the popular associations to carry out a specific revolutionary task. Moreover, orientations are delivered only after prior face-to-face consultation with mass organization officials.

The FSLN frequently proposes that the mass organizations meet certain goals in carrying out their activities. For example, in February

1984 an FSLN zonal office in Managua called on the Sandinista Defence Committees to recruit 100 additional volunteers from each barrio to carry out 'revolutionary vigilance', a five-hour per night neighbourhood watch programme. But before the FSLN set this goal, it met with the CDS zonal leadership to see if it was a realistic proposition. Only after the CDS officials discussed the proposal and told the party that 100 more volunteers were feasible, did the FSLN issue their orientation to the CDSs.[25]

In an August 1984 interview a Rural Workers' Association zonal secretary described how his organization co-ordinates its work with the FSLN:

> We make a weekly work plan, then try to add to this the tasks that the *Frente* sends us. For example, we set production as a priority and then the *Frente* sends us an *orientacion* asking for 32 volunteers for the reserves and the militia. But we may see that this is not possible because the men are needed for production. So we send a written report to the FSLN explaining why the 32 men cannot be mobilized. This happened only this week.
>
> Each Monday there are zonal meetings with the FSLN secretary of propaganda and political education in the zonal offices of the *Frente*. Representatives from the ATC, CST, AMNLAE, UNAG, CDS, JS 19, FETSALUD, UNE, and ANDEN attend the meetings. Here we discuss the new lines. We may discuss the lack of manpower for the harvest of a product. We discuss what mechanisms can be used to get more workers to participate in the harvest. For example, right now we need more people [to harvest] beans. The Juventud Sandinista will guarantee a brigade of students for a *roja y negra* ['black and red' – a volunteer work day]. After the meeting the *Frente* sends us the orientations based on these discussions.[26]

Popular association officials stress that their organizations do not regard FSLN orientations as orders. As one CDS secretary declared:

> If the *Frente* has a task for us we talk with them and decide whether we can do it or not. We negotiate with them to see whether it's possible. We are an autonomous organization. We don't have a vertical relation with them.[27]

To verify the assertion that the popular associations' relationship to the FSLN is not 'vertical', one need only consider two of the conflicts that have occurred between the party and the grassroots organizations. These disputes have involved key revolutionary policies.

One such conflict occurred in early 1980. In the months following the revolutionary triumph, the Association of Rural Workers engaged in a series of land takeovers of non-Somoza farms.[28] The Association argued that land seizures were the just, heroic response of the rural majority.

The Sandinista leadership, concerned with maintaining the support of the national bourgeoisie and ensuring the survival of the revolution, tended to oppose post-victory land takeovers.

By early 1980, the tensions over land seizures were building towards a dramatic climax. In late 1979, the courts moved to return to owners those farms and ranches spontaneously taken over by peasants and farmworkers, if it could not be shown that the owners had been linked to Somoza. For the ATC, however, any return of land to private owners symbolized an end to the process of agrarian reform at a time when thousands of workers and peasants expected its continued advance.

Carrying banners and machetes, more than 30,000 peasants and landless rural workers from all over Nicaragua converged on Managua's Plaza of the Revolution on 17 February 1980 to present their demands before the Government of National Reconstruction. Edgardo Garcia, Secretary General of the ATC, demanded that all land then under the control of the agrarian reform agency be legally transferred to the Area de Propriedad del Pueblo (Area of Public Ownership – APP). Garcia insisted that 'not one inch of land be returned' to the original large landowners.[29] The ATC also demanded the reduction of land rental prices, the requirement that landlords rent their unused land at these lower rates and a more liberal credit policy for peasant producers.

Shortly before the ATC rally, the FSLN backed down from its previous position and decided to support the Association's demands. Jaime Wheelock, Minister of Agricultural Development and a member of the FSLN's National Directorate, responded to the demonstrators: 'We know that your demands are just, and this march gives us the confidence to advance and make further transformations.' While Wheelock stressed the need for the agrarian reform to follow an orderly path, avoiding 'anarchic and spontaneous actions', he affirmed that 'there are elements among the landowners who must be hit hard if their lands are left idle'.[30] He promised that the state would move quickly to meet the ATC's demands. At the same time, Sergio Ramirez of the governing junta announced that a new decree was imminent. Issued on 3 March, the decree ordered the immediate takeover of all the confiscated lands, excluding those owned by small producers.[31]

Another conflict between a mass organization and the FSLN centred on the law establishing a compulsory draft. Until January 1984, Nicaragua's primary defence had been provided by two volunteer forces: the Popular Sandinista Army and the Sandinista Popular Militias. Although the Sandinistas had been discussing a compulsory draft since the victory over Somoza, they waited until August 1983 to introduce legislation calling for obligatory military service.

All the Sandinista popular associations backed the draft proposal strongly. But AMNLAE objected to that part of the law that made a distinction between men and women, excluding the latter from the draft. The women's association launched an attack against the draft legislation and a rigorous debate ensued. Glenda Monterrey, the General Secretary of AMNLAE, expressed the Association's position on the law:

> We all have limitations, and we run into obstacles. This does not mean that our society can adopt a law that includes discrimination on the basis of sex ... Women are demanding the right to take an active part in the service that is being organized.[32]

During the month of popular debate over the law, AMNLAE members campaigned vigorously for their position. They pointed out that many women participated in a combat role during the struggle against Somoza, and that thousands of women were contributing to the defence of Nicaragua's sovereignty in the war against the counter-revolutionaries; between one third and one half of the militia members are women, and women comprise about 30 per cent of the reserve battalions directly involved in combat with the Contras.[33]

The final version of the military service law reflected a compromise between the position of AMNLAE and that of the FSLN: women won the right to be included in active military service as volunteers, but such service would be compulsory only for men. In November 1983, several thousand women throughout Nicaragua registered for active service.[34]

Thus, the mass organizations, in advancing the interests of the social sectors which they represent, sometimes enter into conflict with the FSLN, which is charged with mediating the interests of the revolutionary process as a whole. Although the party is usually supportive of popular association demands, it withdraws its support when the grassroots organizations press demands that conflict with the Sandinista policy of national unity. For example, some observers speculate that the FSLN opposed AMNLAE's proposal to extend the draft to women because it would have alienated certain Catholic sectors that have so far supported the revolution.

Interlocking Memberships

The FSLN draws most of its new members from the ranks of the mass organizations. For example, in the northern city of Esteli – a Sandinista stronghold – four of the five AMNLAE zonal officers are FSLN militants[35] and six of the eight regional CDS leaders are in the party.[36] Agustin Lara describes the attributes that the party looks for in its recruits:

> The FSLN is a political organization that feeds its ranks with people from different social sectors, but largely from among the peasants and workers. From the mass organizations [we recruit] ... the excellent leaders who wish to join. To be an aspiring member you must be 18,

and be recognized in your sector as being capable, honest, and so on. Without having authority, prestige, and love from the masses you can't enter. You must be an example: last in gaining privileges and first in making sacrifices. These requirements demonstrate to the people that the *Frente* chooses the best people from the masses.[37]

Lara emphasizes that in most cases the new recruits maintain their active participation in the mass organizations.[38]

But because both the party and the popular associations lack sufficient numbers of politically trained cadres, conflict sometimes arises over the recruitment of new members. If the FSLN recruits an ATC activist, for example, and then assigns this person to a task unrelated to the union's activities, the ATC loses a valuable member and must then spend considerable time and effort training a replacement.[39]

The FSLN's continuous recruitment of mass organization activists reinforces the party's close links to the grassroots. But it also poses the danger that the Sandinistas could one day unwittingly control rather than guide the mass organizations. For if the Sandinistas ever lose their close relationship to Nicaragua's popular sectors, they could take advantage of their well-established presence among the mass organization leadership by unduly influencing the popular associations.

Edgardo Garcia is both General Secretary of the ATC and a member of the Sandinista Assembly.[40] When asked whether he thought there was any danger in Sandinistas holding dual memberships, he responded:

> I don't have any fear in the overlap of members of the *Frente* and the mass organizations. I don't have any fear of this. Remember, Nicaraguans of the popular classes don't mind taking on anyone – including militants who have the most experience in the guerrilla and in the FSLN.[41]

Mass organization autonomy will face its greatest challenge as the institutionalization of the revolutionary process unfolds. Until January 1985, the mass organizations maintained their own elected representatives in the Council of State, the nation's legislative body. But because only political parties fielded candidates in the November 1984 national elections, the popular associations lost their power to choose legislative representatives directly. And although many FSLN delegates to the new National Assembly are mass organization leaders,[42] they could face a serious dilemma: a conflict of interests. As FSLN militants and mass organization members, these delegates may have to vote on legislation backed by the party, but opposed by their popular association constituencies. It remains to be seen whether they will be able effectively to represent both the FSLN and grassroots interests.

The Mass Organizations and the State

The relationship between the mass organizations and the state is marked by co-operation as well as conflict. The popular associations officially recognize the revolutionary government as the instrument that directs the administrative policy of the government,[43] and assist the state in planning and executing national policies. Indeed, few government programmes could be implemented without the co-operation of the mass organizations. At the same time, however, the grassroots organizations act as a watchdog over state power. Because the nature of the state requires a bureaucracy, the government tends towards rigidity and inflexibility in reacting to popular demands. Therefore, the mass organizations constantly monitor state activities to ensure that the state responds to the needs of the population.

Immediately after Somoza's overthrow, the new state did not yet exist.[44] Consequently, amid the destruction and chaos in the first days after the war, the Sandinista Defence Committees (CDSs) took upon themselves parastatal functions. Continuing and expanding the tasks they carried out during the insurrection, the CDSs filled the vacuum left by the disintegration of the Somocista state and economy. During this period, the neighbourhood organizations distributed food donated by foreign agencies; treated cases of malnutrition, polio and malaria; found housing for the homeless; and began the process of reconstruction. In addition, the CDSs worked with the militias to organize security on a block-to-block basis, defending against the continuing threat from roaming National Guards as well as common criminals.[45]

Even after the state apparatus began to function, the mass organizations continued to carry out some state tasks. 'They [the mass organizations] behaved as parastatal organs', explains Carlos Nunez of the FSLN, 'because they failed to find in the state the receptiveness, dynamism, and flexibility required to solve real problems'.[46] The Sandinistas have usually supported the mass organizations in conflicts with the state, backing their attempts to streamline government operations and activities. For example, the popular associations have helped increase government efficiency in the supply of basic food products.

Food shortages have been a long-standing problem in Nicaragua. Under Somoza, the development of an agro-export economy forced peasants to seek their subsistence on the most marginalized lands. Inefficient patterns of production and the failure to carry out multi-cropping further aggravated the food problem. Numerous middlemen plagued the transportation and distribution of food, each trying to maximize personal profit.

The Sandinistas face another series of difficulties. The severe shortage of foreign exchange prevents the government from importing food, machinery or spare parts necessary to increase food production. Because the purchasing power of most sectors of the population has greatly expanded, considerable pressure on the market for food products exists.[47] In addition, the government's failure to gain full control over the allocation of basic goods has exacerbated distribution problems – hoarding and speculation are rampant.

The war against the Contras has greatly aggravated the supply problem. As of February 1985, 40 per cent of Nicaragua's resources were devoted to fighting the Contras, leaving few goods available for civilian consumption.[48] Up to 50 per cent of the country's beans and corn is now lost because peasants are unable to plant or harvest in the war zone.[49] In addition, the massive transfer of vehicles to the battle fronts has depleted an already inadequate food transport system.

The government has not ignored these problems. The state institutions responsible for production, sale and distribution have been working with the mass organizations to improve the supply situation. The Ministries of Internal Commerce, Industry and Agrarian Reform deal most directly with the provision of basic goods, but they alone are incapable of normalizing the commerce of staple products. Not surprisingly, the government has turned to the grassroots organizations for assistance with the supply problem.

Since Somoza's defeat, the popular associations have played a direct and leading role in tackling the supply problem. In early 1983 the government and the mass organizations took concrete steps to institutionalize popular participation in the planning, design and implementation of supply policies and programmes. Two co-ordinating bodies have been established to this end: the Councils of Internal Commerce made up of different ministries and the mass organizations, and the Popular Supply Committees comprising representatives of the CDSs, the Ministry of Internal Commerce (MICOIN) and the Sandinista Police. The Councils of Internal Commerce plan global policies, while the Popular Supply Committees attempt to resolve the more immediate local supply problem.[50]

The CDS, as the most widely-based mass organization, plays the major role in the distribution of consumer products. The CDSs work closely with the Ministry of Internal Commerce to secure adequate supplies for the country's thousands of retail outlets. The CDSs also enforce government price controls on certain basic goods, and maintain a distribution coupon system that allows families to purchase fixed quantities of eight basic items each week: rice, beans, sugar, laundry soap, toilet paper, corn, oil and eggs.

The other mass organizations have played a more limited role in assisting the state with supply distribution. The women's association co-ordinates a maternal child programme that aids low-income families suffering from malnutrition. AMNLAE secures medical attention, nutritious foods and social security benefits for these families. In 1982 AMNLAE began a drive to collect containers for preserving fruits and vegetables, and in 1983 launched a campaign to promote the cultivation of family and communal gardens.[51]

Both the Rural Workers' Association and the Sandinista Workers' Federation have worked with the National Basic Grain Marketing Enterprise and the Ministry of Commerce to establish commissaries in work centres. Thousands of urban and rural workers now have better access to basic consumer products; they are able to purchase these goods at official prices and can also buy on credit. The Sandinista Workers' Federation tracks the volume of products at MICOIN distribution points; then unions can make accurate purchase orders for their members. Direct sales from MICOIN to workers prevent goods from entering distribution channels that are subject to speculation and hoarding.[52]

The National Union of Farmers and Cattle-raisers (UNAG) maintains some 300 storage facilities for agricultural products. UNAG farmers are working to overcome the shortage of basic grains, producing more quantities of beans and corn every harvest season. Union lobbying for the repair and construction of roads facilitates the transportation and marketing of its members' goods and products. In some zones, where the Ministry of Construction has been unable to send its crews, UNAG relies on its own membership to repair roads, to maintain clear access in remote rural areas and to provide transport for peasants in isolated areas.[53]

While the CDSs are aware of the effects that the war and the US blockade have on supplies, they cannot overlook state agencies' aggravation of the shortage problem. Defining the neighbourhood organizations' relationship to the Ministry of Internal Commerce, one regional CDS official bluntly proclaimed: 'We maintain a belligerent attitude towards MICOIN. We have to pressure them to send products to retail outlets. For example, if cooking oil doesn't arrive we pressure them for more oil.'[54]

Mass organizations have continued to combat bureaucratic short-comings and negligence. In his major speech of April 1980, Carlos Nunez encouraged the popular associations to take militant action when confronted with governmental inaction:

> The mass organizations should gather and make as their own the demands of the masses, of their social sectors, and struggle for their materialization through all the new mechanisms that the Revolution has instituted. But when these channels are closed, when they knock and nobody answers, whether it be because of bureaucracy, whether it be because of liberal methods, whether it be because the problems of the masses are not taken into account, etc., our organizations must move on to other forms of political persuasion.[55]

Bureaucratic foul-ups and red tape have delayed or prevented the delivery of promised material assistance. UNAG, for example, must frequently pressure the agrarian reform agency to deliver tractors, seeds, fertilizers and other inputs needed to maintain production on agricultural co-operatives. At the UNAG National Assembly in February 1984, union leaders denounced government mismanagement of programmes affecting the small and medium peasantry.[56]

The popular associations and the state have attempted to cut red tape by reordering their structures. In July 1982, the state began to decentralize its authority by placing ministerial delegates in the various regions and zones of the country.[57] At the same time, the mass organizations began to restructure their intermediate bodies – previously established at the municipal and departmental levels – in order to correspond to the new zonal and regional divisions of the country. This new structure provides a direct link between mass organization leaders and government representatives at each level of the state's administrative hierarchy.

For example, if a CDS zonal executive committee wishes to discuss its members' housing problems, the committee will arrange a meeting with its counterpart, a zonal delegate of the Ministry of Housing. Both the zonal CDS representatives and the ministry's delegate may have to appeal to higher levels of their respective organizations. But the co-ordination of structures reduces or eliminates intermediaries between the popular associations and the state bodies, thereby facilitating the implementation of revolutionary projects.

The relationship between the mass organizations and the state contains a fundamental tension. On the one hand, the grassroots organizations aid the government in the design and execution of revolutionary policy; on the other hand, they monitor the state to ensure that it responds to popular needs and grievances. This latter task is difficult because the revolutionary state is plagued by numerous problems: scarcity of material resources, inadequate technical and fiscal capacities, poorly trained administrative personnel and bureaucratic red tape. Facing these obstacles, the popular associations must heed the words of Carlos Nunez:

> The mass organizations, acting in the framework of the general line of the revolution, must have sufficient right to resort ... to private criticism, utilization of all the communications media, and even mobilizations to demand the measures necessary to guarantee that their concerns are heard.[58]

Of course, the elimination of the causes of bureaucratism and other state deficiencies is a distant prospect. Nevertheless, the popular associations possess both the awareness of the problem's existence and the determination to combat it, and will therefore continue to pursue their role as watchdog over the Nicaraguan state.

The Development of Internal Democracy

The Sandinista mass organizations serve as 'schools of democracy' for their members. Since the victory, the popular associations have been experimenting with democratic procedures to select their leaders, to promote effective member participation in decision-making, to ensure that their leaders are held accountable for their actions and to guarantee political equality to all members. These experiments have had mixed results.

The Selection of Leaders

Today all the mass organizations employ democratic procedures to select their leadership, but during the initial period of the revolution it was common to appoint executives from above. This led to a commandist tendency in some mass organizations, alienating sectors of the rank and file. The Sandinista Labour Federation, for example, sometimes appointed advisers to union locals who were unresponsive to rank-and-file concerns. This paternalist practice disenchanted many CST workers during the first year of the revolutionary process.[59]

The Rural Workers' Association managed to avoid the early errors committed by the CST: it was the first mass organization to replace appointed officials with elected ones. In December 1979, 250 farmworkers from across the country gathered in a constituent assembly to draw up the association's statutes and replace the appointed executive with an elected leadership. Prior to the assembly, 660 local assemblies had been held, allowing the entire membership to discuss all the issues before they were raised at the constituent assembly. Through open elections, farmworkers selected delegates to the assembly, as well as local union officers.[60]

In 1983, the CDSs carried out a round of restructuring at the zonal and regional levels to match the state's decentralization process. A regional CDS secretary in Las Segovias explains how the rank and file chose the executive committees in his region:

> We have a system of popular democracy. At the zonal and regional level, we are approved or rejected in public assemblies. Our record of struggle against Somoza is taken into account, as well as our level of acceptance by the people. All block, neighborhood, rural district, and community leaders participate. So in this zone four hundred CDSs and two thousand people can participate. In October 1983 the regional assembly met and chose the regional secretaries. Each zone put forth two or three candidates that were chosen at the base level. Seven people were elected and we then decided among ourselves who should be responsible for each position.[61]

The National Union of Farmers and Cattle-raisers (UNAG), the only mass organization to emerge after the revolutionary victory, established both its original structure and leadership through a democratic process. Until the founding of UNAG, peasants with small and medium plots of land had been organized by the ATC, but by 1980 it became clear to many farmers that the ATC could no longer respond to the needs of both the peasants and landless agricultural workers.[62] Consequently, in late 1980 many peasants began to meet on their own to discuss the establishment of a new organization. Within three months, meetings of hundreds of small and medium campesinos took place in towns and villages throughout Nicaragua. A total of about 10,000 attended five regional assemblies and on 25 and 26 April 1981, 360 delegates met in a constituent assembly to form UNAG. The assembly delegates adopted the resolutions that were first passed at local meetings and regional assemblies.[63]

Participation in Decision-making

How the mass organizations handle decision-making power is another test of their democracy. Are leaders the only ones who set priorities, assign tasks and design the mechanisms used to carry out these tasks? Or is a genuine effort made to distribute responsibility down to the base in order to perform the work of the organization in truly democratic manner?

There is no single answer appropriate to all the mass organizations. The popular associations seek to incorporate Nicaragua's workers, peasants and poor merchants into the decision-making process at all levels. Power-sharing within the grassroots organizations depends on both the leadership and the rank and file. Leaders must do everything possible to encourage the development of those members who are not as self-confident, articulate or politically sophisticated as others within the organizations, while base-level members must constantly monitor the leadership to guarantee that tasks are rotated, debates are open and technical and political training is available to all interested members.

How is decision-making power handled in a Sandinista Defence Committee? The case of the Managua barrio Georgino Andrade provides one answer to this question.[64] Settled in early 1981, the barrio is home to hundreds of working-class and poor merchant families. After the settlement was established, Housing Ministry officials determined that many of the homes in the neighbourhood were sitting on two earthquake faults, and that the design of the barrio failed to meet established urban planning standards. Ministry representatives told the barrio's executive committee that the neighbourhood would have to be reorganized. To meet the Housing Ministry's recommendations, the leadership, in conjunction with the CDS co-ordinators, developed a plan to relocate the affected families.

Both the block and neighbourhood leaders sought to come up with a plan that took into account the well-being of the families and the interests of the entire community. Furthermore,they wanted the entire population in the neighbourhood to participate in the plan's development. A major concern was that 70 families would have to leave the barrio because the required transformations would not leave enough ground space to relocate all the affected families within the boundaries of the neighbourhood. The barrio leadership, after talking to the families, decided that an alternative site would be found for these residents; the executive committee met with MINVAH and received a commitment that the families would be relocated in a new barrio that was to be constructed two kilometres away.

Nearly all the neighbourhood's adult inhabitants participated in the meetings held to plan the renovation process. Long discussions took place concerning building materials, loans for new homes and plans for building a new community centre. Even when most participants were exhausted, barrio leaders never cut off the debates that arose during these discussions. It was evident that in such a situation – in which everyone would be affected by the decisions taken at meetings – all CDS members were anxious to be in on the process.

The Accountability of Leaders

The accountability of leaders is another important element in the building of mass organization democracy. Members of mass organizations can ratify or reject their leadership in assemblies held at the base, zonal, regional and national levels. To assess the behaviour of their base-level executive officers, the membership periodically holds evaluation sessions, in which members raise criticisms concerning the job performances of their leaders and suggest how they can improve their service to the organization.

In principle, all mass organization leaders are subject to immediate recall for abuses of power or negligence, and members do not hesitate to employ this measure when necessary. CDS members, for example, removed many of their leaders at the end of 1982.

In that month Commander Bayardo Arce of the National Directorate sent a letter to all CDS co-ordinators. In the letter Arce conveys the strong belief 'that the CDS leadership and members should express qualities that can be measured by ... their willingness to be the best servants of the people, avoiding and combating opportunism, bureaucracy, favouritism and bossism'. He goes on to describe 'arbitrary attitudes and actions that exert influences which are contrary to Sandinista principles', listing the following cases:

> Withholding the sugar distribution card from someone who still does not understand the Revolution, instead of using the accomplishments of the Revolution to raise his consciousness. We know that this

method is sometimes used to pressure people into doing CDS tasks, which are supposed to be voluntary.

Harassment by words and actions of people who profess another ideology – whether religious or political – or of persons who work with persons or entities not identified with the Revolution.

Falling into an abuse of authority and using a position of responsibility in the Organization as a way to enjoy personal and family privileges.

To allow and lead abuses in carrying out the Voluntary Night Watch, especially in taking repressive measures against those who do not participate in this task. (There are even cases which have gone so far as to break a door or cast a shadow of disconfidence [sic] on someone, ignoring the fact that all CDS jobs are voluntary.)[65]

Between the middle of October and 7 November 1982, an organizational restructuring of the CDSs occurred throughout Nicaragua. During that time, CDS members gathered in elective assemblies to ratify or replace the old leadership at all levels of the organization: block, zone, barrio and municipality. The rank and file frequently cited Arce's letter during evaluations of their leaders' behaviour in office. On 1 November, an election assembly for CDS leaders took place in Ciudad Sandino, a poor barrio on the outskirts of Managua. After reading Arce's letter, one woman asserted: 'We should make copies of that letter and give it to everyone. Here our rights are underlined. And we ought to show it to our leaders often so that they fulfil it faithfully.'[66]

Although the popular organizations have institutionalized recall procedures for their leaders, none of them have yet established fixed terms of office for their representatives. In February 1984, however, Comandante Leticia Herrera, national Secretary General of the CDSs, stated that continuing abuses by CDS co-ordinators had prompted the decision to limit this position to a term of one year.[67] The observers anticipate that other mass organizations will follow the lead of the CDSs.

Political Equality

The issue of political equality raises two questions. First, do the mass organizations provide their members with equal treatment according to the standards of their own internal regulations? Secondly, do the popular organizations grant their members equal opportunity to participate in the political life of these organizations?

These questions are particularly relevant to those mass organizations whose members' political ideologies vary widely. To be a member of UNAG, for example, one need only be a small or medium producer, or someone who doesn't yet own land but is ready to produce should they be given land. While members are expected to support the general goals of the revolutionary process, they do not have to be revolutionaries. Roberto Laguna, UNAG secretary general in Region I, elaborates:

> We have members of different political parties in UNAG. You have to produce efficiently but in UNAG you don't have to participate in revolutionary tasks. We defend members as long as they produce and therefore our members feel represented. So we do have some contradictions with other members of mass organizations who accuse our members of being *contras* because they don't participate in revolutionary activities. But we say that they are not – as long as they don't collaborate with the *contras*.[68]

Within UNAG, therefore, there is an effort to afford full political rights to those who meet the union's fundamental criteria for membership.

Women have had difficulties in participating fully in the activities of all the mass organizations (with the obvious exception of AMNLAE, the women's association). They must confront entrenched sexism within the popular associations as well as in the society at large. For example, although women make up almost half of the rural labour force, only 6 per cent of the agricultural co-operatives' members are women.[69] Further, while a large majority of CDS activists are women, very few women hold leadership positions at the zonal and regional levels of the organization.

At a conference in the city of Granada on 10 April 1983, women from the ATC and AMNLAE representatives met to discuss the conditions of women farmworkers.[70] The meeting focused on the political, organizational, labour and social problems that these workers confront. Delegates pointed out that women's family responsibilities prevented them from participating fully in the life of their union. They also criticized husbands for failing to understand their wives' desire to be involved in union activities. The women explained that union leadership positions were beyond their grasp as long as they remained barely literate. Many women who care for children could not attend adult education classes held at night. Some delegates accused two state farms of failing to grant women equal pay for equal work, a practice contrary to Nicaraguan statutes. Other delegates reported cases of discrimination in hiring and training, and instances where ATC officials prevented women from joining the union. Conference participants also reported that some pregnant women miscarried during the coffee harvest because of the difficult terrain in which they were assigned to work.

Many of the delegates offered suggestions on how to overcome these problems, including an educational campaign to inform women of their rights under the law, and a proposal for women to be guaranteed technical training courses. The ATC studied and debated the concerns raised at the conference, and has taken concrete measures to address some of the problems faced by women in the union. One regional office recently decided to reserve 23 per cent of its leadership positions for women, and to hold training courses only for women, or with women comprising the majority of students.[71] Women at all levels of the ATC are continuing to apply pressure for equal rights.

The Power of the Mass Organizations

The goal of constructing a new society in Nicaragua is a constant theme of the revolutionary process. To make this goal a reality, the mass organizations must become organs of genuine popular power within the revolution. Although they currently remain a junior partner in the Nicaraguan power structure, there are areas in which their ability to influence, change and even initiate revolutionary policies is growing. This section evaluates the power of the mass organizations in the following areas: production policy, the emancipation of women and community development.

Production Policy
UNAG, with 80,000 members, significantly influences government policies affecting Nicaragua's agricultural sector. Farmers and ranchers with small and medium-size holdings represent 66 per cent of the economically active population in the countryside and 28 per cent of the entire economically active population. A total of 259,100 small and medium producers, of whom 157,600 are poor peasants, toil on individual farms and agricultural co-operatives.[72]

Family farmers and small and medium ranchers produce almost all the country's basic foodstuffs. Farmers with small plots grow 80 per cent of all beans and corn and 97 per cent of the vegetables in the country.[73] In addition, they produce substantial amounts of coffee and beef, two of Nicaragua's key exports.

UNAG's primary task is to help peasants gain access to land. The UNAG representatives on the Regional Councils of Agrarian Reform play a decisive role in land adjudication. They have a direct voice in determining the criteria used to decide which land is to be turned over and to whom. If there is a large plot of underutilized or abandoned land, the UNAG regional representative will ensure that it is given to the co-operative movement according to the provisions of the Agrarian Reform Law. Union leaders insist that the primary beneficiaries be poor peasants who have no land or who are exploited by landowners. UNAG representatives also propose that those peasants who want to move from marginalized land in order to join a co-operative be allowed to do so.[74] According to Nicolas Chavez, director of the Co-operative Development Programme in Esteli: 'UNAG is the organization that has the most weight, the most social force in determining the distribution of land because of the great number of peasants it organizes and the overall strength of its organization.'[75]

UNAG also participates in the process of allocating credits to small and medium farmers and ranchers. Union representatives sit on credit committees at the zonal, regional and national levels, airing the union's point of view along with those of the banks and the Ministry of Agricultural Development and Agrarian Reform. Often UNAG delegates are able to secure loans for co-operatives with economic and administrative problems because the co-operatives are union affiliates. If a co-operative is seeking a loan, but also needs more land to thrive economically, UNAG officials lobby for additional land and sufficient credit.[76]

UNAG delegates, along with representatives of various state agencies and the FSLN, participate in the deliberations of the zonal and regional Committees of Small and Medium Production. Committee members attempt to establish fair prices for basic grains in order to ensure the economic well-being of peasant producers. Aware of production costs, UNAG delegates try to set prices at a level which guarantees a decent profit margin to its members.[77]

Finally, UNAG works to gain services and technical assistance for its membership. To determine the needs of co-operatives and individual producers, the union convenes periodic municipal assemblies, in which producers detail their needs for agricultural inputs such as machinery, seeds, fertilizer and irrigation equipment. UNAG municipal councils, in conjunction with UNAG zonal and regional councils, determine a plan of action to secure these inputs, and then present the plan to the Committees of Small and Medium Production.[78]

The Sandinista Workers' Federation (CST), the largest industrial federation in the country, groups together more than 100,000 industrial workers. It has played a key role in reactivating the economy, securing the historical demands of its membership and initiating worker participation in the production process.

From late 1979 through 1981, the Nicaraguan capitalist class waged a decapitalization campaign in order to sabotage the national economy.[79] The CST and the ATC detected most instances of decapitalization and greatly contributed to the implementation of two government anti-decapitalization decrees. In a number of cases CST workers took over factories and ran production themselves.[80]

The CST contributes to raising production and sharing the burdens of austerity by participating in the campaign for weekend voluntary work, devoted especially to bringing in the harvests; in supporting, together with the rest of the labour organizations, the goal of reaching optimal labour efficiency as determined by the National Inter-union Commission; by establishing specific, realizable goals for certain aspects of production in given enterprises; and in backing training programmes for *innovadores* – workers who manage to adapt, refurbish, repair or maintain productive equipment, enabling the production process to continue and saving the country precious foreign exchange.

In Nicaragua the majority of workers were, and still are, deeply immersed in an everyday struggle for material survival. This, together with the historical effects of inadequate educational opportunities, places strict limitations on their ability to take on the tasks of administering production. Nevertheless, a pilot project to increase the level of worker participation in the decision-making process is currently being carried out in eight state enterprises. The project has led to some worker gains, but it is still too early to draw any firm conclusions.[81]

The ATC, with its 40,000 full-time members and more than 110,000 part-time members, makes its organized power felt in the countryside. Under Somoza, agricultural workers received extremely low wages. Shortly after taking power the Sandinista government raised the minimum wage by 30 per cent and fringe benefits contributed further increases. But by 1981 two years' inflation had cancelled out real gains in cash income for most permanent and seasonal workers on the state farms. In 1983 the Ministry of Labour announced that a new minimum wage for rural workers was in the offing, which would boost the previous amount by 30 per cent. And in 1984 and 1985, agricultural workers received substantial pay increases. As of February 1985, the minimum wage was 4,000 cordobas per year.[82]

Aware of the financial constraints on the government, the ATC has pushed for more health and housing improvements and for additional government stores selling basic foods at low fixed prices in the countryside. Gaining such increases in the 'social wage' has become an important goal for ATC activists.

The ATC, like the CST, is involved in a pilot project designed to increase the participation of workers in state farm management. It entails upgrading the level of worker input in reviewing and approving production plans as well as augmenting their ability to understand the technical and financial aspects of the production process. In attempting to increase their participation in administrative tasks, ATC members face the same problems and challenges as CST workers. As one state farm administrator put it:

> These are the first slow steps toward worker participation. We need to develop a series of conditions that will begin to resolve the problems blocking the development of worker participation: the low level of education, the military aggression, and the backwardness of our enterprises and national economy; but we really think that the projects will strengthen the ability of the workers to economically manage this farm, this enterprise, and eventually this country.[83]

The Emancipation of Women

AMNLAE, with a membership of 60,000 women, has had the most influence on revolutionary policies concerning education, child care, family life and employment for women. The association has also challenged the prevailing patriarchal ideology in the country.

AMNLAE works to ensure that the interests of women are represented in government policies. The organization used its seat on the Council of State to introduce and pass legislation that contributes to the struggle againt sexist attitudes and practices in Nicaragua. The Law on Relations between Mothers, Fathers and Children, approved in 1983, requires men who abandon their children to pay child support,and has been very effective. In Esteli, for example, 319 parents – nearly all men – were ordered in 1983 to pay for the support of 515 children.[84] Another law, the 'Law on Nurturance', calls on all family members, regardless of sex, to contribute to household tasks.

AMNLAE activists helped advance the tremendous achievements of the National Literacy Campaign, in which women played a key role, participating as students and teachers as well as co-ordinators and providers of logistical support. Some 60 per cent of the members of the Popular Literacy Army were young women, many of whom taught in the most remote areas of the country. AMNLAE also mobilized 196 Mothers' Committees for Literacy to provide logistical and moral support for the literacy workers.[85]

AMNLAE, in conjunction with the Ministries of Social Welfare, Health and Agricultural Development and Agrarian Reform, promotes an extensive programme to establish daycare centres in city and countryside. By the end of 1983, the programme had created 22 urban and 22 rural child-care centres;[86] both the war against the Contras and the economic crisis have prevented the establishment of more child-care facilities.

AMNLAE helps create agricultural production co-operatives that contribute to the reactivation of the economy and give employment to rural women. In addition, AMNLAE supports artisan co-operatives producing clothes and arts and crafts. To increase the number of women in the professions, AMNLAE sponsors professional development programmes in co-ordination with the National Federation of Professionals.[87]

AMNLAE has made significant contributions to health care in Nicaragua. It plays a leadership role in the Popular Health Campaigns, providing co-ordination at the national, regional, zonal and base levels. In 1981 the women's organization helped mobilize thousands of women for the polio vaccination campaign and the struggle against dengue-fever and malaria. According to AMNLAE, 65 per cent of the popular health educators and 75 per cent of the *multiplicadores* – people who train base-level health workers – are women.[88]

Community Development

The CDS, with about 600,000 members, is the largest mass organization in Nicaragua. Everyone, young and old, men and women, party members and non-members, capitalists and workers, Catholics, Protestants and atheists, can participate in a CDS. Every type of contradiction is found in this organization: class distinctions, differences in education, unequal levels of participation in the insurrection, generational conflicts and different points of view on the problems faced by Nicaragua.

With their large membership, the CDSs are a powerful force in the country. The power they wield is focused on their ability to carry out their fundamental task of defending the revolution in all its aspects: political–ideological, social, economic and military.

In the political–ideological realm, the CDSs must daily confront ideas and attitudes inherited from Somocismo, such as individualism, apathy, authoritarianism and negligence. CDS leaders are expected to explain the serious problems that exist in all areas of national life – problems that have been compounded by the aggression carried out against Nicaragua by the United States and its Central American allies. Throughout the country, the CDSs train leaders to increase their cultural, political and ideological capacities.

Social defence of the revolution is carried out through Vigiliancia Revolucionaria (revolutionary vigilance – VR). The principal objective of revolutionary vigilance is to curtail all activities that harm the revolution. The national office of the CDSs describes harmful activities as follows: activities carried out by enemies of the people who are directly tied to the counter-revolution; and activities derived from isolated or organized delinquency, drug addiction and prostitution.[89] To ensure the effective functioning of revolutionary vigilance, the CDSs collaborate closely with the Sandinista Police and State Security.

Social defence of the revolution also includes the following tasks: aiding the Popular Health Campaigns in their environmental sanitation campaigns, and massive vaccinations against polio, measles, tetanus, diphtheria and whooping cough; helping the programme of Popular Basic Education for Adults, the continuation of the National Literacy Campaign; promoting different projects for the well-being of the community such as road repair, school construction and the installation of electricity and water facilities; and contributing to the solution of housing problems through participation in the priority assignment of lots carried out in co-ordination with the Housing Ministry.[90]

The CDSs' main economic task is to guarantee a just distribution of the basic products of popular consumption: rice, sugar, beans, eggs, salt, oil and laundry soap. To fulfil this task, the CDSs monitor and supervise prices in collaboration with the Ministry of Internal Commerce. As a CDS pamphlet proudly asserts: 'It is the popular inspectors of the CDSs that principally guarantee the fulfilment of the task against hoarding and speculation, in defence of the real salary of the working people.[91]

Finally, the CDSs' primary defence function is to recruit volunteers for the Popular Sandinista Militias, the military organization responsible for local defence. The CDSs work directly with the militias in each neighbourhood and rural district to guarantee that each community has a sufficient number of trained militia members as well as enough arms. CDS activists also work with the militias to organize the people into civil defence brigades to fight fires, administer first aid, care for children and construct bomb shelters.

Conclusion

The mass organizations in Nicaragua constitute an essential element in the revolutionary process. They continue to grow both in numbers and organizational strength; yet they also face numerous obstacles in their bid to increase their participation in the revolutionary process. The conclusion evaluates the extent to which the popular organizations exercise autonomy, democracy and power in the Nicaraguan revolution.

The mass organizations have displayed a considerable degree of autonomy from the FSLN, sometimes even opposing the FSLN and the state in order to meet the demands of the sectors they represent. For the most part, the Sandinistas have encouraged the autonomous development of the mass organizations, preferring to let these organizations play an independent role in the revolution. But when the grassroots organizations press demands that conflict with the party's policy of national unity in the face of continued aggression and economic crisis, the FSLN withdraws its support. For example, some observers speculate that the FSLN opposed AMNLAE's proposal to extend the draft to women in 1983 because it would have alienated certain Catholic sectors who have so far supported the revolution.

The party's stance concerning independent action by the mass organizations is contradictory. Jaime Wheelock warned the ATC in February 1980 against 'anarchic and spontaneous actions' in pressuring for agrarian reform. Two months later, Carlos Nunez stressed that the popular associations must assert their demands in the face of state inflexibility. On the one hand, the FSLN urges the mass organizations to employ all means at their disposal to back their demands, but on the other, it cautions them against unsanctioned actions. While this seems contradictory, it also revals the Sandinistas' simultaneous commitment to the primary position of Nicaragua's workers and peasants *and* to the preservation of a broad class coalition.

Mass organization autonomy could be significantly bolstered if the Constituent Assembly formally recognizes their independent status in the new constitution. This would give the popular organizations greater legitimacy and strengthen their hand in the political process. It would also protect them from any political forces that might one day challenge their independent status.

The mass organizations have made significant advances in democratizing their internal structures. All the grassroots organizations employ democratic procedures to choose their leaders and assess their behaviour in office; but they have not yet implemented fixed terms of office. That the CDSs will soon limit their co-ordinators to one-year terms is an important precedent; the other mass organizations will need to consider this measure as a means to check the power of incumbents.

Lack of political equality within the popular organizations is a major problem. Due to the 'double shift' and unequal access to education, many women are unable to participate fully in the life of the grassroots organizations. Inequality within these organizations also stems from educational differences among members. The vast majority of popular association leaders possess sufficient formal education to write reports and conduct meetings. The mass organizations must work constantly to raise the capacities of their least educated members and afford them access to leadership positions.

There are signs that the mass organizations are aware of this need, for they have established study circles and training workshops for both rank-and-file members and leaders, in which popular association activists study the history, structure and functions of their organizations. This educational process is designed to broaden the participation of the entire membership and, in the long run, extend the democratization process.

Even though hundreds of thousands of Nicaraguans are newly literate and possess only a short history of political experience, they have felt the exhilaration and power that comes from direct involvement in the revolutionary process; they will not accept anything less than political equality within their organizations.

The mass organizations have demonstrated their power to the extent that they have been able to win some of the demands of their membership and influence certain revolutionary policies; but there are three basic reasons why the power of the popular associations remains somewhat circumscribed.

First, the limited development of the productive forces in Nicaragua acts as a brake on all social and political organizations in the country. Generally, mass organizations operating in societies that have the most meagre resources of capital, technology and skilled personnel face tremendous obstacles in developing their capacity to act as a counterweight to state and party organs; and they inevitably have to compete with these power centres in a situation of scarcity.

115

Second, to the extent that they subordinate their tasks to those set by party policy and mobilize their constituencies only to fulfil state goals, the popular associations will be unable to realize their full potential in influencing the revolutionary process. This is especially obvious in the case of AMNLAE. Despite AMNLAE's deliberate efforts to avoid the path taken by women's organizations in the socialist countries, its priorities tend to reflect party policies only.[92]

This is not to deny AMNLAE's contributions to health campaigns, women's education, child care and so on; but AMNLAE's projects remain firmly tied to women's prescribed roles. For example, the organization's long-range goal of socializing domestic work does not address the fundamental problem: the equalization of male and female responsibilities for domestic labour.

Finally, the power of the mass organizations is limited to the extent that they lack full representation throughout the various levels of the state apparatus; their representation on some bodies is merely token. The continued advance of the revolutionary process is best guaranteed by the constant expansion of mass participation in all aspects of public life.

The first six years of the Nicaraguan revolution have been marked by an incredible explosion of popular mobilization and organization. The central question is whether the country's peasants, workers, artisans and merchants will continue to consolidate and expand their participation in every aspect of revolutionary life. To achieve this objective, mass organization members will have to rely on their capacity for creativity and organization that led them to victory.

Notes

1. In this essay 'mass organizations' is used interchangeably with 'popular associations' and 'grassroots organizations'.

2. The *July 19th Sandinista Youth – JS 19*, although often referred to as a mass organization, is the youth wing of the FSLN. It has strict membership requirements and does not consider itself a mass organization.

3. See Carol Pateman, *Participation and Democratic Theory* (Cambridge: Cambridge University Press, 1970), pp. 22-45.

4. In US Out of Central America, *Declaration of Managua* (San Francisco, n.d.), p. 14.

5. George Black, *Triumph of the People: The Sandinista Revolution in Nicaragua* (London: Zed Press, 1981), pp. 79-80.

6. Humberto Ortega Saavedra, *Cinceunta anos de lucha sandinista* (Habana: Editorial de ciencias sociales, 1978), pp. 166-7.

7. Among the population over ten years of age illiteracy was more than 50 per cent and was higher than 85 per cent in some rural areas. See Ministry of Education, *La Educacion en el Primer Ano de la Revolucion Popular Sandinista* (Managua: Junta del Gobierno de la Reconstrucion Nacional, 1980), p. 31.

8. The following discussion is based on Anne Foster, 'A History of the Mass Movement among Women in Pre-Revolutionary Nicaragua' (unpublished mimeo, July 1983), pp. 1-2.

9. Black, *Triumph of the People*, pp. 79-80.

10. Pilar Arias, *Nicaragua: Revolucion* (Mexico: Siglo XXI Editores, 1980), p. 34.

11. *Nicaragua: A People's Revolution* (Washington: Epica Task Force, 1980), p. 23.

12. See Michael Dodson and T.S. Montgomery, 'The Churches in the Nicaraguan Revolution', in *Nicaragua in Revolution*, ed. Thomas Walker (New York: Praeger Publishers, 1982), pp. 170-2.

13. Epica Task Force, p. 26.

14. Quoted in ibid.

15. Black, *Triumph of the People*, p. 273.

16. Elizabeth Maier, *Nicaragua, La Mujer en la Revolucion* (Mexico, D.F.: Ediciones de Cultural Popular, 1980), p. 85.

17. Quoted in Borge, et al., *Sandinistas Speak*, ed. Bruce Marcus (New York: Pathfinder Press, 1982), p. 71.

18. The following statement taken from AMNLAE's 'Declaration of Principles' is typical of official mass organization statements concerning the FSLN's vanguard role: 'We recognize the FSLN as the indisputable vanguard that led the people to its liberation and that today leads the construction of the new society. AMNLAE will work toward the fulfilment of the historical program of the FSLN and the decisions of its National Directorate.' AMNLAE, *Documentos de la Asamblea Constitutiva*, n.d., p. 12.

19. The mass organizations are financed by members' dues and non-governmental aid from organizations abroad. Their financial resources are extremely limited.

20. Quoted in Roger Burbach and Tim Draimin, 'Nicaragua's Revolution', *NACLA Report on the Americas*, 14 (May–June 1980), p. 21.

21. *El Papel de las organizaciones de masas en el proceso revolucionario* (Managua: SNPEP del FSLN, 1980), p. 16.

22. Interview held in Esteli, 20 January 1984.

23. Quoted in Burbach and Draimin, 'Nicaragua's Revolution', pp. 29-30.

24. Quoted in ibid., p. 30.

25. Interview held with zonal CDS official in Managua, March 1984.

26. Interview with Vivian Peres, ATC zonal secretary of political education, in Esteli, 13 August 1984.

27. Interview held in Esteli, 18 February 1984.

28. The following account draws on Joseph Collins, *What Difference Could a Revolution Make?* (San Francisco: Institute for Food and Development Policy, 1982), p. 82.

29. ATC, *El Machete* (February 1980), p. 11.

30. Quoted in Collins, *What Difference?*, p. 82.

31. Ibid.

32. *Barricada*, 18 August 1983.

33. Instituto Historico Centroamericano, *Envio* (January 1984).

34. *Barricada*, 5 December 1983.

35. Interview in Esteli, 20 January 1984.

36. Ibid.

37. Interview with Javier Molina, member of ATC national training staff in Esteli, November 1984.

38. Interview with AMNLAE zonal secretary, in Esteli, August 1984.

39. Interview with CDS regional secretary, in Esteli, August 1984.

40. An advisory body to the FSLN's national leadership.

41. Interview in Managua, 22 March 1984.

42. For example, Lucio Jiminez, Secretary General of the CST, Leticia Herrera, General Secretary of AMNLAE, and Daniel Nunez, President of UNAG, all have seats in the National Assembly.

43. See, for example, AMNLAE, *Documentos de la Asamblea Constitutiva*, p. 12.

44. For a fascinating account of the situation in Nicaragua during the first few days after the triumph, see Borge et al., *Sandinistas Speak*, pp. 102-3.

45. Epica Task Force, p. 79.

46. *El Papel*, p. 16.

47. Instituto Historico Centroamericano, *Envio*, 27 (September 1983), p. 3c.

48. *Barricada Internacional*, 14 February 1985.

49. E.V.K. Fitzgerald, government economic adviser, in Latin American Studies Association, 'The Electoral Process in Nicaragua: Domestic and International Influences' (19 November 1984), p. 6.

50. *Barricada*, 26 December 1983.

51. Ibid.

52. Ibid.

53. Ibid.

54. Interview with CDS regional secretary in Esteli, 18 February 1984.

55. *El Papel*, p. 21 (my translation).

56. *Barricada*, 15 February 1984.

57. As Philip Martinez notes: 'The goal [of the decentralization] was to reduce the dependency of regional and local government on the national structure in Managua. In the event of an invasion . . . each region was to have the ability to function independently' ('Five Years of Agrarian Reform in Nicaragua: The Case of the Noel Gamez Cooperative', [MA Thesis, University of California, Berkeley, 1985], p. 34).

58. *El Papel*, p. 13.

59. See James Petras, 'Nicaragua: The Transition to a New Society', *Latin American Perspectives*, 29 (Spring 1981), p. 89.

60. Burbach and Draimin, 'Nicaragua's Revolution', pp. 22-3.

61. Interview held in Esteli, 18 February 1984.

62. See Carmen Diana Deere et al., 'The Peasantry and the Development of Sandinista Agrarian Policy, 1979-1984', *Latin American Research Review* (forthcoming).

63. Matilde Zimmermann, 'Nicaragua's Farmers and Ranchers form Union', *Intercontinental Press* (25 May 1981), p. 552.

64. The following discussion is based on the author's observations at barrio meetings in July and August 1983.

65. Quoted in Instituto Historico Centroamericana, *Envio*, 16 (15 October 1982), p. 10.

66. Quoted in ibid., p. 13.

67. *Barricada*, 19 February 1984.

68. Interview held in Esteli, 16 January 1984.

69. CIERA, *La Mujer en las Cooperativas Agropecuarias en Nicaragua* (Managua, April 1984), p. 26.

70. The following discussion draws from Jane Harris, 'Women Farm Workers Meet', *Intercontinental Press* (16 May 1983), p. 257.

71. ATC, *El Machete* (December 1983).

72. UNAG, *Las Pequenas y Medianos Productores Agropecuarios* (n.d.), p. 1.

73. UNAG Bulletin, September 1984.

74. Interview with Roberto Laguna in Esteli, 16 January 1984.

75. Interview held in Esteli, 27 January 1984.

76. Ibid.

77. Ibid.

78. Ibid.

79. See Gary Ruchwarger, 'Workers Control in Nicaragua', *Against the Current*, 2 (Winter 1984), pp. 18-20.

80. See, for example, Matilde Zimmerman, 'An Example of Workers Control in Nicaragua', *Intercontinental Press* (February 1980), p. 88.

81. See Ruchwarger, 'Workers Control', pp. 21-2. Cf. Carlos Vilas' essay in this volume.

82. *Barricada*, 18 February 1985.

83. Interview with Alcides Montoya, director of zone 2 of the Oscar Turcios tobacco enterprise, held in Esteli, 23 January 1984.

84. Interview with Arquimides Colindus, delegate from the Ministry of Social Welfare and Social Security to Region I, held in Esteli, 30 November 1984.

85. AMNLAE, *Documentos*, p. 7.

86. Interview with AMNLAE secretary conducted by Sally Barros, in Managua, March 1984.

87. AMNLAE, *Somos* (November 1983).

88. AMNLAE, *Documentos*, p. 8.

89. CDS, *Los CDS Somos: Poder Popular* (n.p.), p. 3.

90. Ibid., p. 4.

91. Ibid.

92. Although for obvious reasons Maxine Molyneaux does not include an analysis of AMNLAE in her recent article, 'Socialist Societies Old and New: Progress Toward Women's Emancipation', her comments on women's organizations in socialist societies can be applied to the Nicaraguan women's organization: '[T]hese organizations do not generally encourage radical thinking or action, and many of the more subtle discriminatory structures are not tackled unless they are considered to be survivals from the pre-revolutionary period and obstacles to development', *Monthly Review* (July–August 1982), pp. 93-4.

Author's Note
I am indebted to Margaret Bergamini for her contributions to the overall conception of this paper as well as for her extensive editorial assistance.

5 The Workers' Movement in the Sandinista Revolution

Carlos M. Vilas*

In one of his best known works, General Sandino states that: 'only the workers and peasants will stay with the struggle until the end; only their organized force will achieve victory.'[1] Those who have studied his thought and practice agree that this passage reveals Sandino's recognition of the class content of his anti-imperialist struggle.

The present stage of the Sandinista revolution does not yet reveal this class content. This does not mean that it does not exist as a *project* within the FSLN, or at least in some of its elements, but the revolutionary vanguard characterizes the present stage of the revolution as popular, democratic and anti-imperialist, based upon a schema of national unity and a mixed economy. The FSLN accepts the coexistence of antagonistic classes and groups within the sphere of production and, as a consequence, the class struggle *within its project of national unity*.

Under these conditions, what is the situation of the workers' movement? How does it reconcile the doctrine that it is one of the two fundamental social forces of the revolution with the necessity of maintaining a mixed economy? What kind of relationships have developed between the unions and the state, which is committed to promoting national unity? How do the perspectives of the working class fit into this complex matrix of forces and contradictions? This essay attempts to answer these questions, taking into account the limitations which arise when dealing with such an extremely dynamic situation which does not yet appear to have reached a state of equilibrium.

We begin with a brief presentation of the quantitative aspects of the development of the working class and the union movement in Nicaragua; we will then analyse the way in which the FSLN characterizes the role of the workers' movement in the present stage of the revolution and how this has conflicted with that of certain workers' organizations, especially those of the left. This will be followed by a discussion of the experience to date on workers' participation in the management of the economy. The reader will note that for the sake of brevity we have omitted a discussion of the historical development of the working class in Nicaragua. We prefer to devote attention to less analysed subjects such as the actual problematic of the workers'

* *Translated by R.L. Harris.*

Figure 5.1 Nicaragua's Unions in Numbers

Central Organization	No. of Unions or Locals	Membership	Political Affiliation
Sandinista Workers Federation	504	111,498	FSLN
Farmworkers Association	480	42,000	FSLN
Health Workers Federation	39	15,613	FSLN
Independent General Labour Confederation	19	17,177	Socialist Party
Trade Union Action and Unity Federation	15	1,939	Communist Party
Workers Front	Not released	2,000	Marxist–Leninist Popular Action
Confederation of Trade Union Unification	17	1,670	Democratic Co-ordinating
Workers Confederation of Nicaragua	21	2,734	Social Christian Party
Nicaraguan Teachers Association	1	16,000	FSLN
National Employees Union	1	17,000	FSLN
Nicaraguan Journalists Union	1	300	FSLN
Total	1,099	227,931	

During the dictatorship
133 unions
27,000 members
161 contracts signed

Since 1979
1,099 unions and locals
227,931 members
Over 1,000 contracts signed, benefitting nearly 292,000 workers. For the first time in Nicaragua's history, agricultural workers, fishermen, miners and domestic workers have been organized.

Source: *Barricada Internacional,* 7 February 1985, p. 6.

121

movement, and refer the reader to the existing literature for background on the contemporary situation.[2] Finally, in spite of the broad scope of the title of this essay, we will deal almost exclusively with the industrial workers' movement.

The Recent Development of the Workers' Movement

By the end of the 1970s, the Nicaraguan working class appears to have consisted of between 230,000 and 240,000 workers, or slightly less than 30 per cent of the economically active population (estimated at almost 800,000).[3] In so far as the proletarianization of the countryside and the cities was concerned, the urban proletariat for this same period is estimated to have been between 75,000 and 80,000 people (about 20 per cent of the non-agricultural EAP), whereas in the countryside the numbers fluctuated between 110,000 and 130,000 salaried workers (one-third of the agricultural EAP). However, the situation of the rural proletariat is complex; only between one-third and one-half of this number had a steady job throughout the year, while the rest served as an itinerant proletariat moving between different jobs and different regions of the country.[4] To this panorama must be added a large rural semi-proletariat (approximately two-fifths of the agricultural EAP) made up of *minifundista* peasants seasonally involved in wage-earning relations, and a mass of artisans and salaried employees in the cities (almost two-thirds of the non-agricultural EAP).

The Nicaraguan working class has a complex set of linkages with the non-proletarianized masses, especially in the cities. The studies available on this question reveal that the working-class family – as relative a concept as this may be in the Nicaraguan economy – does not reproduce itself exclusively or even principally from wage-earning. Income contributed by members of the family engaged in peddling, providing personal services and petty commercial activities often surpasses the income of the wage-earning workers in the family.

These structural aspects, combined with the political repression characteristic of the Somoza regime, account for the relatively underdeveloped nature of the union movement prior to the revolutionary triumph. In July 1979, there were only 138 registered unions in the country, totalling only 27,000 affiliated workers. This is equivalent to a rate of unionization of about 11 to 12 per cent of the salaried population (quite a bit more than the conventional estimate of between 6 and 7 per cent.)[5] Many of these unions had a merely formal existence, having been inactive for years.

Since the revolutionary triumph, the unionization of the workforce has increased rapidly. Between August 1979 and December 1983, almost 1,400 unions were registered at the Ministry of Labour, with more than 120,000 members. Almost half of these new organizations are in the agricultural sector, and a little less than 20 per cent are in the industrial sector. The predominant form of union is that organized by all the workers in a single enterprise. Over 75 per cent of all the unions fall into this category. However, since 1981, the main union confederations and the FSLN have been pushing the formation of unions on an industry-wide basis. During 1983, three of these types of unions were created – in the construction, food and textile industries respectively. And the process is underway for forming a single union for the agro-industrial sugar sector.

Almost 90 per cent of the new unions and the new union members are affiliated with the Central Sandinista de Trabajadores (the Sandinista Trade Union Confederation, known generally as the CST) or with the Asociacion de Trabajadores del Campo (the Sandinista Association of Agricultural Workers or ATC). In 1979–80, 75 per cent of the new unions affiliated with the CST, reflecting the high-point of the unionization of urban and industrial workers. In contrast, almost 80 per cent of the new unions in the period 1981–2 affiliated with the ATC, since this was a period of rapid unionization in the countryside. Although there are several union confederations besides the CST and ATC, together they account for little more than 10 per cent of all the unions and union members.[6]

At the moment it is not possible to determine what the overall rate of unionization is for the workforce as a whole. The records kept by the trade union confederations often differ from the information possessed by the Ministry of Labour.[7] Moreover, estimates of the total number of salaried workers vary according to the source and the methodology used. Without disclaiming the speed and massive extent of unionization that has taken place since 1979, it seems safe to say that the current figures are exaggerated and lack statistical reliability.[8] According to our own estimates, based on information from the Ministry of Labour, it appears that by late 1983 the total number of workers affiliated with unions was between 130,000 and 135,000. In other words, this represents between 35 per cent and 40 per cent of the total salaried workforce. These estimates are approximations, since the unions do not always inform the ministry about changes in the total number of their affiliates.

Aside from differences in the estimates, it is evident that in the last five years the union movement in Nicaragua has acquired an unprecedented impetus and growth in magnitude among the working class. The determining factor for this rapid increase in unionization within a country as economically backward and unevenly developed as Nicaragua is the support accorded to mobilizations of this sort by the revolutionary state and the FSLN.

Union Action as Political Struggle

The stage that began on 19 July 1979 was characterized not only by the growth in unionization but also by a marked change in the conception of a union and the role it should play in the revolutionary process. This change in conception of the union's political role took place in the midst of an intense struggle within the union movement and the revolution as a whole, and forms part of the process of the consolidation of Sandinista hegemony in this area.

From the viewpoint of the FSLN, the unions should not be viewed only as organizations which make demands. This activity has to be linked to the advancement of the revolutionary process on all fronts,and the workers must be trained in increasingly more complex forms of participation. In particular, immediately following the overthrow of the dictatorship, the FSLN demanded that the union movement make an active contribution to the country's economic recovery. From the FSLN perspective, this not only implied careful vigilance of the entre-preneurial behaviour of the bourgeoisie, but also the strengthening of labour discipline and the subordination of wage demands to the reconstruction of the country.

This approach dealt a severe blow to widespread popular expecta-tions that there would be a rapid improvement in wages and caused a certain amount of initial disorientation. The FSLN argued that the state of the war-torn economy, the destruction and disarticulation of the productive apparatus made it nearly impossible to satisfy the monetary aspirations of the workers. Production had declined sharply, the mechanisms of distribution were disrupted,[9] and under these conditions, it was felt that a rapid increase in wages would reinforce inflation, already very high due to the consequences of the civil war. It is possible that many Nicaraguan revolutionaries remembered the tragic end of Chile's Popular Unity government, in which an uncontrollable inflation-ary process, together with a decline in production, facilitated the deterioration of the popular government and hastened its downfall.

The economic policy put forward by the revolutionary state tended to respond to popular demands not through increasing wages but through subsidizing basic consumption and expanding social services – referred to at this time as the 'social wage'. This approach generated conflict within the workers' movement and within the political domain generally. In essence, this contradiction between workers' demands and the reconstruction of the economy reflected the contradiction within the revolutionary camp of the class interests inherent in the historic trajectory of the FSLN and the presence of bourgeois elements and the recognition of the legitimacy of their interests within the framework of national unity and a mixed economy. The manner in which the different forces in play reacted to this contradiction reflected their position at that stage of the revolution.

The strong emphasis placed upon bread-and-butter issues by the Central de Accion y Unidad Sindical (the Confederation of Trade Union Action and Unity, CAUS) and the Frente Obrero (Workers' Front) was due both to their policy of rapidly winning over the rank and file and their characterization of the stage that had just begun. Both organizations recognized the FSLN as the vanguard of the struggle against the dictatorship, but they rejected it as the vanguard of the working class and of the process of revolutionary transformation. They insisted on criticizing the ties between some sectors of the FSLN and certain fractions of the bourgeoisie, and they interpreted the initial presence of some capitalists in the governing junta and the state apparatus as proof of the bourgeois character of both. As a result, they viewed Sandinista requests that the workers moderate their demands as having the effect of protecting capital's rate of profit and consolidating bourgeois political influence. What was for the FSLN 'national reconstruction' was interpreted by CAUS, the Frente Obrero, the Partido Comunista de Nicaragua (the Nicaraguan Communist Party, PCN) and the Movimiento de Accion Popular (leftist Popular Action Movement) as the promotion of the interests of the bourgeoisie. And labour discipline was perceived as exploitation of the proletariat. In response to the political line of the FSLN, these organizations made radical labour demands and strongly attacked the CST and ATC for their lack of combativeness.[10]

The Central de Trabajadores de Nicaragua (Workers' Confederation of Nicarague, CTN) and the Consejo de Unificacion Sindical (Council for Union Unification, CUS), which are linked to political organizations opposed to the revolutionary regime, followed a strict trade-unionist line which reduces unions to the pursuit of categorical interests. This line coincided to a certain extent with the position of the leftist organizations mentioned above, in that they too attempted to undermine the working-class support of the FSLN – built during the heat of the revolutionary struggle in which all of these organizations had played a marginal role. The remaining labour organization, the Confederacion General de Trabajo – Independiente (the Independent General Confederation of Labour, or CGT-I, which is tied to the Partido Socialista de Nicaragua or PSN), took a less belligerent position with respect to the FSLN. Without prejudicing its differences with the CST on specific issues, it agreed to join with it and form a co-ordinating body called the Comision Nacional Intersindical (the Inter-union National Commission, CNI).

Thus, the final months of 1979 saw an escalation of the political tensions in the workers' movement. Work-stoppages, strikes, the takeover of factories and large estates, and mobilizations during this period reflected the struggle for political control of the unions that was taking place in the context of their rapid expansion. In these confrontations, each of the participants mobilized all the forces at its

125

command. Thus, the FSLN used the prestige it had gained in the struggle against the dictatorship, its broad base of mass support and the power of the revolutionary state. Actually, at this initial stage, the organic position of the FSLN seems to have been less consolidated among the proletariat than that of other organizations with much less participation in the war for liberation. This appears to have been due largely to the fact that the political work of the FSLN among the working class started much later than its efforts among the students, peasants and urban poor. At this moment, therefore, it had not yet reached the same level as among these other sectors.[11] In the first months following the revolutionary triumph, the Sandinistas' political presence in the workers' movement was confined basically to the agricultural workers in the agro-export sector, and was not yet obvious in the urban sectors of the economy. The position of the FSLN in these sectors of the workforce appears to have been consolidated only after a fraction of the PSN, which originally had broken away from that party in 1977, joined with the FSLN a few months after the revolutionary triumph. This fusion gave the CST a group of experienced union leaders and their rank-and-file followers.

In the development of these contradictions, the FSLN combined its ideological struggle with its economic policies and its use of the state apparatus. This made it possible for the FSLN to win over progressively the rank and file of these other competing organizations – as well as quite a few of their cadres – and at the same time neutralize or divide their leadership. The imprisonment of the leaders of the Frente Obrero and the PCN in early 1980, the closing of the daily newspaper *Pueblo* (published by the Frente Obrero) and the PCN's newspaper *Avance*, were carried out in conjunction with the expansion of the CST's support among the working-class base of these organizations.

This process was closely linked to the development of contradictions between the FSLN and the bourgeoisie. The FSLN had expected heavy investments from the sector of the bourgeoisie represented within its ranks to boost the reactivation of the economy. By the end of 1979, the members of this sector holding ministerial positions were displaced almost totally from the state apparatus, leaving Alfonso Robelo as the only visible figure of the grand bourgeoisie in the Sandinista government. The contradictions between the class fraction led by Robelo and the revolutionary regime were increased after this 'Sandinization' of the state took place. This also coincided with the growing rigidity of Washington's policy towards Nicaragua. The FSLN manoeuvred to isolate Robelo from the bourgeoisie; in this strategy, control over the workers' demands, labour discipline, etc. constituted a vital element in avoiding excessively alarming the capitalists and delaying their displacement to the opposition.

Between Workers' Demands and Political Power

The FSLN's views with respect to the workers question appears to be the product of the relation of forces between the revolutionary block and the bourgeoisie, the limitations arising from the productive apparatus and international pressures – all within a framework that defines the worker–peasant alliance as the fundamental base of the revolutionary process and which is aimed at bringing about profound social transformations.

As a consequence, the FSLN argued that in the stage which began with the victory of July 1979, *popular power* could not be reduced to *union power*; rather, it encompassed all spheres of revolutionary construction, and particularly that having to do with the revolutionary state. The autonomy of the unions to make demands, therefore, had to be subordinated to the strategic interests of the larger revolutionary project. This was not meant to negate the legitimacy of union activism, however, nor the pursuit of worker demands within this framework. The document submitted by the CNI at the Assembly for Trade Union Unity on 13 April 1980,[12] was representative of the FSLN's position on this subject during this period; and the speech by Comandante Carlos Nunez on 20 April was a further example.[13]

The CNI document proposed that the unions had to act within the following two guidelines of the Sandinista popular revolution: (1) to work hard for the consolidation of the revolution and to be willing at any moment to defend it economically, politically and militarily; and (2) to lead the way in expressing the workers' most deeply-felt demands, to make those demands their own, channel them and do their best to see that they were satisfied and translated into the material practices of the revolution. This document saw the need to reach a point of equilibrium – not without contradictions – between immediate bread-and-butter demands and the long-range political project.

In some cases, their emphasis on the economic recovery of the enterprises – both those belonging to the new state sector and those in the private sector – led some unions to neglect the task of articulating the demands of their members. This left a gap, in certain cases, which was exploited by the union confederations competing with the CST for leadership of the workers' movement. Moreover, the sacrifice of the workers contrasted with the attitude of many entrepreneurs, who made no effort to revive the productive process, while rejecting their workers' demands on the grounds of the prevailing poor state of the economy.

Comandante Nunez's speech brings out these aspects of the situation, in support of the legitimacy of the workers' demands:

> We wanted to raise awareness within the mass organizations that
> while it was true that we should work for the revolutionary political

project, they should also be instruments that were capable of expressing with autonomy the demands of the social sectors they represented, and as such they would have to use both the usual as well as unusual means.

At the same time, he criticized those who wanted to postpone the satisfaction of popular demands.

Thus, the National Directorate of the FSLN announced that there should be relative autonomy between the mass organizations and the state. In the same document, Comandante Nunez goes on to state:

> Should the mass organizations resort to their own force, means of expression and mobilization, when their demands are not heeded, when the doors are closed on all sides? We believe that they must ... The mass organizations must collect and make their own the demands of their members, they must struggle to see them materialized through the new mechanisms that the revolution has established. But when these channels are closed, when they knock and no one listens, when nothing happens after using these channels, whether because of bureaucratism or liberal methods, or because the problems of the masses are not being taken into account, etc., then our organizations must use other forms of political persuasion. This means that when these channels are closed to them, the mass organizations have the right, within the general framework of the revolution, to resort to internal criticism, the utilization of all the means of mass communication, and even mobilization – to demand that the necessary measures be taken to guarantee that their concerns are heard.

The battle plan put forward by the CST in February 1980 can be considered as an example of putting this political line into practice. The basic points of this plan included: an increase in the minimum wages of the lowest-paid workers; a revision of the wage scale; the reform of the Labour Code (enacted during the period of Somoza Garcia); improvement of the social wage; and promoting workers' participation in the management of enterprises through the establishment of Consejos de Produccion (Production Councils). Moreover, the CST advocated the creation of occupational health committees to watch over working conditions and promote safety in the enterprises, as well as the systematic denunciation of owners and managers involved in the decapitalization of their enterprises or who did not contribute to the reconstruction of the productive apparatus and the normalization of the channels of distribution and supply.

In late 1980, the FSLN began to emphasize the need to promote workers' demands in a manner that did not interrupt the production process, leaving shutdowns and strikes as measures of last resort. For example, Comandante Victor Tirado made the following statement around this time:

> labor conflicts must be solved without stopping production, it is evident that strikes at this time not only harm the economy in general but also the workers in particular. On the basis of these points, we must make one thing clear: restrictions on wage increases and the right to strike must be seen as measures adopted freely, voluntarily, and consciously by the workers themselves due to the situation that the country is going through at this time. It is a matter of defending the economy and consciously assuming the sacrifices and efforts this implies.[14]

This represents a limitation on the position taken in April of the same year, although there is still an appeal to persuasion and the receptivity of the masses.

This reorientation took place in the context of a process in which the different union confederations were drawing closer with the aim of unifying the workers' movement. By this point, it was clear to the FSLN that the organizations representing the large bourgeoisie, particularly the Consejo Superior de la Empresa Privada (Superior Council of Private Enterprise, COSEP), had adopted a position of open opposition to the revolutionary regime.[15]

It is clear that the election of Ronald Reagan prompted some elements of the bourgeoisie to involve themselves in openly counter-revolutionary activities. The FSLN sought to create rifts and to promote political differences within this class, while it was promoting the unification of the workers' movement. At this point, the Coordinadora Sindical de Nicaragua (the Co-ordinating Labour Council of Nicaragua or CSN) arose, formed by the CST and ATC joining with the CAUS, CGT-I, Frente Obrero, CUS and the Federacion de Trabajadores de la Salud (Federation of Health Workers or FETSALUD), the Union de Periodistas de Nicaragua (Journalists Union of Nicaragua or UPN) and the Asociacion Nacional de Educadores Nicaraguenses (National Association of Nicaraguan Educators or ANDEN). Only the CTN, linked to the Partido Socialcristiano (rightist Social Christian Party) remained outside the Coordinadora, although the CUS soon withdrew.

Thus, the CSN represented the first step forward in the efforts to constitute a broad-based union movement with a class perspective. With regard to the relationship between worker demands and reconstruction, the platform of the Coordinadora explicitly adopted the FSLN's position:

> In every case of labour conflict, an effort should first be made to resolve the conflict without resorting to a work stoppage. This does

not mean, in any sense, renouncing the right to strike, rather that we want to affirm that strikes must be the last resort for the workers; that all other measures must be exhausted before resorting to this, since every shutdown reduces production and hinders the fulfilment of the plans and programmes of the Government of National Reconstruction and the strategic project of the Sandinista Popular Revolution.[16]

The battle plan of the CSN, of which the above statement is a part, represented a considerable effort to combine the positions of the minority union confederations with the strategy of the FSLN.

The objectives of this plan included: the support, strengthening and defence of the revolution; increasing production and productivity and the fulfilment of the goals of national reconstruction; promoting the participation of the workers in the Milicias Populares Sandinistas (Sandinista Popular Militias, MPS); the elaboration of a new wage scale 'in accordance with the country's economic conditions'; increasing real wages; improving general working conditions and in particular those affecting occupational hygiene and safety; opposing indiscriminate wage increases which represent 'obstacles to the economic reconstruction of the country'; reforming the Labour Code; fighting against bureaucratism, abuses of power, negligence and waste in the enterprises of the APP; preventing the flight of capital and damage to the productive capacity of private enterprises; stimulating the initiative of the workers; organizing voluntary work; strengthening labour discipline in both the APP and the private sector; and promoting the enactment of a 'democratic, anti-feudal, anti-oligarchic and anti-imperialist agrarian reform'.

Sandinista hegemony over the union movement, and over the revolutionary process as a whole, was manifested by the CST and ATC. The period beginning in late 1980 was marked by intense mass mobilization, led by the CST and the ATC, against the opposition parties, and especially against the decapitalization measures taken by the owners of certain private enterprises. The formation of the Coordinadora was thus not only an important step in the unification of the workers' movement, but also the explicit recognition of the leadership of the Sandinista unions.

The main document of the Coordinadora, although it considers strikes and other direct actions as measures of last resort, does recognize a certain autonomy on the part of the workers' organizations to make demands, and the legitimacy of such actions. However, the development of the economic crisis – aggravated by the bourgeoisie's refusal to expand production, by external military and economic aggression, and by the inevitable dislocations associated with major social transformations – curtailed labour demands as a result of state policies, while the class orientation of the unions increased.

The main document of the Second Assembly for Worker Unity makes this orientation clear, by emphasizing the following:

> the class independence of the proletariat in the light of revolutionary doctrine ... the consequent practice of proletarian internationalism; the hegemonic role of the working class in our revolutionary process; the unity of the workers' movement, all workers, and the people under the banners of the struggle for scientific socialism; the unity of the union movement in a Single Workers' Confederation around the fundamental principles and historic tasks of the working class ... to sustain categorically the revolutionary alliance of the workers with the poor peasants; the determining role played by the popular masses in all political, economic, and social transformations; ... the unity of all revolutionary forces around the theory of the Proletarian Revolution [and] ... to sustain and develop the genuinely democratic and anti-imperialist struggle of our people for the defence of national sovereignty and the social and economic development of Nicaragua.

The document goes on to state that these principles will serve as guidelines 'in the struggle for the profound democratization of the country, its definitive liberation from the yoke of North American imperialism, and for making the right steps towards the victory of socialism in Nicaragua'. The document also asserts that 'the social contradictions in our country have been exacerbated to such an extent that it is not possible to draw a veil over the antagonisms between the classes'.

Based on this perspective, the CSN called for greater worker participation in the global management of the economy as well as in the operations of each enterprise; effective political control over the capitalists on the part of the revolutionary state; strengthening of the union movement and the rejection of class reconciliation; the adoption of a global wage policy based upon increased production and productivity, together with wage adjustments to face the increasing cost of living; the organization of unions by industry rather than enterprise; the strengthening of national defence and the incorporation of the workers into the militias; and the immediate confiscation of the enterprises of capitalists who engage in decapitalization practices.

It is interesting to note that the whole document has the revolutionary government as the implicit or explicit instrument of its proposals. The government reacted to these proposals in a balanced way. Its policies against decapitalization and the flight of capital were strengthened considerably; various measures were adopted to prevent employers from taking reprisals against workers who joined the militias; the organization of unions on an industry-wide basis was stimulated; the Ministry of Labour began to foster the progressive institutionalization of worker participation in the management of enterprises through collective bargaining agreements. At the same time, the state enacted an Economic and Social Emergency Law on 10 September 1981 which provided for three years of imprisonment for: those who incite, help or participate in the initiation or continuation of a strike, shutdown or takeover of a work centre; as well as those who promote or participate in land invasions or takeovers that contravene the provisions of the Agrarian Reform Act.

The worsening economic crisis led the FSLN to strengthen the control of the revolutionary state over the antagonistic classes in Nicaraguan society. It was evident to the Frente that a strategy based on exhorting greater labour discipline was not having the desired effects, as the following statement by Comandante Luis Carrion reveals.

> as a circumstantial factor which has had a very grave and important effect on this crisis, we have to mention the lack of labour discipline. In these two years of revolution, due to the time lost by the workers, the country has lost $150,000,000 – as a result of strikes, stoppages, and various forms of disruption of production. In essence, because of a generalized lack of labour discipline, we have lost $150,000,000 or the equivalent of 30% of our total annual export earnings. This is too heavy a figure for our country to bear.[17]

Finally, in December 1981, the Council of State modified the respective articles of the Labour Code, suspending the right to strike.

The reformulation of the role and tasks of the union movement in accordance with the needs of the present stage of the revolution has involved a combination of persuasion and repression – although the latter is more of an ultimate threat than an effective practice. When coercion has been used, it has been directed against the leaders, whereas political persuasion and propaganda have been used with regard to the rank and file of such unions.

Workers' Participation in the Management of the Economy

As soon as the revolutionary war had ended, it was evident that the resumption of productive activity and the recovery of the economy depended upon the active participation of the workers. A major part of the industries and agricultural enterprises had been destroyed or seriously damaged. In some regions, the insurrection had coincided with the agricultural cycle and many tasks of production could not be undertaken. And many agricultural estates and enterprises had been abandoned by their owners, who had fled the country. In these conditions, the workers dedicated themselves to the urgent tasks of preserving the existing means of production, repairing the equipment that could be salvaged, advising the inexperienced technicians and managers of the newly created enterprises of the APP, and forcing capitalists to reactivate their paralysed companies and to resume investments.

As mentioned above, workers' participation in the global management of the economy as well as in the direct management of enterprises is one of the permanent demands of the union movement, and particularly of the Sandinista unions. The concept of workers' participation, as a dynamic axis of Sandinista democracy, has undergone a continuing process of definition. The Assembly for Union Unity in April 1980 put forward workers' participation in production and in the transformation of the state. Participation in production was defined in a generic sense, and involved increasing production and productivity, voluntary work and emulation, guarding facilities and protecting machinery against sabotage, preventing decapitalization of their enterprises, struggling for the fulfilment of the Labour Code as well as measures affecting industrial safety and occupational hygiene, strengthening the APP and preventing the paralysis of production.[18]

In other words, participation was defined with regard to production largely in terms of the function of watching over the owners of private companies and involvement in the tasks of production per se, rather than as effective involvement in the economic decisions of the enterprises in which the workers were employed. On the other hand, union participation in the transformation of the state was characterized as involving the selection of representatives who could convey to the state agencies the needs, point of view, recommendations and criticisms of the workers. They were also expected to monitor the implementation of the Plan of Economic Reactivation; to combat bureaucratism, wastage, embezzlement and inefficiency; to eliminate authoritarian worker–employer relationships in the APP; and to inform the state about decapitalization practices and violations of the Labour Code.

Workers' participation appears here as fundamentally the effective fulfilment of production goals, as political surveillance, as collaboration with state agencies in the supervision of the behaviour of both the bourgeoisie and the managers of state enterprises. It does not imply the involvement of workers in the decisions affecting the basic operations of their units of production, that is, decisions about investments, production goals, costs and the organization of the labour process. However, it is not confined solely within the limits of each enterprise, nor does it reduce the unions to mere transmission belts for passing state information to the rank and file. The unions are more than this. They are assigned the functions of vigilancia revolucionaria (revolutionary vigilance) over the production process, the progressive transformation of the relations of production and the labour process in the APP, the elimination of bourgeois criteria of labour discipline, struggling against bureaucratism and upgrading the technical, cultural, political and ideological level of the workers. Thus, workers' participation is seen as oriented towards the economy and the state, and not only towards the level of the units of production. It is seen as more political than technical or economic – more macro-political (that is, concerned with the global transformation of society) than micro-political (concerned with production goals, investment decisions, etc., at the level of specific units of production).

The Second Assembly for Workers' Unity, based upon the experience of over one year, and in the context of the worsening economic crisis, emphasized the linkages between participation and the advancement of the process of economic recovery. In the base document of this assembly, participation in the management of the economy encompasses both global economic planning and the direct management of enterprises – in the APP and in the private sector. It concerns the planning and programming of production, workers' control over the normal operations of their enterprises, effective representation by the union leaders of the interests of the rank and file, vigilance against corruption and the squandering of resources, and the rejection of class reconciliation.

Participation is put forward, therefore, as a dimension of the class autonomy of the workers' movement and of the democratization of the unions. It is evident that the CSN was concerned with differentiating its conception of workers' participation from that put forward by the opposing unions and even by certain sectors of the bourgeoisie. In the early period of the present stage of the revolution, these opposition forces tried to win over elements of the rank and file from the FSLN by proposing co-determination, profit-sharing, etc., at a time when the Sandinista organizations had not yet defined their position on workers' participation.

On the first anniversary of the revolutionary triumph, a group of industrial entrepreneurs in Granada, who were tied to the Conservative Party, took the initiative in instituting a form of workers' participation based on profit-sharing in their enterprises. This move was denounced by the FSLN unions as devationist.[19] The Sandinista unions pointed out that these same entrepreneurs had refused to pay the wage increase decreed by the governing junta on Labour Day (1 May 1980), and had boycotted meetings summoned by the Sandinista unions. The latter also denounced the project because it had been formulated with the advice of officials of the US embassy.[20] The minority union confederations, especially the CTN, were enthusiastic about this strategy for undermining the FSLN unions. On 19 July, the CTN published in the opposition newspaper, *La Prensa*, an extensive manifesto where it advocated an independent and classist union movement and the establishment of what it called 'the social property of the workers'.[21]

Undeniably, these proposals went beyond the type of participation advocated by the CSN and the FSLN. They were based on a different type of unionism and a different conception of society. They were intended to generate around them an alternative political project less objectionable to the bourgeoisie. Although technically they seemed to offer the workers much more than the Sandinista conception of workers' participation, in fact these opposition proposals were custom-made to suit the employers and to subordinate the unions. In this sense, the 'classism' that they advocated reduced the class interests of the workers to achieving a portion of capital's profits.

Participation in the management of enterprises, which started as a result of *de facto* initiatives on the part of the workers, has been progressively institutionalized by means of collective bargaining agreements. The latter have become increasingly important since the revlutionary triumph, starting with the law creating the agrarian reform enterprises, which included provisions regarding the participation of agricultural workers in the administration of these enterprises.

By the middle of 1983, out of a total of 718 collective bargaining agreements, 422 or 59 per cent included clauses on union participation in the administration of the enterprises concerned. The proportion of agreements with this type of clause is slightly greater in the APP than in the private sector – 61 per cent for the APP enterprises and 58 per cent for the private enterprises. And it is clear that the labour confederation that has been most active in promoting these types of agreements has been the CST – more than 75 per cent of its agreements.

Clauses referring to participation in these agreements encompass different levels and intervention in different areas of operation – labour discipline, the administration of the labour force, evaluation of production, training, etc. The unions have gained participation in the elaboration of the internal regulations of enterprises, control over hiring and promotional procedures as well as lay-offs and transfers, access to information on production goals and costs as well as the right to be consulted on both, and they have secured resources for the technical and political training of their members (for example scholarships, subsidies, time off, etc.).

As regards vigilance over the production process and participation in the general operations of the unit of production, revolutionary Nicaragua has gone through different phases in a process which appears to be still evolving. The first attempt to generalize participation in the operations of enterprises took the form of Asambleas de Reactivacion Economica (Assemblies of Economic Reactivation, ARE). These assemblies were formed by all the personnel, the directive council of the union and the directors of each enterprise, and eventually the corresponding minister or vice-minister for the economic sector concerned. In certain enterprises, because of their economic import-ance or for other reasons, representatives of the governing junta or the FSLN also participated.

The AREs began to operate in 1980. Discussions in these assemblies focused on the problems of the economy, issues connected with the productive process in each enterprise and matters involving the linkage between both of these types of concerns – the shortage of spare parts, the lack of foreign exchange, the supply of raw material and other inputs, etc. The AREs sought to break with the tradition that bound workers exclusively to their immediate sphere of work, and to expand their horizons of participation and interest. In this regard, they aimed at several objectives: to ensure that the workers in every section and department of each enterprise were informed about the enterprise's production plan; to make sure that the progress of production was continuously evaluated in terms of the goals of the plan by each section, department and/or work brigade; to ensure that problems were identified, tools and machinery properly maintained and the resources of each enterprise rationally utilized; and to extend the AREs to the branch level of production.[22]

The achievements of these assemblies depended upon the way in which they were conceived and carried out. The AREs which functioned best, in terms of workers' participation in the discussion of important issues, were those which were set up at the urging of the local union, where the union carried out effective political work among the rank and file, and where the latter demanded, sometimes belligerently, information on and discussion about issues which up to this time had been closed to them. In other words, the existence of a strong union, with a firm base in the rank and file, proved to be the main condition favouring the development of genuine participation. In contrast, where the AREs were vertically organized from the top by management, the results were poor and tended to hinder the development of the process of workers' participation.

Experience in the AREs made it clear that the prevailing technical and cultural level of the workers was such that participation should be developed first in the immediate sphere of the workers and in accordance with the technical division of the labour process, that is, at the section and departmental level. In general, the best assemblies were those which started at this level. They made it possible for the workers to engage in a more informed discussion on subjects about which they had better knowledge.

The AREs made the workers see that the management of an enterprise was not something mysterious or remote, and contributed to their understanding of the importance of organized labour in achieving the objectives of the revolution within their sphere of production. But at the same time, they revealed that there needed to be more continuity to the process of participation – not just one or two moments in the annual production cycle. Thus, Asambleas de Produccion Permanentes (Permanent Production Assemblies) were established as organizations charged with constantly evaluating the performance of the various sections of the enterprises in relation to the goals set by the AREs. These new assemblies worked well with regard to matters of production, but they tended to distance the workers from the framework of administration, and separate management from production.

On the other hand, in many cases it was clear that workers' expectations about the level of participation and the efficacy of the latter clashed with the reticence of many administrators with regard to workers' participation. This tended to generate strong tensions between the workers, who demanded a share in the administration of the enterprise, and the management, who resisted their demands. The initial response to this situation was to incorporate some of the members of the directive council of the union in the management of the enterprise. The union would then begin to function as a transmission belt between workers and management. This made it possible to improve the performance of the production process in some enterprises, but it also created a process of bureaucratization of the union leadership, leading to the desertion of the rank and file. Very soon, it was clear that this process had one of two results. Either the union leadership, in trying to solve problems of production, became progressively detached from the rank and file and assumed the perspective of management, or, in an attempt to maintain its representative function, the union leadership abandoned the management of the enterprise and adopted a belligerent attitude towards it – thus worsening the problems which in principle it had tried to solve.

Both the achievements and limitations of the AREs led to a search for other forms of participation, starting with the immediate sphere of work – the section or department. As a result, Consejos de Produccion (Production Councils) were established. In general, these bodies are formed by each work section electing, after prolonged discussion, a representative – not necessarily on the basis of political criteria, but rather from the point of view of being the most representative as a productive worker (vanguard worker). The Production Council for each enterprise consists of the representatives of the workers from every section or department, as well as the representatives of the administration, also on a sectional or departmental basis.

The Production Councils study and discuss the enterprise's production goals, the difficulties that arise in meeting them as a result of internal problems or the effects of the national economic situation and ways of dealing with these problems. They draw up the enterprise's internal regulations, set guidelines for improving the general working conditions and occupational safety, etc. In the beginning, the councils ran up against the indifference of the workers towards participating in these discussions, and political education on the part of the union was essential in overcoming this attitude. In TEXNICSA (an APP textile enterprise), for example, the plant union, affiliated with the CST, organized weekly meetings to inform the workers of the plant's progress,

137

of the opportunity for participation afforded by the Production Council, etc., as part of an effort to stimulate their active partipation. Similar meetings were organized by the union with personnel from each production section in the Benjamin Zeledon Sugar Mill (also an APP enterprise). The results were generally successful; workers' representatives started participating in the council, and the members of each section began to demand that they be informed of the matters discussed in the council meetings.

The experience of the Production Councils allowed workers to consider issues such as labour discipline that until then had been the exclusive prerogative of the management of their enterprises. One outcome was the creation of Comites de Disciplina (Discipline Committees) in each enterprise, charged with combating the attitudes of workers and technicians which are detrimental to the maintenance of production and increasing productivity, such as negligence, absenteeism, wasting resources, etc. These committees are made up of representatives of the workers. Instead of repression or sanctions, they function through persuasion and political discussions with each worker concerning his or her faults, the causes, the impact on the performance of the enterprise and on the morale of his or her fellow workers – all within the context of the revolutionary process. If, despite these discussions, the indiscipline continues, the committee finally considers this must be a deliberate attempt to act against the interests of the working class, and only then is some sanction applied.

In order to systematize and consolidate the accumulated experience to date, a pilot project in workers' participation is currently being carried out in eight major state enterprises, promoted by the CST and supported by the Corporacion de Industrias del Pueblo (Corporation of People's Industries or COIP). It involves three levels of participation. First, there is the Enterprise Committee, which is a collective management body formed by the director of the enterprise, section managers and the union leadership (the secretary general, the secretary of labour affairs, the secretary of propaganda and the secretary of production). This committee discusses production goals, their linkage to the overall economic process, difficulties that may arise, etc. Agreements reached are sent to the Production Committees, which are formed by the union leaders, union representatives for each section of the enterprise, the director of the enterprise and the section managers. The goals set by the Enterprise Committee are discussed by the Production Committee from the standpoint of each section. New points of view, criticism and workers' initiatives are also included in these discussions. Afterwards, the goals are discussed in what are called Commitment Assemblies, where the management of the enterprise and the union leadership take up problems of supply, the costs of production, efficiency etc.

The Enterprise and Production Committees meet every 15 days to evaluate the progress of the production process, the fulfilment of goals, the solving of supply problems, etc. There are three types of Commitment Assemblies, each one with its own schedule of meetings. There is a monthly assembly, made up of the management of the enterprise, the union leadership and representatives from the CST. There is also a tri-monthly sectoral assembly above the enterprise level, composed of the COIP director for the respective branch of industry (e.g. metal products or textiles, etc.), the union leaders in this branch, representatives from the CST and occasionally representatives from government ministries related to the branch of production involved, as well as representatives from the FSLN. Finally, there is a half-yearly assembly for evaluating the entire sector of the economy, which is attended by the COIP directors for the branches involved, the general secretaries of the unions involved in the sector, the vice-ministers of the Ministry of Industry, the directors of all the enterprises concerned, representatives of the CST and possibly the Regional Directorate of the FSLN.[23]

The experimental character of the project makes it difficult to arrive at conclusions about its scope and impact, both at the level of effective worker participation and the incorporation of worker initiatives from the base in enterprise decisions, as well as the level of its effects upon the evolution of the production process in each enterprise.

Here it is also relevant to mention several other instances in which the unions participate in decisions regarding the social and economic policies of the revolutionary state. Both the CST and the ATC participate in the formulation and implementation of sectoral policies – in a consultative capacity. This is the case with regard to the Commission on Employment and Living Standards, the Hygiene and Occupational Safety Commission, the consultative commissions on agricultural policies (in cotton, coffee, livestock, rice, bananas, sugar, basic grains, etc.), the different inter-ministerial commissions that participate in drafting the annual national economic plan, etc.

The scope and effectiveness of union participation at this level is uneven. Receptivity towards their initiatives is greater in some state sectors than in others. Not all state functionaries are willing to accept discussions with union representatives, and they do not always offer the most propitious conditions for carrying out discussions – such as making information available in time for it to be thoroughly analysed by the union representatives, etc. In other instances, the paternalism of some state organizations and functionaries leads them to pay less attention to the union representatives, or the technical framework for discussions is so unnecessarily obtruse that it makes effective participation by the workers' delegates difficult.

The Scope and Limitations of Participation

Contrary to what is sometimes thought – especially outside of Nicaragua – workers' participation is not a gift of the revolutionary regime, but a right which the workers have won through their own struggle. This does not just refer to the support the workers provided the FSLN in the struggle against the dictatorship, or to its character of an exploited class, but to the development of its effective participation in the current stage of the revolution. The unions and the union confederations had to fight private owners and also certain APP administrators as well as state functionaries for the incorporation of organized workers in the management of the economy.

The union organizations of the FSLN have generally formed the vanguard in this struggle. They have progressively broadened the space for workers' participation through their mobilizations, internal and public criticism, denunciations, etc. Naturally, the greatest resistance was encountered in the private sector. In a capitalist milieu such as that of Nicaragua, the workers' demands rapidly acquired what the bourgeoisie regarded as a subversive character. Participation in the administration of enterprises, the development of the union movement and the support for workers' demands in certain sectors of the state apparatus all implied the rupture of bourgeois principles of authority within the enterprise, just as the revolution ruptured bourgeois authority within the society at large. This has been particularly evident in the rural sector. If collective bargaining agreements transformed worker–employer relations in the urban sector of the economy, in the countryside they represented a veritable revolution. The unions of the workers in the haciendas achieved through this means the establishment of internal labour regulations, which they participated in drawing up, and a say in the administration of recruitment, lay-offs, etc.

But there has also been resistance to workers' participation in the state. In late 1980, for example, the CSN strongly criticized the functionaries of the Ministry of Planning for not taking into account the opinions of the workers in the drafting of the 1981 Plan of Economic Reactivation, despite the fact that a group of unions had requested meetings with ministry functionaries. On other occasions, the criticisms refer to the lack of firmness on the part of some state institutions in facing the obstacles to union participation placed in their way by the owners of private enterprises.

In 1983, the ATC publicly denounced the passivity of some state functionaries in the face of the systematic failure of certain employers to comply with their obligation to permit the unions access to their records. According to the ATC:

> There are cases of inspectors who will not make an inspection, if we do not provide the transportation. The inspectors lack adequate

contact with rural work and agricultural workers. They should know the work centres better, and they should organize themselves better, so that they can enforce compliance with the labour legislation.[24]

It is clear that the type of participation promoted by the ATC and the CST challenges bourgeois principles of authority more than the traditional forms of participation in profits, permitting the workers to be minority stockholders, etc.

Workers' participation in the APP has also run up against managers and administrators who tend to reproduce in the state sector the pattern of employer–worker relations in the private sector – authoritarian behaviour, refusal to discuss matters with the workers, etc. In these cases, the position of the unions has been as belligerent as in the private sector. The workers of the Plywood enterprise – a wood manufacturing enterprise under COIP – used the occasion of a visit by Comandante Victor Tirado (one of the members of the FSLN National Directorate) to organize an improvised assembly where they criticized the administration of the enterprise for violating the collective bargaining agreement, disregarding the functions of the union, failing to support the technical innovations proposed by the workers, for being ideologically confused, setting inflated commissions and expense accounts for management personnel, etc.[25] On another occasion, the workers at a COIP plastics factory denounced excessive expenditures on the part of the administrators for fuel and repairs of their own vehicles, as well as for not controlling the use of raw materials.[26] In early 1983, the workers of a COIP spinning and weaving factory accused the management during an assembly of being responsible for the enterprise's poor performance.[27] There have been other similar cases.

In general, the criticisms and demands of the workers have been well received by the management of COIP. One illustrative case is that of the PLASTINIC enterprise, the main producer of plastics in the state sector. In August 1982, more than 350 workers and the union leadership informed the Junta de Gobierno of a series of problems in the enterprise, including: inadequate maintenance of the plant, the shortage of spare parts, no encouragement of worker innovations, the administrator's refusal to deal with the union and obstruction of worker participation, etc. In October, an agreement was reached between the union and COIP that the plant administrator would be replaced. However, the administrator was not replaced, and the workers raised their demands again. Following these renewed pressures, they managed to have the administrator dismissed in late January 1983. As on other occasions, the entire episode was given broad coverage in the pages of *Barricada*, the official daily newspaper of the FSLN.[28]

The Sandinista triumph on 19 July 1979 has not eliminated the union struggle – rather it has provided this struggle with a receptive state as

141

part of the historic project of the revolution. For the time being, workers' participation appears to be more a function of the unions than the workers themselves. This is particularly obvious in terms of the structure that has been erected by the revolutionary state – political commissions and state councils where union representatives are designated by the union confederations without the participation of the rank-and-file union members. On the other hand, at the enterprise level, the union leaders are elected by the workers in assemblies, and the same generally takes place in terms of the delegates to the Enterprise Committees.

In many cases, however, there is still a fairly low level of participation by the union cadres and the workers. The weight of illiteracy, cultural backwardness and authoritarianism left by years of dictatorship has not been completely erased, and is responsible for the reduced level of workers' participation in the management of the enterprises. One factor that is not always taken into account is that effective participation requires certain minimum qualifications as well as the investment of time and energy. It represents an additional task beyond that of paid work, and as a result requires political conviction and training. An important part of union activity today still consists of motivating the rank and file to involve themselves in the forms of worker participation that are available – attending assemblies, participating in discussions, demanding reports from delegates, monitoring the production process, etc. For example, during a production assembly held by the 600 workers of the Oscar Benavides Enterprise (one of the agrarian reform enterprises), the ATC representatives present urged the workers to adopt a more belligerent position with regard to management, to increase their participation and to take a more active role in the armed defence of the enterprise. At one point, the following comments were made by an ATC official: 'Let's realize once and for all that these enterprises are ours. Therefore, we all have an obligation to learn about and direct them, as well as to defend them.'[29]

The unions as well as the FSLN are undertaking the task of promoting participation and training the rank and file so that they will be able to improve their participation. This task is not simple since in many instances the union leadership itself is not exempt from the limitations that we have noted in the case of the workers. There is a shortage of experienced cadres; their level of training is not the best; they have to perform a multiplicity of tasks, etc.[30]

These conditions have created a context within which paternalistic practices have developed among certain sectors of the state apparatus and the administration of the APP, as well as among the union leaders themselves. There is a tendency towards leadership by substitution, that is, decisions are made for the workers instead of by them. Or participation is omitted in an effort to avoid overloading the workers or their organizations; or because the functionaries have better technical knowledge; or because of the slowness of the union's response due to the factors we have already mentioned – all of which in the end leads to decisions being taken at the top, leaving the workers' representatives simply to endorse the decisions.

The Workers' Movement and the State

One question which is raised every time that the subject of workers' participation is discussed concerns the type of relations that have developed between the unions and the state, particularly the extent of autonomy the unions have *vis-à-vis* the state. It was noted earlier that the position of the FSLN and its unions is that of conferring on the unions the role of transmission belt between workers and enterprises – within the framework of the policies and guidelines set down by the revolutionary state. Some observers have criticized the initial manifestations of this approach, noting that in practice it could reduce the unions to mere instruments or apparatuses of the state, with no real autonomy.[31]

Undeniably, such tendencies do exist in certain sectors of the state, and even within the FSLN, and they have been repeatedly denounced by the FSLN.[32] However, our opinion, on the basis of many interviews with union leaders and rank-and-file workers and as a result of following the union movement over four years, is that in practice the unions have effective autonomy from the state, and their adhesion to a common political project reinforces this autonomy. This is not a mechanical question nor are we trying to assert either that there are no tensions or contradictions in the relations between the state and the unions or that one cannot detect overlap and confusion between these elements.

The intense worker mobilizations that took place during the first half of 1981 around the issues of decapitalization and depletion of the inventories of the enterprises of certain sectors of the bourgeoisie offer a good opportunity to examine a concrete example of the relations between the state and the unions. In March 1980, the Junta de Gobierno issued a decree that attempted to put an end to the decapitalizations, divestments, the clandestine export of assets, etc. – all aimed at sabotaging the recovery of the economy. This measure was adopted as a result of union mobilizations and the FSLN's concern with rapidly reactivating the productive apparatus of the country. The evaluation of the 1980 economic plan revealed that private enterprise was generally not fulfilling the role expected of it, and that decapitalization was increasingly being used as a measure by the bourgeois opposition to the revolution.

By the beginning of 1981, CST and ATC denunciations, mobilizations, occupations and takeovers of both factories and agricultural

143

estates were on the increase. They demanded the modification of the March 1980 decree, and the confiscation of all enterprises where decapitalization was evident. The FSLN responded to these actions in various ways. For example, in June, Comandante Jaime Wheelock denounced several notorious cases of decapitalization, charging that:

> the anti-patriotic attitude of some sectors of private enterprise is endangering the survival of this type of [mixed] economy. If we are going to have an economy that robs and capitalizes, we prefer to close down completely this type of economy.[33]

A few days later, at the end of a workers' assembly, Comandante Bayardo Arce charged that the decapitalization activities of many businessmen conformed to imperialism's programme of destabilizing the revolution.[34]

In other words, the FSLN leadership responded to the demands and mobilizations of the workers by raising them to a new level. The issue was no longer just a question of sabotaging the plan for reconstructing the economy, but of manoeuvres promoted and inspired by imperialism. Thus, they brought into question the legitimacy of the mixed economy and the existence of the bourgeoisie within this economy.

The workers' organizations responded immediately to this situation. Mobilizations, land seizures, the occupation of factories and direct management of production by the workers increased. The Sandinista mass organizations joined the ATC and CST under the banner of immediate confiscation of those engaged in decapitalization. Huge marches were organized to press this demand before the offices of the Junta de Gobierno. The four Sandinista union confederations – the ATC, CST, FETSALUD and ANDEN – added the demand that all technicians and administrators in the APP who squandered resources or neglected their responsibilities should be dismissed. In the province of Matagalpa, all the mass organizations called upon the revolutionary government to confiscate the land of all those landlords guilty of decapitalization. In the province of Granada, something similar occurred: the ATC and the CST published long lists of the enterprises and haciendas where decapitalization, abandonment and similar practices had taken place. In the majority of cases, these organizations proceeded to take over these entities. In a joint declaration, the ATC and the CST stated that the choice was between decapitalization or workers' control. The Ministry of Justice backed up the popular demands by making it known that in meetings with business organizations outside the country, Nicaraguan businessmen had drawn up plans for facilitating the decapitalization of their holdings.[35] In the cotton-producing province of León, the ATC demanded the immediate confiscation of the property of all those involved in decapitalization or who refused to put their land into production. They announced that 'the workers will take the initiative in order to make them produce'.[36] And the Second Assembly for Workers' Unity demanded that all enterprises where decapitalization was suspected should be taken over immediately while an investigation was in progress.[37]

During a workers' assembly organized around the slogan 'To Combat Decapitalization; We Demand Confiscation', CST Secretary General Lucio Jiminez stated that:

> We workers could not stay on the defensive ...; we had to pass immediately to the offensive, in a clear fight, not against just this or that element or against one or two administrators of the bourgeoisie, or against one or two employers, but rather to go to an immediate struggle aimed at striking decisively against the bourgeoisie as a class.[38]

Shortly afterwards, he denounced the perfunctory manner in which some state functionaries dealt with the problem. He stated that 'there are state organisms whch seem to be accomplices to the decapitalization; they give the owners time to falsify their accounts'.[39]

This rapid increase in the level and political scope of the union mobilizations alarmed the bourgeoisie, and they denounced what they called an FSLN campaign against the private sector and the mixed economy project.[40] At one point, a certain disjuncture developed between the evolving popular protest and the state. The Ministry of Labour issued a communique prohibiting work stoppages, strikes and occupations connected with the protest against decapitalization.[41] The CST opposed this statement and made public its disagreement.[42] The Junto de Gobierno, however, proclaimed its 'categorical support' for the position of the Ministry of Labour.[43]

Meanwhile the climate of labour and political agitation over the issue of decapitalization had been reinforced by the announcement of the impending enactment of a new law against decapitalizations. This law included several of the proposals put forward by the workers' organizations. This climate was also created by the impending execution of the new Agrarian Reform Law. Finally, in August, the Council of State approved the new law against decapitalization. However, while this law incorporates the proposals of the popular organizations on confiscation, preventative measures, etc., it also prohibits 'any action aimed at forcibly modifying the relations of production in enterprises'.[44] Even though the wording of this law is only declarative and does not include any penalties for failure to comply, it elicited the open opposition of all the union representatives in the Council of State, including the CST and the ATC, despite the fact that it was fully supported by the FSLN.[45] Since the law took effect, denunciations of instances of decapitalization have continued, but they have generally been carried out without any intense mobilizations or resort to direct action.[46]

We have dedicated a considerable amount of space to this particular case, because it reveals clearly the form in which workers' mobilizations on fundamental issues are articulated with the general orientation of the revolutionary vanguard. From specific demands directed against certain sectors of the bourgeoisie, the process moved to a higher political level, in which these demands took on both an anti-imperialist as well as a class character. At some moment, the workers' mobilizations brought into the process all the popular organizations, which further sharpened the fundamental class contradictions involved. These contradictions involved technical and professional sectors which shared a certain ideological solidarity with those sectors of the bourgeoisie involved in decapitalizing their holdings. The expansion and depth of the popular mobilizations put pressure on the mixed economy project and the alliance with certain sectors of the bourgeoisie promoted by the FSLN. The state then intervened to restrain the activism of the workers and popular organizations, while giving institutional priority to their fundamental demands.

Final Considerations

Other examples could have been presented,[47] but what has been mentioned is sufficient to demonstrate that the reality is too fluid and complex, and the participants too active, to enable the formulation of definitive conclusions. In any case, it would be pure speculation to assert that, on the basis of the evidence available, there is in existence a type of local stalinism which could stifle the capacity for criticism and autonomy possessed by the unions. As we mentioned previously, if there is any conclusion to be drawn from the experience so far of the Sandinista revolution, it is that the advances and consolidation of this process are based upon the capacity for mobilization and organized struggle possessed by the popular classes. The latter appear to have a dialectical articulation – which by definition does not exclude contradictions – with the political organization that on a daily basis proves itself to be their vanguard, precisely as a result of the unfolding of this relationship.

In this sense, the relations between the unions, the FSLN and the revolutionary state can be interpreted as different levels of instances of the unfolding and concretization of the same project of social transformation. At each of these levels, the strategic and conjunctural elements, the sectoral and political components, acquire different weight. Naturally, the issue is complex and changing, since the limits of the proletarian–popular project are circumscribed during the present period by the scheme of national unity and a mixed economy that expresses the alliance between the FSLN and certain fractions of the bourgeoisie within the context of the present stage of national reconstruction.

To the extent that the demands of the workers form an integral part of the Sandinista project for the transformation of Nicaraguan society in terms of a popular and anti-imperialist perspective, the position and role of the workers' movement exceed that of mere trade unionism. Union demands involved both the short-term improvement in living and working conditions, and direct workers' participation in the management of the economy and the political direction of the society. Moreover, this participation is not defined in sectoral or categorical terms, but rather in political terms. Therefore, it is not a matter of the sociological representativeness of an organization – the greater or lesser proportion of workers in its base or leadership cadres – but the class character of the political project that the organization promotes. While these two considerations are not independent of each other, the latter cannot be reduced to the former.

It is worth stressing once again that this process, which is always complex and full of tensions, is much more complicated and difficult in a society such as Nicaragua, which does not have a democratic tradition, has very little previous experience in union organizing, a working class that until six years ago was largely illiterate and a primitive and deformed economy. Moreover, it is a society which, precisely because it is undergoing a revolutionary process, must confront in precarious conditions the increasing aggression of the United States government and the military attacks of the counter-revolutionary forces supported by it.

Notes

1. Cf. A. Sandino, *Pensamientos* (Managua: Ministerio de Educación, 1979), p. 8.

2. Cf. for example G. Gutiérrez, 'El reformismo artesanal en el movimiento obrero nicaraguense', *Revista del Pensamiento Centroamericano*, 159 (April–June 1978), pp. 2-21; O. Guevara and C. Perez Bermudez, *El movimiento obrero nicaraguense* (Managua: Ediciones Davila Bolanos, 1981); etc.

3. The most recent population census was carried out in 1971. Therefore, all data regarding total population, economically active population, etc., after that year are estimates.

4. Our estimates regarding the class composition of Nicaraguan society differ from those of other authors. A larger development on this theme can be found in C.M. Vilas, *Perfiles de la Revolucion Sandinista* (Buenos Aires: LEGASA, 1984), ch. II. Due to the limitations pointed out in note 3, the term 'economically active population in agriculture' is used as an equivalent of 'economically active population in rural areas'.

5. The estimate of 6 per cent corresponds to *Barricada* (16 March 1980) and was reproduced by M. Perez-Stable, 'The Working Class in the Nicaraguan Revolution', in Thomas Walker (ed.), *Nicaragua in Revolution* (New York: Praeger, 1982), pp. 133-45. The estimate of 7 per cent was made by Ronald

Membreño, of the CST National Executive, in an interview with the author on 12 May 1981.

6. These are: The Central General de Trabajo – Independiente (Independent General Confederation of Labour, CGT-I), created in 1963, and tied to the Nicaraguan Socialist Party; the Central de Accion y Unidad Sindical (the Confederation of Trade Union Action and Unity, CAUS), formed in 1973 and tied to the Communist Party of Nicaragua; the Central de Trabajadores de Nicaragua (the Workers' Confederation of Nicaragua, CTN), created in 1972 and associated with the Social Christian Party; and the Consejo de Unificacion Sindical (Council for Union Unification, CUS), created in 1972. For general information on this subject, see *Envio*, no. 12 (June 1982).

7. For example, according to the Ministry of Labour, the CTN had 40 unions and 3,511 affiliates in mid-June of 1982. But according to the directors of the CTN, there were as many as 65,000 workers affiliated. See *Envio*, ibid. At present, the CTN has only 19 organizations: *Barricada*, 6 June 1983.

8. According to Perez-Stable, 'The Working Class in the Nicaraguan Revolution', by July of 1980, over 200,000 urban workers belonged to Sandinista unions, as well as some 100,000 rural workers. If true, these figures would indicate an urban unionization rate of 74 per cent, and a corresponding rate of 77 per cent for salaried workers in the rural areas, this despite the fact that we have already seen that rural unionizing took on its strongest push during 1981. The average figure for all salaried workers would be 75 per cent. All this only refers to Sandinista unions. According to the Managua daily *El Nuevo Diario* (20 June 1981), the Association of Rural Workers (ATC) had 100,000 affiliates in mid-1981. None the less, in an interview with the author on 20 September 1983, Denis Chavarria, member of the ATC National Executive, cited the figure of 43,000.

9. In 1979, due to effects of the war, Nicaragua's GDP fell nearly 25 per cent in relation to the previous year, and the consumer price index grew by 70.3 per cent.

10. W. Villagra, 'Las posiciones politicas de las corrientes sindicales nicaraguenses', *Anuario de Estudios Centroamericanos*, 6 (1980), pp. 83-94. In the case of the CAUS, some demands went as far as pushing for a 100 per cent salary increase.

11. The hostility of the traditional left towards the FSLN was extensive. According to one member of the FSLN National Directorate, 'those who felt like they had a strong position within the unions, once they understood the political orientation of our organizers, didn't hesitate to single them out in public assemblies as FSLN militants who intended to, as they put it, "carry the workers to a sure death, to an adventurous method of struggle". In this way they were able to, in some cases and at a given time period, deter the integration of the workers into the revolutionary process.' Commander of the Revolution Bayardo Arce C., *El papel de las fuerzas motrices antes y despues del triunfo* (Managua: Secretaria Nacional de Propaganda y Educacion Politica del FSLN, 1980), p. 19.

12. *Barricada*, 14 April 1980.

13. Commander of the Revolution Carlos Nunez, *El papel de las organizaciones de masas en el proceso revolucionario* (Managua: Secretaria Nacional de Propaganda y Educacion Politica del FSLN, 1980).

14. Commander of the Revolution Victor Tirado, speech at the inauguration of the First Assembly for the Unity of Workers, Managua, 15 November 1980.

15. Speech of Commander of the Revolution Jaime Wheelock in the Plaza of the Revolution, Managua, 19 November 1980. *Barricada*, 20 November 1980.

16. *Los Trabajadores*, 16 July 1981.

17. Commander of the Revolution Luis Carrion, *Austeridad: Principio y norma de nuestro pueblo* (Managua: Departamento de Propaganda y Educacion Politica del FSLN, 1981).

18. *Barricada*, 14 April 1980.

19. *Barricada*, 11 July 1980.

20. *La Prensa*, 2 July 1980.

21. *La Prensa*, 7 June 1981.

22. A general evaluation of the experience can be found in *Nueva Economia*, 8 (*Barricada*, 29 December 1980).

23. *Barricada*, 29 June 1982, and interview by the author with Alberto Alvarez, responsible for production matters on the National Executive of the CST, on 7 September 1983.

24. *Barricada*, 27 January 1983.

25. Ibid., 9 July 1982.

26. Ibid., 24 July 1982.

27. Ibid., 16 February 1983.

28. Ibid., 2 September 1982; 26 January and 27 February 1983.

29. Ibid., 7 September 1983.

30. For example, *Barricada*, 1 October 1982.

31. For example, Henri Weber, *Nicaragua: la révolution sandiniste* (Paris: F. Maspero, 1981), ch. 6.

32. For example, Commander Carlos Nunez (see text cited in note 13, p. 16): 'We find that sometimes, they try to use the masses to put out fires when there are conflicts, and as static instruments when there are none.' See also speech of Commander of the Revolution Tomas Borge during the celebration of the Second Anniversary of the Revolutionary triumph (*Barricada*, 20 July 1981).

33. *El Nuevo Diario*, 13 June 1981.

34. *Barricada*, 25 June 1981.

35. For example, *Barricada* following editions: 20, 22, 26 and 29 of June, and 1 and 2 of July 1981.

36. *Barricada*, 2 July 1981.

37. *Los Trabajadores*, 16 July 1981.

38. *Barricada*, 2 July 1981.

39. Ibid., 16 July 1981.

40. *La Prensa*, 27 June and 1 July 1981.

41. *El Nuevo Diario*, 27 July 1981.

42. *Barricada*, 27 and 31 July 1981.

43. Ibid., 28 July 1981.

44. *La Gaceta, Diario Oficial*, 199 (3 October 1981).

45. *El Nuevo Diario*, 31 July 1981.

46. For example, *El Nuevo Diario*, 26 June 1982; *Barricada*, 11 July and 9 September 1982; 15 September 1983.

47. For example the recent public polemic between ANDEN – the teachers' union – and the Ministry of Education regarding the quality of education and delays in salary payments to teachers. Both the Secretary General of ANDEN and the Minister of Education are officially classified as

militants within the party structures of the FSLN. This fact has not stood in the way of the frankness of the polemic – in which both participated directly – nor of the firmness and diversity of the respective positions. *El Nuevo Diario*, 4 and 5 August 1983; *Barricada*, 4, 5 and 6 August 1983.

6 Ideology, Religion and the Class Struggle in the Nicaraguan Revolution

Luis Serra*

Introduction

In this brief essay we provide an analysis of the basic aspects of the religious phenomenon in the Nicaraguan revolution. Our theoretical framework is based on the Marxist conception of ideology, enriched by the contributions of the sociology of religion.[1] Moreover, our perspective is based upon an active five-year commitment as a Christian and a revolutionary in Nicaragua.

In the first part of the essay we deal with the phenomenon of Christian participation in the revolutionary process. This phenomenon started in the late 1960s, and adopted a massive character in the insurrectional stage and after the triumph. In the second part of this essay, we focus on the association of certain religious elements with imperialism and with the right-wing bourgeoisie. After the revolutionary triumph, this religious sector became a fundamental domestic ally of US imperialism and the counter-revolutionary forces which it backs. In the third section, we analyse the FSLN and the revolutionary government's position on religion. We will consider both the unique character of this position and its contradictions. In the final section, we will delve deeper into the dynamics and the future prospects of the religious phenomenon in Nicaragua.

Christian Participation in the Revolution

Christian participation in the revolutionary mobilization of the masses began in the late 1960s. This phenomenon has its origins in a Christianity committed to the cause of the poor. This tendency has been in the past relatively impotent against its opposite, the ecclesiastical institutions which have been the accomplices of those who have wielded power for the benefit of local and foreign minorities.

A study on the functioning of the Catholic Church in Nicaragua, carried out in 1969, revealed its main characteristics at that time.[2] This study concluded that: (1) The hierarchy and clergy were out of contact

* Translated by R.L. Harris with the assistance of Mark Nechodom and Lorena Martos.

with the people and more concerned with their own personal well-being. (2) The clergy were concentrated in colleges, schools and in parish churches within the urban areas. (3) Many religious associations were ineffective and tied to ritualism. (4) Catechism was reduced to mere memorization. (5) The prevailing Thomist theology was divorced from the existing social reality. (6) The religious population was devoted to ritual practices and to religious festivities involving alcohol and games. However, ten years later there was massive Christian participation in the revolutionary insurrection against Somoza. What were the main factors which accounted for this process of growing Christian integration into the revolutionary movement?

Starting in 1965, the formation of Comunidades Eclesiales de Base (Ecclesiastical Base Communities or CEBs) began among the population of the marginalized urban areas and the rural zones, as a result of the new evangelical orientation initiated by the Second Vatican Council and developments in other Latin American countries such as Brazil and Panama. There were five basic characteristics of these CEBs: (1) The study of the Bible was linked with critical reflection on the existing social reality. (2) All evangelical activities were based on the church's new preference or 'option' in favour of the poor. (3) The liturgy was simplified and popular language and music were introduced. (4) Impetus was given to organizing the lay community so that they could deal in a collective manner with the problems that surrounded them. (5) Responsibility for evangelical work was assumed by laymen as well as the clergy.

In the city of Managua, CEBs were developed in poor barrios such as '14 de Septiembre' by Father Jose de Lara, in 'El Riguero' by Father Uriel Molina, in 'Open 3' by the Maryknoll Sisters, in 'San Judas' by the Sisters of the Assumption. In the rural zones, CEBs flourished in Zelaya as a result of the work of the Capuchin monks, in Solentiname as a result of the efforts of Father Ernesto Cardenal, and in Matagalpa under Mgr. Calderon y Padilla. As of 1979, the number of CEBs in Nicaragua was estimated to be more than 300.[4]

Due to the scarcity of priests, the training of laymen for catechism and the administration of the sacrament was encouraged in this period, particularly in the rural areas. Delegados de la Palabra (Delegates of the Word, DPs) were chosen from the most respected persons in each local community, and charged with carrying out the arduous tasks of evangelization and community development. Training of the DPs included, in addition to biblical teachings, the subjects of health, literacy, agriculture and politics. The application of the consciousness-raising method originated by Paolo Freire in Brazil contributed to the development of the critical awareness and the political commitment of the DPs. The multiplication of the number of DPs was impressive in all regions of the country, amounting to approximately 5,000 by 1979. Their major contribution was the development of both Christian practice and a reading of the Bible based upon the perspective of the oppressed. Because of this, the DPs were victimized by the National Guard. With the intensification of repression in 1974, there were many victims among the members of the rural CEBs. This was publicly denounced by the Capuchin monks in 1976.

Alongside the CEBs there developed Christian student movements, such as the Movimiento Cristiano Revolucionario (Revolutionary Christian Movement), the Juventud Obrera Catolica (Catholic Workers' Youth), the Movimiento de Jovenes Cristianos (Movement of Young Christians) and the Movimiento Estudiantil Cristiano (Christian Student Movement). These student movements gained importance because of their combative mobilizations, church takeovers and propaganda efforts, which denounced the repression and injustices of the Somocista regime. Many of their members joined the FSLN.

The Cursillos de Cristianidad (Short Courses on Christianity), which were organized around the focus of the theology of liberation, also contributed to raising the consciousness of the middle and upper strata of the population. The same thing happened as result of the work of organizations such as the Centro de Educación y Promoción Agraria (Centre for Agrarian Education and Promotion, CEPA), the Instituto Juan XXIII (John XXIII Institute), the Instituto Nicaraguense de Promoción de Derechos Humanos (Nicaraguan Institute for the Promotion of Human Rights, INPRHU), the Comite Evangelico Por Ayuda al Desarrollo (Evangelical Committee for Development Aid, CEPAD) – which trained Christian leaders, printed materials, promoted community development and supported Christian organizing and consciousness-raising efforts. Magazines such as *Testimonio* and *Diakonia*, the pamphlet *Cristo Campesino*, and the Escuelas Radiofonicas (Radio Schools) spread the Latin American Bible and the voice of the revolutionary clergy.

Some try to explain the phenomenon of Christian participation in the anti-Somocista struggle as primarily the result of organizational and theological changes fostered by the Catholic and Protestant Churches. This point of view emphasizes the influence of the Second Vatican Council, the Medellin Conference (Ecuador, 1968), the progressive Encyclicals of Paul VI and the theology of liberation. We believe that these were *not* the major reasons. Rather it was the confluence of the structural crisis of dependent capitalism in Nicaragua together with the repressive character of the Somocista regime and the revolutionary actions of the FSLN, which gave impetus to the popular insurrection and the incorporation of Christians into this struggle. It is important to remember that the religious phenomenon we are discussing developed within a society marked at the time by the intensification of the antagonistic contradiction between the popular movement and the Somocista dictatorship.

In this social context, the people became the conscious authors of history and they also appropriated the religious domain by interpreting and practising religious matters in a revolutionary manner. The Delegates of the Word and the clergy committed to the poor became organic intellectuals of the people who knew how to unmask the religious teachings and practices influenced by bourgeois ideology. Their aim was to develop an alternative evangelical praxis that reflected their own level of political consciousness and organization. In this task these organic intellectuals saw the original intent of Jesus' message to be the expression of the oppressed in a hierarchical society subordinated by imperialism. Christian values of justice, equality, the sharing of goods, defence of the meek, etc., they interpreted as the interests of the exploited classes against slavery, feudalism and capitalism.

The frequent testimony by Sandinista Christians that they became involved in revolutionary politics because of their faith, is a subjective perception which hides the objective causality of a social context politicized by the popular struggle led by the FSLN. The theology of liberation, which provides a critical perspective on social reality, served as an important link between the objective and subjective conditions present. The presence of progressive clergy living among the people served to transform their religiousness, while at the same time the people educated the progressive clergy. Conversion and evangelization were mutual. The reformist efforts of the charitable religious elements aimed at minimally fulfilling popular needs were frustrated by the suffocating power structure. They were confronted with a clear dilemma: they could be accomplices of exploitation through their passivity and silence, or they could be faithful to the poor by joining their struggle to overthrow the dictatorship. These Christians, motivated by an evangelical and ethical imperative and aware of the causes of the social problems around them, had no choice but to help the people. In Nicaragua, the dictatorship did not leave any other option but armed struggle to bring about social and spiritual change. Joining the insurrection was the next logical step.

In Nicaragua, the religious renewal promoted by the progressive clergy went beyond the framework of the social doctrine of the church. Christians joined the guerrilla struggle or provided the logistical support and spiritual encouragement which were indispensable to achieving victory.

For these people, the struggle against Somoza was a struggle against sin. This is exemplified in the words of Father Gaspar Garcia Laviana, the revolutionary priest who joined the FSLN and was killed in battle. He stated:

> Somocismo is sin, and to liberate ourselves from oppression is to get rid of sin. With rifle in hand, full of faith and love for the Nicaraguan people, I shall fight to my last breath for the advent of the kingdom of justice in our

homeland, that kingdom of justice announced by the Messiah under the light of the Star of Bethlehem.[5]

As a logical continuation of Christian participation in the overthrow of the dictatorship, many Christians joined in the tasks of the revolutionary process after the triumph over the dictatorship. However, after 19 July 1979, a sector of the clergy and the bourgeoisie began to distance themselves from the revolutionary process. The efforts of this minority, even though it controls the hierarchy of the Catholic Church, have not succeeded in preventing Christian participation in the revolution.

After the triumph, most lay Christian leaders, and many religious persons, became cadres of the state, the mass organizations or the FSLN, as a result of their participation in the anti-Somocista struggle, their political commitment and their level of education in a country characterized by a scarcity of technical cadres and a largely illiterate population. The most well-known examples are the priests in top government positions: Miguel D'Escoto as Foreign Minister; Ernesto Cardenal, Minister of Culture; Edgar Parrales, Minister of Social Welfare and Representative of Nicaragua to the OAS. Fernando Cardenal was co-ordinator of the Cruzada de Alfabetización (Literacy Crusade), subsequently deputy co-ordinator of the Juventud Sandinista (Sandinista Youth) and now Minister of Education. In the Consejo de Estado (Council of State), the Asociación del Clero Nicaraguense (Association of Nicaraguan Clergy, ACLEN) was represented by Father Alvaro Arguello.[6]

A large number of clergy and countless laymen are involved in other spheres of the state apparatus; participation in the mass organizations is extensive. Many leaders of these organizations have been DPs. Christian participation in the FSLN is widespread, and at all levels, from the National Directorate down to the Base Committees. For instance, Comandante Luis Carrion, a member of the National Directorate, is a member of the Movimiento Cristiano Revolucionario and the CEB in the barrio of Riguero in Managua. Fathers Miguel D'Escoto, Fernando Cardenal and Ernesto Cardenal are members of the Sandinista Assembly. And several comandantes and sub-comandantes of the FSLN have been active members of Christian organizations in the past.

The National Literacy Crusade, which took place a few months after the triumph, had the enthusiastic participation of thousands of young people from religious schools and more than 200 members of the clergy. In addition to their personal participation, these clergymen were important because of the material and financial resources as well as the spiritual support they contributed to the mobilization of Nicaragua's young people. In the words of Father Fernando Cardenal, 'The Crusade was an act of love by the entire population toward those who were most forgotten . . . it was the great novitiate of our Sandinista youth.'[7]

In the Popular Health Campaigns and in other health-care tasks, the active participation of clergy and laymen has been important. An illustrative case is the donation by the Oblate Sisters of the Heart of Jesus of their school as the site of the National School of Health. Another example is the formation of a health brigade in the rural district of El Viejo, Chinandega, by the Mercedarian Sisters.

Christian participation has also been notable in the Voluntary Work Campaigns which are periodically carried out to improve local neighbourhoods, to harvest crops, to repair roads and build community halls. Christian participation in the different forms of civil defence has also been extensive, as proven in the May 1982 flood and in response to the counter-revolutionary attack on the Port of Corinto in 1983, which caused a major fire and the evacuation of the entire population.

Christians are involved in the defence of the country through their participation in revolutionary guard duty, the Milicias Territoriales (Territorial Militias), the Batallones de Reserva (Reserve Battalions) and the Servicio Militar Patriotico (Patriotic Military Service or the draft). In the words of Roberto Flores, a DP and President of the Co-operative 'Ulises Rodriguez' of Esteli: 'A true Christian will defend his home and does not think only of himself, because if one sees that they come to kill children as the Contras do, the Christian must fight. Just like Jesus, we have to feel the pain of those who suffer aggressions in the mountains and that is why we have to thrust our chest forward'.[8]

Revolutionary Christians have also been crucial in the ideological defence against the efforts by US imperialism to depict the revolutionary government as atheist and anti-religious. Revolutionary Christians have been a very important channel for the international dissemination of the truth about the Nicaraguan revolution. They have also been very effective at obtaining financial support for the reconstruction of the country. And recently, Christians have expressed their support for the new electoral process in the following terms: 'We as Christians acknowledge the liberating presence of God in the middle of our process, and especially in this stage of free and honest elections'.[9]

There are two essential aspects of the revolutionary process where Christian participation has been outstanding: in the construction of the moral values of the new revolutionary man and woman and in the critical and creative analysis of Nicaragua's social reality. Revolutionary Christians have assumed these two tasks in an explicit and responsible manner in a variety of circumstances.

Numerous Christian newspapers, magazines, weekly bulletins, posters, books, seminars and conferences have been directed at analysing Nicaragua's social reality from the standpoint of the theology of liberation's preferential option for the poor. The document *Fidelidad Cristiana con el Proceso Revolucionario* (Christian Fidelity to the

Revolutionary Process), adhered to by all revolutionary Christian organizations, is a clear example of this constructive critical analysis. This document states the following concerning the bourgeoisie:

> The new Nicaragua must achieve progressive economic independence, which does not favor the excessive foreign financing demanded by the bourgeois class for its economic security and for the satisfaction of its luxury consumption ... this call is an evangelical invitation to the members of the capitalist class for them to let their class interests die and for them to live in solidarity with the popular majorities.

Concerning the state, this document continues:

> The support we give the state must contribute at the same time to the revolutionary vigilance against bureaucratic excesses ... As Christians we must remember that no state apparatus has in itself its reason for being and that its continued structural temptation is to exist for itself. Its sole reason for being is that of service...

And concerning the FSLN, it suggests that:

> Continuous receptivity to the criticisms of the popular majority, cofraternity and living with them, serene and objective explanations – this more than slogans, are the means of maintaining a dialectic complementarity between the vanguard and the masses.

Finally, with regard to the churches, it states:

> Christian opinion on the revolutionary process cannot be measured primarily in terms of the well-being of our churches as institutions. What is decisive are the consequences the process has for the hopes of the poor.[10]

Constructive criticism made from a revolutionary standpoint by these committed Christian groups has been scarce but at times necessary in the last five years of the revolution, when the ideological debate has become polarized between bourgeoisie critics and Sandinista apologists.

The triumph of 1979 brought an end to the repression against the DPs, CEBs and the revolutionary clergy, and it has given them freedom of action. In contrast, since 1979, repression has come from the religious hierarchy, not from the state apparatus. The CEBs have consolidated into an important force in the rural areas. One of the best examples is that of the Inter-Community Bloc for Peasant Welfare in Chinandega.[11] The CEBs continue to be important in the urban zones, and in Managua they have established a co-ordinating network.

The short courses or Cursillos de Cristiandad have continued under the auspices of Cristianos en la Revolución (Christians in the

Revolution), which is an organization composed mainly of Christians who hold top posts in the revolutionary state. And university students are organized into the Universitarios Cristianos Revolucionarios (Revolutionary Christian University Students, UCR).

Consciousness-raising and the formation of progressive Christian leaders through Bible studies and the diffusion of publications have been carried out by Christian organizations such as the Centro Antonio Valdivieso (Antonio Valdivieso Centre), the Centro de Educación y Promoción Agraria (the Centre for Agrarian Education and Development), the Eje Ecumenico (Ecumenical Axis) and the Instituto Histórico Centroamericano (Central American Historical Institute). The efforts of these religious organizations have supported deep-seated theological renewal which has responded, on the one hand, to the challenges posed by the revolutionary process and, on the other, to the challenge posed by religious leaders opposed to the revolution. The main themes of this theological renewal have been the relationship between faith and politics, church unity and authority, Christian identity, productive work, agrarian reform and national defence.

The role played by numerous Christian leaders in the absorbing tasks of building a new society has produced a new form of Christian practice and reflection. Many of these leaders have not been able to continue participating in the CEBs, in priestly functions, or in other ecclesiastical activities. However, their Christian faith is expressed in their tenacious labour on behalf of a revolutionary process which aims at fulfilling the evangelical command to 'give food to the hungry, give drink to the thirsty and clothe the naked'. For these Sandinista Christians, the Gospel has become a point of reference for their work in their CDS and their party. If this way of living the teachings of Christianity is continued, it will bring about important transformations in the religious sphere in Nicaragua.

In the first place, this type of religious practice calls into question the need for a religious institution which administers and monopolizes religious services and which develops a specific space for religious practice. Secondly, the integration of Christianity into the revolution replaces the earlier idea of a 'strategic alliance' between religious and atheist revolutionaries. In its place, it substitutes an intimate, practical and theoretical amalgam found in the same persons and organizational structures. Finally, it will be hard for the church to replace these religious leaders, especially in view of the fact that the mass organizations have become the main channels of popular education and community life: the reactionary religious leaders who are left in the churches have alienated the increasingly more conscious youth.

Christian Participation in the Counter-revolutionary Project

Historically, the vast majority of the Catholic and Protestant clergy helped legitimize the system of political domination imposed by the conservative bourgeoisie and US imperialism. Until 1893, the Catholic Church was acknowledged as the 'religion of the state' and it enjoyed an ideological monopoly. After the brief interlude of the liberal reforms around the turn of the century, Liberal President Zelaya was overthrown in 1909 by the Conservatives with US support and with the blessing of the Catholic hierarchy. Those were the days in which Archbishop Mgr. Lezcano, who was a Conservative Party member of the National Congress, used the pulpit to urge the people to participate in the electoral farces staged by the Conservative oligarchy. The Catholic Bishops' Conference in Nicaragua also tried to dissuade the people from participating in the anti-imperialist struggle led by Sandino. After Sandino was murdered, the Catholic hierarchy legitimized the Somocista dictatorship through its blessings and participation in public acts. In fact, they honoured Somoza with the title of 'Prince of the Church' after the first Somoza's assassination in 1956. The church hierarchy justified its support for the dictatorship with statements such as the following, from 1950: 'For Catholics it must be a true and extolling doctrine that all authority comes from God . . . and that when they obey the government they do not debase themselves, but rather they perform an act which deep down constitutes a compliance with God'.[12]

The Protestant missions located on the Atlantic Coast were part of the British and North American penetration of that zone. These missions conveyed a spiritualist, pietistic and puritanical religious orientation. They also induced an admiration for the Yankee model of living and a fear of all revolutionary thought. Their anti-communist preachings grew noticeably stronger after the Cuban revolution, when new evangelical missions began to appear all over Nicaragua.

After the late 1960s, popular opposition to the dictatorship began to grow and the role of the churches as ideological apparatuses of the dictatorship began to change. The majority of Christians took the road towards a revolutionary position, whereas the rest either identified with the bourgeoisie opposed to Somoza or continued to support the Somocista dictatorship.

The attitude of the Catholic hierarchy was a clear example of the second position. It harshly criticized the dictatorship, but it did not identify itself with the revolutionary project of the FSLN. Thus, Archbishop Obando was involved in the various negotiations proposed by the bourgeois parties and by US imperialism which were aimed at forcing Somoza to leave the country. These negotiations were intended to prevent a popular takeover of the government and the destruction of the National Guard. As late as 17 July 1979, when Somoza was fleeing

159

from Nicaragua. Mgr. Obando supported the efforts of the bourgeois-dominated Frente Amplio Opositor (Broad Opposition Front), which sought to broaden bourgeois participation in the new government.

After the triumph, the Nicaraguan bourgeoisie increased their opposition to the revolutionary process when they saw that it did not coincide with their project of establishing a liberal capitalist state subordinate to the United States. At this time, a convergence occurred between the bourgeois opposition and the leadership of the churches.[13]

In May 1980, when the Consejo de Estado (Council of State) was established with a majority of popular representatives, Alfonso Robelo, Violeta Chamorro and other bourgeois members of the government resigned. At the same time, most of the staff of *La Prensa* were fired because of political divergences with the board of directors. In this conjuncture, the Catholic Bishops' conference called for the resignation of all those priests who held government positions. This request coincided with the interests of the pro-imperialist bourgeoisie who sought to weaken the revolutionary government by undermining its image of pluralism and respect for religion.

A year later, the request by the Bishops' conference was turned into a forceful ultimatum.[14] This aggravated the conflict between the revolutionary government and the Catholic hierarchy, as well as the growing separation between the hierarchy and the lay population, who mobilized in favour of the Sandinista priests. Through the mediation of the Vatican, the conflict was temporarily solved by an agreement which allowed the temporary continuation of these priests in their positions, on condition that they abstain from their priestly duties.

A second breaking point occurred during September and October 1980, when the bourgeois parties began an offensive in favour of the rapid promulgation of a law on political parties and the call for elections. At the same time, they launched a propaganda campaign against what they called 'the atheist and communist totalitarianism that threatens Nicaragua'.

In these circumstances, the FSLN set the electoral calendar for 1985, defined its conception of democracy and stated its official position with respect to religion. In response, the Bishops' Conference systematized for the first time its main arguments against Sandinismo, which would be repeated later on numerous occasions. These arguments are as follows: (1) in Nicaragua there is a totalitarian, atheist and materialistic state; (2) the FSLN has established the dictatorship of one armed party; (3) the state and the FSLN are manipulating religious people and religion for political purposes; (4) divisions within the churches are being promoted by revolutionary infiltrators; (5) class hatred, violence and militarism are being promoted by the state and the FSLN; (6) the people are being indoctrinated with materialistic and atheist ideologies; and (7) Cuba and the USSR are taking over the reins of the new government.[15] A few days later, in another pastoral letter, the Catholic bishops reaffirmed their interest in maintaining their control over education when they called for 'the right of parents to educate their children according to their Christian conviction'. The bishops also stressed the need for unity within the church through the obedience of its members to the hierarchy.[16]

In the evangelical Protestant sector, there was a notable expansion of different sects and denominations after the triumph. A systematic propaganda campaign was conducted by means of bumper-stickers, murals, posters, loudspeakers and fliers, which bombarded the Nicaraguan people with slogans such as 'Only Christ Saves', 'Get Ready, Christ is Coming', 'Only Jesus Liberates', 'We have to be Militiamen of Peace not of Hatred', 'Repent' and , in contrast to the popular Sandinista slogan, 'Sandino, Yesterday, Today, and Always', they substituted the slogan 'Christ, Yesterday, Today and Always'. Groups of promoters travelled to the most remote places in the country. Musical bands with professional entertainers sought to attract young people by cleverly mixing music with political and religious slogans. Thousands of pamphlets produced in Mexico, Uruguay and Guatemala flooded the country. Well-known evangelical speakers were brought into Nicaragua. Some were denied entry, such as Morris Cerrulo, who had stated before arriving in Nicaragua that 'he was coming to help in the great and urgent task of annulling the satanical work which is palpable in that nation'.[17]

These campaigns sought to prevent popular participation in the Sandinista mass organizations, to cultivate fatalism and passivity, to encourage people to disobey the authorities and revolutionary law, and to undermine popular participation in the defence of the homeland. The old anti-communist fears inculcated for decades by Somoza were given new vigour by these pseudo-religious preachings. The opposition between good and evil was translated into capitalism versus 'Sandino-Communism'. The tasks of health care and economic reconstruction were systematically discouraged and subordinated to 'God's plan'.

With the strategic objective of weakening the revolutionary government, of estranging the people from the FSLN, and of lessening Christian participation in the revolutionary process, this reactionary religious sector has used a variety of methods in the last five years, including: (1) the transfer out of the country of religious leaders committed to the revolution (in the Catholic Church alone, more than 20 cases of this nature have occurred); (2) the creation of organizations which extend the influence of this sector, such as the Centro de Estudios Religiosos (Centre for Religious Studies, CER) which is supposedly responsible for the interpretation and diffusion of the Bible; the Comisión de Promoción Social Arquidiocesana (Commission of Archdiocesan Social Promotion, COPROSA) which is responsible for social projects aimed at broadening the church's social base in the poorer zones, and the Union de Padres de Familia de Escuelas Catolicas (Union of Parents of Catholic Schools, UPACEF); (3) the articulation of a neo-spiritualist theological discourse in the political sphere, openly anti-Marxist and, in the Catholic case, linked to the 'Social Doctrine of the Church'; (4) the fostering of ritualistic and miracle-faking practices, centred in processions, festivities and charismatic acts, which seek to mobilize the people in ways that are alien to the tasks and values of the revolutionary process; (5) the reinforcement of ecclesiastical authority through disciplinary and coercive actions aimed at enforcing the 'necessary unity' of the church; (6) the participation of the reactionary clergy in public and private acts promoted by political parties, entrepreneurial groups and embassies connected to the imperialistic project. A prime example in this regard has been the actions of the bishop of Managua, Mgr. Obando, who has closely associated himself with the right-wing political opposition in Nicaragua;[18] (7) the diffusion of an internal propaganda campaign against the revolutionary government, the FSLN and the mass organizations–developed through pastoral letters, sermons, pamphlets, radio programmes and newspaper articles in *La Prensa*; (8) the signing of agreements for the receipt of funds from organizations connected with US imperialism, such as USAID, the CELAM (Latin American Bishops' Conference), and the US-based Institute for Religion and Democracy; (9) the condemnation of laymen, religious leaders and organizations which are committed to the revolution; (10) explicit opposition to key policies of the revolutionary government such as the state of emergency decreed in the face of escalating US aggression, the relocation of the frontier population away from the war zones, the establishment of compulsory military service, state control over education, etc.

In relation to the above, it should be noted that the Rockefeller Report (1968) specifically acknowledged the need for US foreign policy to use religious institutions to offset popular revolutions. The CIA's infiltration and manipulation of religious organizations in recent decades reveals that this is indeed the case.[19] The infamous 'Santa Fe Report', which has served as the basis for the Reagan administration's foreign policy, states that:

> The foreign policy of the US must begin to confront and not simply to react to the Theology of Liberation as it is utilized in Latin America ... Unfortunately, Marxist forces have utilized the Church as a political weapon against private property and the capitalist system of production by infiltrating the religious community with ideas which are less Christian than Communist.[20]

Thus, for US imperialism, the church should defend the capitalist system; those who oppose this idea are 'communist infiltrators'. These very arguments have been voiced by the Nicaraguan bourgeoisie and their religious spokesmen.

The articulation between US policy and Nicaragua's reactionary religious sector has been manifested in the following ways: (1) The United States has financed and trained pastors from different evangelical sects who have since 1979 gone to the most remote corners of Nicaragua.[21] (2) The mass media in the United States have distorted the religious conflict in Nicaragua. (3) The United States has financed community development projects and the training of religious leaders in towns where popular or government organizations have not been consolidated, with the purpose of creating support for the counter-revolutionary forces. (4) The United States has provided technical and financial assistance for the production of anti-Sandinista pamphlets, posters, radio messages and the right-wing newspaper *La Prensa*.[22] (5) The US-sponsored Institute for Religion and Democracy has tried to stop the backing which the Sandinista revolution has received from a broad range of progressive Christian groups in the United States.[23]

The reactionary and authoritarian position of the religious hierarchy in Nicaragua has posed a difficult challenge for revolutionary Christians. This challenge is greatest for the progressive clergy, who are constrained to obey their religious superiors, but who feel their faithfulness to Jesus necessitates their identification with the poor and the Sandinista revolutionary project.

Christian laymen, especially the youth, have overcome this difficult situation by abandoning the ecclesiastical sphere and by living their Christianity in their revolutionary tasks. However, their abandonment of the ecclesiastical sphere has made it easier for the bourgeoisie to associate the religious institutions more closely with the counter-revolution and US imperialism. This phenomenon may result in a self-fulfilling prophecy, since the political shift to the right on the part of most of the religious institutions in the country may lead to the expulsion of their leaders by the Sandinista government at a critical conjuncture for the defence of the revolutionary process.

This convergence of the position of the reactionary religious sector with the imperialist project cannot be reduced to either mere manipulation or to an explicit agreement between both parties. Nor can it be explained by the idea expressed in the famous dictum 'religion is the opiate of the people'. This idea has been extrapolated from a much richer text by Marx and nowadays must be qualified by the blood which revolutionary Christians shed every day in the anti-imperialist struggle of the Latin American peoples.

Since the 4th Century, the Catholic Church has been the accomplice of the exploiting classes – slave-owners, feudal lords and capitalists. The same thing happened to the Protestant churches in relation to capitalist development. Over the centuries Christianity has assimilated a series of concepts, values and beliefs which constitute the dominant ideology of the exploiting classes. Key elements of bourgeois ideology, such as private ownership of the means of production, unrestricted individual freedom and the idealist conception of social reality, have been assimilated by the Christian churches as essential elements of their religious thought and tradition.

The great majority of the Nicaraguan clergy have been trained in this ideology. Their education is encyclopaedist, abstract and alien to the advances of the social sciences. It only prepares them for ritualistic tasks and for moralizing as the remedy against social or individual evils. The stress they place on the other life, which relegates man to a passive role in history and which seeks to harmonize class struggles, has made them an irreplaceable ally of bourgeois domination.

To this must be added the relationship between the churches operating in Nicaragua, and their parent institutions, which have definite political positions. It should be remembered that the Vatican and some Protestant churches have investments in transnational companies. The *tercerista* (third way) line of the Vatican is known to be based on the advocacy of certain reforms aimed at strengthening capitalism; this is reflected in the so-called 'Social Doctrine of the Church', as updated by John Paul II.

Undoubtedly the negative experience of other contemporary revolutions with respect to church-state relations and freedom of worship constitutes a very real source of anxiety for certain religious groups. The anti-religious position in the Soviet literature which has been widely distributed among revolutionary cadres reinforces this fear on the part of the churches. Another important factor has been the skilful work of the pro-imperialist bourgeoisie in winning over the ecclesiastical hierarchies through personal relations, banquets, kinship ties, participation in liturgical services and the personality cult around hierarchs such as Mgr. Obando.

The Position of the FSLN with Respect to Religion

Just as in other aspects of Sandinista ideology, the background to the FSLN's position on religion can be found in the praxis of General Sandino. He was a believer, but his religious practice and reflection were radically different from the religiosity which predominated in Nicaragua during the 1920s. Sandino anticipated the position which would be adopted decades later by revolutionary Christians and by the theology of liberation movement in Latin America. In his writings, Sandino identifies God with Love, and the basis of all things. Thus, he believed that:

> Social injustice comes from the ignorance of divine laws. Injustice has no reason for being. In order to destroy injustice it has been necessary

to attack it, and that is why we have seen many men come to earth with that mission, among them Jesus, and every man who struggles for the freedom of the people is a follower of these doctrines.[24]

In his celebrated manifesto *Luz y Verdad* ('Light and Truth'), Sandino regarded the final judgement as: 'the destruction of injustice on earth and the reign of the Spirit of Light and Truth, that is to say Love'. Sandino believed that when the final judgement comes, 'the oppressed peoples will break the chains of humiliation which the imperialists on earth have used to keep us prostrated . . . We have the honour, brothers, of being in Nicaragua the ones chosen by Divine Justice to begin the judgement of injustice on earth'.[25]

Various testimonies have indicated that Sandino's Army for the Defence of National Sovereignty was characterized by an atmosphere of religiousness and of conviction that God was on their side. From the perspective of the exploited people, Sandino represented someone with strong faith. And for Sandino, the true Christians in Nicaragua were those who struggled against injustice. That was his answer to the illustrious prelates who tried to prevent the people from joining his anti-imperialist struggle.

Carlos Fonseca, who founded the FSLN, provides us with a second antecedent to understand the present position of the FSLN on religion. The personal contact that Carlos Fonseca had with revolutionary Christians such as Camilo Ortega and Mgr. Arias Caldera greatly influenced his position on religion. He maintained that: 'unity between true revolutionaries and true Christians is fundamental in the Sandinista Front. It is the unity forged with rifle in hand by Comandante Ernesto Che Guevara and Father Camilo Torres who fought to liberate the oppressed in Latin America.'[26] Carlos Fonseca clearly believed in the compatibility between Marxism and Christianity, and that there could be unity between believers and non-believers in the revolutionary struggle to liberate the Nicaraguan people.

Many revolutionaries who joined the FSLN were motivated by their Christian faith, and as they developed their political commitment and their knowledge of revolutionary theory they contributed to breaking down the atheist dogmatism of a certain sector of the Sandinista movement. This practical and authentic unity within the FSLN of believers and non-believers has been and continues to be a key to its strength and to its ties with the masses. In addition, it offers an important lesson to other Latin American revolutionaries.

One year after the triumph, the National Directorate of the FSLN issued a document in which it clearly defined its official position on religion. In the introduction, the document refers to the different forms of Christian participation in the struggle against the dictatorship and proposes that this very original phenomenon must be maintained in the future. Other basic aspects of the document are: respect for freedom of religion; the acknowledgement that there is no contradiction between being a believer and being a revolutionary; the right of believers to join the FSLN, on condition they do not engage in religious proselytism; the need to safeguard popular religious festivities from corruption or political manipulation; and abstention by the FSLN from involvement in the internal divisions of churches or from voicing its opinion on strictly religious matters.

The substance of this document, which has subsequently been reaffirmed on various critical occasions, has been of major importance in dissipating the doubts and fears created by the counter-revolutionary groups at the national and international level about religious persecution in Nicaragua. It has also been important for other Latin American revolutionary movements, since it goes well beyond the establishment of a strategic alliance between Christian and atheist revolutionaries in order to take power. The document expresses the position of a Marxist-like vanguard party, already in power, which advocates unity between both sectors, without any terms. The Leninist conception of the party is modified by accepting believers into its ranks, and by considering the religious beliefs of its militants to be a private matter.

The integration of Christians into the Nicaraguan revolutionary process has made an important contribution to the ideology of the Sandinista movement. When Comandante Daniel Ortega recently stated that 'Christianity and Marxism are a part of Sandinista democracy',[27] he was referring to the confluence of the three main ideological currents of the Sandinista revolution: revolutionary Christianity, historical materialism and the thought of Sandino. With regard to ultimate ends, the Sandinista leadership considers that there is a clear identity between these three currents of thought. For instance, Comandante Victor Tirado declared at the centennial of Marx's death: 'The Gospel, Sandinismo and Marxism coincide in their central goals. They are in agreement as to the need for upgrading the condition of the poor, of the marginalized classes'.[28]

The ethical contribution of Christianity has been noted on various occasions. Based on his own personal experience, Comandante Luis Carrion has stated: 'I drew near the revolution through a religious experience ... My first encounter with the concept of justice, my first search for identification with the people, took that road.'[29] And Comandante Tomas Borge has said:

> When we talk about respect for others, when we talk about personal integrity, about honesty, we are coinciding with the moral postulates of Christianity ... In the use of criticism, for instance, what is confession? Confession is self-criticism ... We are in favour of respect for human life ... of international solidarity ... which is what missionaries do when they go to help other peoples.[30]

Biblical interpretation, as used by the proponents of the theology of liberation, has frequently been utilized as an explanatory framework for the revolutionary process by the Sandinista leadership. In part this is probably due to didactic motives and to political calculations, but it also responds to a deeper ideological influence which goes beyond the conscious will of the individuals involved. For instance, in reference to the celebrated passage of the Gospel according to St Matthew, Comandante Borge has stated that: 'to give food to the hungry and to clothe the naked is only possible by carrying out deep economic transformations ... the true historical project of Jesus Christ is resurrection and life. And here we proclaim the right to life.'[31]

The traditional religious sector in Nicaragua, which stands for a ritualistic, idealist and charismatic Christianity, has its counterpart in a sector of the revolutionary movement which is atheist, and which stresses economicism and metaphysical materialism. Their anti-religious polemic has objectively fulfilled the ends of imperialism by identifying Sandinismo with Marxism, and then equating Sandinismo with atheism. However, the representatives of this dogmatic Marxist sector represent a small minority. At least five different positions can be found within the FSLN on religion: (1) Christians who do not attend liturgical practices except the christening of their children; (2) Christians who actively practise their faith without renouncing their condition as Marxists; (3) those who are indifferent and have taken no clear position with respect to religious problems; (4) those who take a pragmatic atheist position and who do not consider it to be good politics to confront religion at this stage of the revolution; and (5) those who take a militant atheist position against religion.[32] These last two groups have not been dominant, but they have tended to grow in strength as a result of the courses and texts used in various types of political and ideological training.

Undoubtedly some attitudes associated with these two last sectors have been an irritating factor in the relations between the FSLN and religious institutions. However, they do not have much weight among that sector of the top leadership who assimilated Marxism in the course of the revolutionary armed struggle. They exist among the recent cadres who have learned Marxism through theoretical studies and the memorization of Soviet manuals. These textbooks oppose a scientific, materialist, revolutionary and proletarian conception of the world to the idealist, religious, reactionary conception of bourgeois ideology. This bipolar interpretative framework helps very little to understand Nicaraguan reality. On the contrary, it creates theoretical confusion among the Christian revolutionaries and threatens the practical unity between Marxists and Christians within the revolutionary movement.

The words of Carlos Fonseca have an unquestionable relevance to the present conjuncture:

> We must be careful that our theoretical progress is linked to our concrete practice, since otherwise we fall into sterile dogmatism. In this sense the very modest theoretical tradition of our organization can help: our theory, fundamentally, has been linked to the practical problems of the movement ... Nicaraguan national reality has to be read with the eyes of Marxist theory and Marxist theory has to be read with Nicaraguan eyes.[33]

The FSLN's declaration on religion has served as a political guideline for the handling of religious problems, but its application has been difficult. On the one hand, it has been difficult because of the utilization of religious institutions by the counter-revolution for its ideological offensive and, on the other hand, due to mistakes in the political treatment of religious questions by some revolutionary leaders.

There are, of course, positive aspects of this difficult relationship between religion and politics: mutual collaboration in the Cruzada de Alfabetización, the operation of religious schools with state support, the legal prohibition of the commercial use of Christmas festivities, the control of alcoholic beverages and other vices in patron-saint festivities, the integration of Christians at different levels into the government, the FSLN and the mass organizations, the donation of 112,637 manzanas of state land for ecclesiastical buildings and the continuing dialogue between the government and the churches. In fact, it is common to see top Sandinista leadership participating in religious meetings, seminars, celebrations and other instances where there is a direct communication between both.

The main issues of conflict have been the mass media, education, youth and the defence of the homeland.[34] With regard to the mass media, the first conflict arose in 1980, when the broadcasting of Sunday mass by Mgr. Obando was suspended because he did not accept the proposal of the Sandinista TV service of alternating with other bishops and priests. Subsequently, state control of the media became stricter when the state of emergency was decreed in 1982. Also a letter from Pope John Paul II condemning the 'Popular Church' in Nicaragua was censored by the government, although some months later this censorship was lifted.

In other areas of conflict, such as the attempt to remove priests from government positions, the Sandinista mass media and the mass organizations have mobilized the people against these measures. This has to some extent served the counter-revolution, since the confrontation between these Sandinista organs and the church seems to confirm the allegations that the FSLN is totalitarian and atheistic.

Another source of irritation is the pro-Sandinista humour magazine *La Semana Comica* and the radio programmes *El Tren de las Seis*, which have repeatedly treated ecclesiastical individuals in a vulgar manner. But the most offensive episode was the TV coverage given to the crude exposure of the naked figure of the Vicar of the Diocese of Managua,

Mgr. Bismark Carballo, when the Sandinista police found him involved in a sex scandal.

The revolutionary government has established a single unified educational system for both public and private schools. This state control of an area which was traditionally dominated by the churches has been a continuing source of conflict. The immediate causes have been various: the materialist approach of some textbooks, political conflicts between teachers and school directors, the organizational efforts of the Sandinista Youth Organization in the religious schools, and in some cases conflict over the use of schools for the activities of the opposition parties.

An illustrative case was the takeover of four religious schools in August 1982 by students protesting the government's handling of the Father Carballo affair. These students were led by groups opposed to the Sandinistas and a confrontation with the Sandinista Youth Organization and the local branches of the Sandinista mass organizations quickly took place, thus worsening the conflict. Then several CDSs occupied various local churches and several incidents took place, involving religious leaders opposed to the revolutionary process. The worsening crisis was ended by the forceful intervention of the Direccion Nacional of the FSLN, which reiterated its 1980 declaration and called for a halt to the confrontations.

In sum, a political protest in several religious schools evolved into a serious conflict when some Sandinista militants allowed themselves to be provoked into using force to solve an ideological problem. This converted a secondary contradiction into a principal contradiction and confused the issues. It allowed the conflict to be presented by the reactionary opposition as proof of religious persecution by the Sandinistas.

The general offensive launched by the Reagan administration against the Sandinista revolution has given rise to various defence and security measures. This has been another source of conflict with religious institutions who have opposed the integration of their members into the national defence structure, the transfer of people from the border areas, the restrictions on mobility and the controls established in the war zones. When any religious leader has assumed a public and intransigent position against these defence measures, the government has first resorted to dialogue, but in the case of foreign clergy who continue to cause problems it has then proceeded to expel them from the country. These cases have amounted to no more than ten in five years, but their repercussions have been quite negative in terms of the government's relations with both the Catholic and Protestant Churches.

An important source of conflict has been religious opposition to compulsory military service. In 1983, the Catholic hierarchy issued a public letter opposing compulsory service and claiming the right of conscientious objection for young Christians who did not want to serve in the armed forces. Reactionary elements in the church planned the takeover of churches and protest mobilizations, but these activities were physically blocked by the Sandinista mass organizations. The reactionary elements rapidly protested at the national and international level that this was 'another instance involving the violation of religious freedom in Nicaragua'.

Another famous case has been the transfer of the Miskito Indians away from the frontier war zones. The justifications for this move, based on defence and security grounds, were blurred by the brusque manner of the transfer, the burning of homes, the slaughter of cattle and the prohibition against travel on the Coco River, which caused considerable discontent among the Miskito population. Reactionary religious leaders took advantage of the situation to denounce what they alleged to be ethnic and religious persecution by the Sandinistas, and through skilful propaganda convinced thousands of Miskitos to flee the country and go into exile in Honduras, where they have been recruited by the CIA to the Contra forces.[35]

The Sandinista principle, that 'in Nicaragua there is freedom of religion but there is no freedom to make counter-revolution through religion', has been simple to adopt theoretically, but very difficult to apply correctly, especially if the popular and international image of religious freedom in Nicaragua is to be preserved. The official declaration of the Sandinista leadership provides a solid and unquestionable basis for establishing harmonious relations with Nicaragua's religious institutions. However, in practice, serious conflicts with these churches have resulted. The basic reason for these conflicts has been the counter-revolutionary use of religion and religious institutions in the context of an open war against the revolutionary government. It is difficult, for instance, to tolerate a brazen sermon against the defence of the homeland when every day those men and women who guarantee the freedom and peace enjoyed by the people are falling in combat.

There appears to be a lack of consensus and understanding among the rank and file of the FSLN concerning the National Directorate's position on religion. The reactionary behaviour of some religious leaders has confirmed for some Sandinistas that religion is the opiate of the masses and that the time has come to use the churches for schools and health centres. The practical consequences of such dogmatic Marxist views have proved to be more dangerous than their theoretical weakness.

Mistakes have been made because of the lack of foresight or the use of incorrect methods in the treatment of religious problems. At times there has been a failure to understand that changes in the religious and ideological field cannot be achieved rapidly and that the correct response to an ideological offensive is not always to be found in taking direct action against the perpetrators. In this case, the right-wing opposition to the revolution has revived in its favour the martyrdom and persecutory tradition of Christianity.

Nevertheless, these critical reflections should not lead us to forget the important phenomenon discussed earlier, that is, Christian participation in the revolutionary project. Moreover, we cannot attribute to the FSLN the full responsibility for conflicts which are the product of the counter-revolutionary opposition and US imperialism.

The Dynamics and Prospects of the Religious Phenomenon

Religion and religious institutions in Nicaragua are criss-crossed by the acute class struggle which characterizes the present revolutionary period. On 19 July 1979 the popular revolutionary block of forces managed to gain political and military power, leaving the conquest of economic and ideological hegemony on the agenda.

An adequate understanding of the religious problem in the Sandinista revolution necessarily leads us to the global social context, to the dynamics of the revolutionary process marked by its antagonistic contradiction with imperialism and the local mercenary bourgeoisie. The fundamental contradiction between the Nicaraguan people and US imperialism has set the pace and the dynamics of the revolutionary process. The escalation of US aggression has affected all aspects of Nicaraguan social life and has forced the government to decree a state of emergency, to delay the reconstruction of the country and to restrict the opposition. This restriction has further worsened the conflict with the bourgeoisie, which has found in religious institutions their most effective avenue of expression. The advantages of this channel of expression are clear: national coverage, an effective communications apparatus, a discourse already steeped in bourgeois ideology, the ability to mobilize a large number of people and, finally, the angelical disguise of religion with which to conceal their class interests.

Identification with or against the revolutionary project cannot be hidden or postponed when it is a public and daily subject in popular discourse. If the ecclesiastical authorities choose to identify themselves with the imperialist project, as in the case of the Catholic Church, then the other members of the church have the right to identify themselves with the Sandinista project. This conflict over political identification has broken the unity and cohesion of both the Catholic and Protestant Churches within Nicaragua.

On the one hand, the people have gradually moved towards greater democratization in their work centres, in the mass organizations and in the state. There is growing political participation and they have a say in the decisions which concern them. On the other hand, in their religious institutions, especially the Catholic Church, there has been a gradual

171

hardening of authoritarianism, a demand for submissive obedience and compliance with doctrinaire orthodoxy.

Logically, the religious population have asked for more participation within their religious institutions. Unfortunately, this attitude, which is a product of the objective process of democratization, is perceived by the ecclesiastical authorities as an ominous consequence of the revolutionary process. For the religious hierarchies, the problem of unity and ecclesiastical obedience is their fundamental concern. They consider other political and ideological concerns in relation to the institutional interests of their churches. In contrast, for revolutionary Christians, church unity is not built on the indisputable authority of the hierarchy but through service to Jesus as embodied in the service of the oppressed and humiliated peoples of Latin America.

Another consequence of the revolutionary process is that the people are gradually acquiring a critical and scientific consciousness, thanks to the tremendous increase in public education. However, the bourgeoisie and its ecclesiastical allies are moving towards mysticism and irrationalism, expressed in charismatic experiences, miraculous apparitions and the apology of idealism.

The tendency towards mysticism can be seen as an escapist route for the bourgeoisie in the face of a revolutionary process which undermines both the material and ideological bases of their identity as a superior social class. Their search for shelter in irrationalism reflects their desperate need for some form of psychological compensation and their need to escape from the reality of their inexorable disappearance as a ruling class. It is interesting to recall that it was the bourgeoisie who, several centuries ago, defeated the feudal lords by raising the banner of the 'God of Reason' against 'medieval religious obscurantism'. Now that the reason of force and the force of reason have been appropriated by the social classes they have exploited, we see the bourgeoisie returning to the irrationalism they themselves once condemned.

The vitality shown by the bourgeois conception of Christianity in these last six years of revolution is linked to the existing lag between the revolutionary advances in the political and military spheres and the still very backward nature of the ideological sphere. This has been skilfully utilized by the counter-revolution, which has found the ideological domain, especially religion, to be a weak flank of the Sandinista revolution. In addition to this, some Sandinista leaders have made mistakes in the understanding and handling of religious problems.

It is difficult and risky to predict the future development of the religious phenomenon in Nicaragua. The majority of the Nicaraguan people have no difficulty combining their Christianity with the revolution. However, much more needs to be done in order to create an adequate expression of this reality. This is a challenge which must be met in order to consolidate the unity between Christians, Marxists and

Sandinistas that has been a key aspect of the originality and strength of the Nicaraguan revolution.

The religious elements identified with the pro-imperialist project will have the same fate as the *vende-patria* (sell-out) bourgeoisie in the conflict between imperialism and the Sandinista revolution. Subtleties in the different motivations which have prompted certain religious sectors to follow the designs of imperialism do not lessen their undeniable objective connivance in the effort to destroy the Sandinista revolution. However, it will not necessarily be the FSLN or the revolutionary government who judge these religious sectors – it will be the people themselves. This will not result in the disappearance of the churches; rather it will force them to adapt themselves to the conditions of the revolutionary process. Nor will Christianity be weakened: it is deeply rooted in the revolution.

Notes

1. Otto Maduro, *Religión y conflicto social* (Mexico: Centro de Reflexió Teológica, 1980); and Giulio Girardi, *Marxismo y Cristianismo* (Barcelona: Laia, 1977).

2. Noel Garcia, 'La realidad de la iglesia en Nicaragua', in *De cara al futuro de la iglesia en Nicaragua* (León: Editorial Hospicio, 1969).

3. Felix Jiménez, 'Formas especificas del proceso secularizador en los católicos de Managua', monograph (Managua: UCA, 1977); and Juan Vega, 'Movimientos y agrupaciones de laicos en Nicaragua y su insercion en la pastoral', monograph (Managua: UCA, 1977).

4. Magazine of the Centro Regional de Información Ecuménica (CRIE), no. 32, Mexico.

5. Manuel Rodriguez, *Gaspar vive* (Costa Rica: Artes Gráficas, 1981).

6. As of 1983, there was an estimated total of 240 Catholic priests in Nicaragua; 61 per cent were foreign. The number of known evangelical pastors was estimated at 1,600 excluding a fair number of itinerant preachers.

7. *Informes CAV*, June 1981. Centro Antonio Valdivieso (Managua).

8. Based upon a personal interview on 24 March 1984.

9. From a document entitled 'Los cristianos ante el proceso electoral', 7 March 1984 (Managua).

10. From a document entitled 'Fidelidad cristiana en el proceso revolucionario de Nicaragua', March 1984 (Managua).

11. Jorge Cáceres, et al., *Iglesia, politica y profecia* (Costa Rica: EDUCA, 1983).

12. Jorge Arellano, *Breve historia de la iglesia en Nicaragua* (Managua: 1980).

13. The point at which the Catholic hierarchy drew closest to the revolutionary process was the pastoral letter of November 1979, which was an isolated and 'miraculous' act.

14. The Bishops' Conference was not monolithic. There was a minority which refused to identify itself with counter-revolutionary and imperialist

positions, although its conduct has since been vacillating and weak.

15. Conferencia Episcopal, 'Pronunciamiento sobre el comunicado del FSLN acerca de la religión', 17 October 1980 (Managua).

16. Conferencia Episcopal, 'Jesuscristo y la unidad de su iglesia en Nicaragua', 20 October 1980 (Managua).

17. Ana Maria Ezcurra, *Agresión ideológica contra la revolución sandinista* (Mexico: Nuevomar 1983); and Giulio Girardi, 'Marxismo y cristianismo en Nicaragua hoy', *El Nuevo Diario*, 13 March 1983.

18. Mgr. Obando has received countless honorific and material rewards from these organizations. His saint's day has been ostentatiously celebrated every year; in 1981, *La Prensa* published a special edition with 43 photographs of his career and congratulations from all the entrepreneurial groups in the country.

19. Phillip Agee, 'La Acción de la CIA en las iglesias latinoamericanas', lecture at Centro Antonio Valdivieso, Managua, 16 October 1981.

20. Spanish translation of the 'Santa Fe Report' in the Nicaraguan magazine, *Soberania*, Managua, September 1980.

21. Debora Huntington, 'The Salvation Brokers: Conservative Evangelicals in Central America', *NACLA Report on the Americas*, January 1984.

22. Somocista bands were distributing posters and painting walls with messages such as 'Con Dios y Patriotismo derrotaremos al Comunism' (With God and Patriotism we will defeat Communism), 'Decidase: Iglesia o Sandino-Comunismo?' (Decide: Church or Sandino-Communism?) and 'El Papa está con Nosotros' (The Pope is with us).

23. The sector opposed to the revolution has been estimated as 54 per cent of the Catholic clergy. See *Envio*, December 1983 (Managua), Instituto Histórico Centroamericano. This estimate did not consider, however, the existence of a large and vacillating sector of those who identify neither with the reactionaries nor with the revolutionary sector.

24. Sergio Ramirez, *El Pensamiento vivo de Sandino*, 5th edn (Costa Rica: EDUCA, 1980), p. 205.

25. Ibid., p. 213.

26. Carlos Fonseca, *Bajo las banderas del sandinismo* (Managua: Nueva Nicaragua, 1981), p. 199.

27. Public speech by Daniel Ortega, Managua, 22 February 1984.

28. This speech was given to a conference of the ATC in March 1983.

29. Centro Antonio Valdivieso, *Informes CAV* (Managua), June 1982.

30. Instituto Histórico Centroamericano, *Fe Cristiana y Revolución Sandinista en Nicaragua* (Managua, 1979).

31. As reported in *El Nuevo Diario*, 1 June 1982.

32. César Jerez, *Diakonia*, March 1984 (Managua).

33. Fonseca, *Bajo las banderas del sandinismo*.

34. The two TV channels, two of the country's three main newspapers and half of the radio stations are pro-Sandinista, while the newspaper *La Prensa* and the remaining half of the radio stations are in private hands and opposed to the Sandinistas.

35. 'Los Miskitos y el caso de Mons. Schlaeffer', *Envio*, January 1984 (Instituto Histórico Centroamericano, Managua).

7 Miskito Revindication: Between Revolution and Resistance

Gillian Brown

Considering that the indigenous masses of America, traditionally exploited, oppressed and subjected to the rigours of a brutal internal system, now look with hope to the Sandinista Revolution, we cannot betray this hope.
FSLN, Declaration of Principles with regard to the Indigenous Communities of the Atlantic Coast, 12 August 1981 [1]

Introduction

For centuries the indigenous people of the Americas have suffered the impact of the drive for progress by more highly developed societies. Forced from their lands, massacred and victimized, the indigenous people have struggled to defend their traditional life-style and protect their ancestral practices in the face of adventuristic expansionism.

In Nicaragua, the Spanish conquistadores enslaved the aboriginal populations of the Pacific Coast, sending more than 400,000 Indians to work in the mines of South America. The British, without colonizing the region, eventually established a Protectorate on the East Coast, and through the supply of political and military aid, ensured the ascendency of the Miskito people over other ethnic groups. British mercantile influence finally gave way to United States domination, and a series of transnational companies proceeded to strip the land of its natural resources, exploiting the local population as a workforce, yet establishing little of permanent benefit to the native population.

The Sandinista revolution brought an end to the unrestrained profiteering of the foreign companies, and established as its objectives an end to the exploitation of the indigenous people, respect for their ancient traditions and economic assistance to break the crippling poverty of the region. It was thought that through incorporation into the revolutionary structures, the ethnic minorities would, for the first time, become integrated into Nicaraguan national life.

Yet from the beginning, despite efforts to encourage indigenous participation in the revolutionary process, the Sandinista government

Figure 7.1   The Atlantic Coast of Nicaragua (Ethnic Population and Towns)

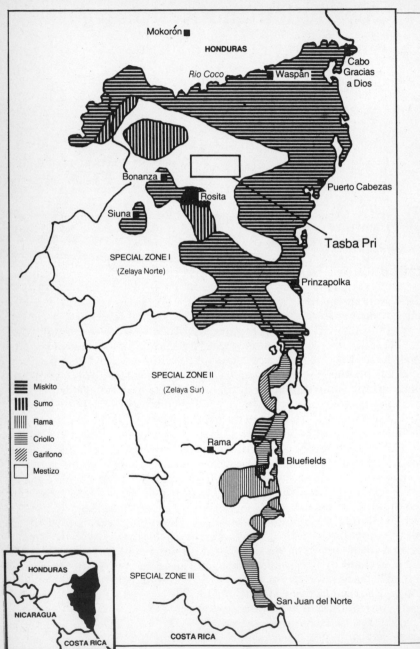

encountered serious resistance. The charismatic Miskito leader, Steadman Fagoth Müller, soon began to agitate for Miskito autonomy. The situation rapidly polarized, precipitating the sudden relocation of Miskito communities close to the Honduran border, as armed clashes threatened to escalate into a serious insurrection.

Many disaffected Miskitos crossed into Honduras, where they joined the counter-revolutionary forces or Contras, backed by the United States to destabilize and overthrow the Sandinista revolutionary government. With anti-Sandinista Miskito groups operating from both Honduras and Costa Rica, the indigenous people rapidly became the object of an intense campaign of propaganda to portray the Sandinistas as guilty of widespread repression, in an attempt to justify the escalating military agression.

Incursions into Nicaragua by Contra groups to evacuate whole villages, and escort the inhabitants willingly or under force of arms to Honduras, have divided families and deepened the rift between the Sandinistas and the Miskitos. Projects for regional development have been thwarted as a result of the conflict, and security measures imposed by the Sandinistas in response to the mounting aggression are often felt by the Miskitos to be unnecessarily repressive.

The Sandinistas have continued their attempts to expand the productive capacity of the Atlantic Coast, to improve standards of health care and education, and to involve the Miskitos more deeply in the revolutionary process. Yet, struggling to regain the confidence of the indigenous people, the government has found its efforts continually undermined by a mounting military offensive, launched under the banner of native rights and regional autonomy, while the Miskitos, caught between the revolution and the counter-revolution, have suffered the brunt of a conflict which they neither understand nor can avoid.

Exploitation and Marginalization of the Indigenous Peoples

The Atlantic Coast, sometimes described as the Miskito Coast or Mosquitia, differs from the rest of Nicaragua, both geographically and ethnically. The area, covering 56 per cent of the national territory, consists of the humid coastal plains, the eastern ranges of the central highlands and, to the south, the Rio San Juan river basin. This area has been divided by the Sandinista government into three administrative regions, designated as Special Zones – Zone I (Zelaya Norte), Zone II (Zelaya Sur) and Zone III (Rio San Juan). The majority of the population of the Atlantic Coast are mestizo (of mixed Indian and Hispanic origin). The English-speaking Black and Creole minority, whose ancestors came from Jamaica and the Cayman Islands, are predominantly

Table 7.1   Races in the Atlantic Coast of Nicaragua

Races	Population	% of total	Languages	Origin
1. Mestizos	182,377	64.5	Spanish	Country's inland
2. Miskitos	66,994	23.8	Miskito	Pre-Hispanic
3. Creole Blacks	25,723	9.1	English	Caribbean/African
4. Sumo	4,851	1.7	Sumo	Pre-Hispanic
5. Carib	1,487	0.5	Garifundi	Belize
6. Rama	649	0.2	Rama	Pre-Hispanic

Source: CIDCA (Centro de Investigaciones y Documentación de la Costa Atlántica – Research and Documentation Center of the Atlantic Coast), 1983.

centred in the port towns. The largely rural population of Miskito Indians inhabit small villages along the banks of the major rivers and at the river mouths. A small remnant of the Sumo Indians remain along the upper reaches of the coastal rivers and the central highlands. The Rama Indians are found in small villages close to Bluefields. Apart from a few North American missionaries, there is also a small population of Chinese merchants in the major towns.

In 1633, British traders from the Isle of Providencia initiated commercial links with the Sumos in the north-eastern area of Cabo Gracias a Dios. Meat, fish and turtle were exchanged for firearms, metal tools and other manufactured goods. After a ship carrying African slaves sank in the region in 1641, the survivors and subsequent slaves brought to the region interbred with the Indians, creating a phenotypically diverse population, who by the end of the 17th Century had become known as Miskito or Mosquito. According to legend, they acquired this name because of the muskets supplied to them by the British.

Aided by access to firearms, the Miskitos succeeded in dominating other indigenous groups in the region, and were often employed by the British in armed incursions into the Spanish colonies of the Pacific. In contrast with the Spanish conquistadores, who virtually eradicated the indigenous population of the Pacific Coast of Nicaragua, the British tended to exploit the existing social, religious and political structures through a policy of 'indirect administration' and the establishment of the 'Miskito Kingdom' as a British Protectorate. In 1687, tribal chief Jeremy I was crowned the first Miskito king in a ceremony held in Jamaica, and over a period of 200 years the Miskitos extended their political influence from Laguna de Chiriqui in Panama to Rio Chamalecon on the Honduran/Guatemalan border.

The discovery of gold in California and the need for an inter-oceanic transit route precipitated a conflict between England and the United States for ascendancy over the region; a series of treaties were signed between the two countries without consultation with the Nicaraguan government. In 1853, US Marines landed in Greytown (San Juan del Norte) to protect the property of the Accessory Transit Company, owned by US nationals. The town was shelled and razed to the ground in the ensuing conflict. Plans for a canal route through Nicaragua were eventually rejected in favour of Panama. But by 1860, under pressure from the United States, Britain renounced jurisdiction over the Atlantic Coast, designated the region a 'Miskito Reserve' with the right to self-government, and recognized Nicaragua's sovereignty over the area in the Treaty of Managua.

In 1894, Nicaragua's Liberal President José Santos Zelaya militarily occupied Bluefields and removed the right of self-government from the Miskitos. His government announced that it had 'reincorporated the Moskitia' as part of the Nicaraguan nation. This marked the first time that the government in Managua achieved political and military control over the Atlantic Coast. This was resented by the indigenous people who saw it as domination by the 'Spaniards' of the Pacific.

During the Zelaya presidency, concessions equivalent to 10.3 per cent of the land were given to North American companies, which had a free hand in exploiting reserves of valuable minerals, forest land and marine life. Many Miskitos and Sumos were displaced from their lands, others were temporarily employed by the companies during their precarious 'boom and bust' existence. For some employees it meant the possibility of obtaining foreign exchange and access to imported goods. The speculative ventures of the transnational corporations continued throughout the 45 years of the Somoza family dictatorship, only to be opposed by General Augusto C. Sandino, who in April of 1931 practically destroyed the installations of the Standard Fruit Company and the Bragman Bluff Lumber Company, and who conceived of establishing large agricultural co-operatives on the Rio Coco.

Ideologically, the Moravian Church, and to a lesser extent the Catholic Church, exercised considerable influence, and were responsible for the building of schools and hospitals, and for providing social services, which successive Somoza governments ignored. Generally regarded as community leaders, the Moravian pastors and Catholic priests tended to lend tacit support to the North American and European exploitation of the region. As the foreign companies withdrew from the Atlantic Coast they left little of benefit to the indigenous people, and the Sandinistas arrived on the coast to face a legacy of serious decapitalization, high unemployment, a lack of skilled technicians and semi-destroyed and abandoned infrastructure. Vast areas of land had been denuded of valuable wood by companies such as the US Nicaraguan Longleaf Pine Lumber Company (Nipco) and Magnavox. There had been no reforestation, and the mines had been seriously over-exploited.

A Capuchin priest, Agustin Sambola, after working in the region for seven years, evaluated the situation encountered on the Atlantic Coast in 1979:

> What did North American imperialism leave on the Coast? It left hundreds of Miskitos without lungs, victims of the exploitation of the mines; it left thousands of manzanas without pines, deforested. It left old machinery, no decent airport to the mines. It left a population chronically infirm; and the saddest thing is that these thousands of Miskitos didn't understand that with their lungs they enriched others, and that their gold helped the development of another country. This is the inheritance that imperialism left to the revolution on the Coast.[2]

The Revolution Meets Resistance

As the Sandinistas surveyed the situation they encountered on the Atlantic Coast, it was anticipated that the most marginal sector of society, the Miskito, Sumo and Ramo Indians, would be readily amenable to revolutionary change. As noted in the 1981 *Report of a Rural Investigation on the North Atlantic Coast*:

> Due to the low development of the forces of production, the class struggle is based on ethnic affirmation. In order to bring about popular mobilization in the region, it will be necessary to re-evaluate the historic project of Miskito liberation, which is compatible with the objectives of the Sandinista revolution and the construction of a new society.[3]

One of the first steps was the expropriation of the few remaining foreign companies, in an effort to eradicate the last vestiges of the capitalistic structures of exploitation. While recognizing the communal lands of the indigenous people, it was recommended that the means of production should be collectivized through the formation of co-operatives.

Plans were elaborated to develop agricultural, cattle-ranching, fishery and forestry projects, emphasis was placed on the elimination of racial and ethnic discrimination, and efforts were made to encourage the indigenous people in the rediscovery of their historical cultural traditions. It soon became clear, however, that the Sandinistas, rather than being met as 'liberators', were frequently regarded with suspicion as 'los del Pacifico', 'Españoles' who were seen as new colonizers, while Somoza and the North American companies, which had brought a temporary influx of imported goods, were often regarded with esteem.

For their part, the Sandinistas attributed the lack of receptivity to a reduced political awareness and the lack of involvement of the indigenous people in the struggle against the Somoza dictatorship.

The Miskito opposition initially became manifest during the literacy programme. Carried out at first in the Spanish language, and later in Miskito, the drop-out rate was high as the Miskitos reacted to the intensely political nature of the programme, and strong anti-communist sentiment instilled throughout the Somoza era began to surface.

Earlier, attempts to disband the indigenous organization, the Alliance for Progress of Miskito and Sumo Indians (ALPROMISU), formed during the Somoza presidency, and to replace it with local branches of the Sandinista mass organizations, had been rejected by the ALPROMISU leadership, and the attempt was abandoned. In November 1979, more than 700 Indian delegates, representing 112 communities, met with Junta co-ordinator, Daniel Ortega, and a new organization, MISURASATA, was formed to represent the Miskito, Sumo and Rama communities. This new organization was formed under the leadership of Miskito leader, Steadman Fagoth Müller. As MISURASATA representative, Steadman Fagoth was also given a seat on the Council of State in Managua. Initially, MISURASATA collaborated with the government in the implementation of literacy and health campaigns, and a law was passed authorizing education in Spanish, English and Miskito in the Indian and Creole communities.

Yet frictions arose in the spring of 1980, as the government announced plans for the implementation of an agrarian reform programme under the organization of the Nicaraguan Institute for the Atlantic Coast (INNICA). These plans included the development of new agro-forestry and fishing enterprises, which involved the integration of the Atlantic Coast resources and labour force into the national economy. A petition was sent to the Council of State requesting an investigation into the territorial claims of the Miskitos, and on 5 August 1980, the government agreed to permit MISURASATA to present a map indicating the territorial demands of the indigenous peoples. However, at the same time, the government allotted 9,000 sq. kilometres of virgin forest land to the Nicaraguan Institute of Ecology and Natural Resources (IRENA), designated for the establishment of a forestry reserve in the Boswas region of northern Zelaya, with the intention of protecting the environment and benefiting the indigenous communities. The project was, however, considered by MISURASATA leadership to be a violation of the government's agreement to consider indigenous land claims, and the beginning of an attempt by the government to nationalize the natural resources of the Atlantic Coast.

Reviving earlier Miskito hopes for regional autonomy, Steadman Fagoth began pressing for extensive land rights, and political independence. A study of native land titles was carried out, which resulted in a claim for some 38 per cent of the national territory. MISURASATA also began to demand five seats on the Council of State, and one in the government junta, besides an autonomous role in the appointment of local officials.

Fearing that MISURASATA had pushed their demands to the point of subversion, the Sandinista government acted to bring an end to what was rapidly becoming a secessionist movement. On 28 February, a few days before a regional meeting was to have taken place to discuss the land problem, armed soldiers forced their way into a Moravian church in Prinzapolka, with orders to arrest two Miskito leaders. In the ensuing scuffle, four Miskitos were killed, and the parishioners retaliated by killing four soldiers. Steadman Fagoth was arrested in Managua, and another 32 MISURASATA leaders were also rounded up on charges that they were militarily training Miskito followers with the intention of fomenting a separatist uprising. In Waspan, Miskitos protesting the arrests held a two-month vigil of 200-1,000 people on the grounds of the Catholic and Moravian churches, and demonstrations also took place in Puerto Cabezas, until most of the imprisoned Miskitos were released.

The government revealed intelligence information that Fagoth had collaborated with the Somoza regime as an informer, infiltrating the student movement under the pseudonym Saul Torres, and that he was continuing to conduct subversive activities to destabilize the government in accordance with a scheme named 'Plan '81'. Fagoth was, however, released on 7 May on a conditional pardon, with the proviso that he would leave Nicaragua to study in the Soviet Union or Bulgaria. Returning to Waspan on the Rio Coco, Fagoth immediately fled to Honduras, followed by some 3,000 Miskitos, and by June he was known to be collaborating with Nicaraguan exiles in Miami planning to overthrow   the Sandinista government.

In an attempt to clarify the government's position with regard to the indigenous communities a 'Declaration of Principles' was issued in Managua on 12 August 1981, which reaffirmed that 'the Nicaraguan nation is one nation, territorially and politically, and cannot be dismembered, divided or reduced in terms of its sovereignty and independence'. Guaranteeing the participation of the communities of the Atlantic Coast in all social, economic and political affairs, the Declaration further stated:

> The Sandinista Popular Revolution guarantees, and will legalize by means of issuing titles, the property of the lands where the communities of the Atlantic Coast have lived, whether in communal form or as co-operatives.

The natural resources of our territory are the property of the Nicaraguan people, represented by the revolutionary state which is the only entity capable of establishing their rational and efficient exploitation, recognizing the right of the indigenous communities to receive a quota of the benefits that derive from the exploitation of the forestry resources for the purpose of financing projects of communal and municipal development in conformity with national plans.[4]

This document, based on the principles of popular democracy, and anti-imperialism, and designed to guarantee the recovery of the natural resources of the region from foreign control, while also initiating the emancipation of the ethnic minorities, was, however, not well received by many Miskito leaders, who saw in it a justification for the seizure of their lands by the Sandinista government.

By the end of 1981 relations had further deteriorated, and in September one of the few remaining MISURASATA leaders, Brooklyn Rivera, left the country to join Steadman Fagoth in Honduras, where Fagoth was using the clandestine Radio 15 September to call upon the Miskito community to flee the country, claiming the Sandinistas were establishing a 'communist' regime under Cuban and Soviet domination. Inciting the Miskitos to participate in a 'Holy War' for regional autonomy. Fagoth succeeded in deepening the rift between the indigenous people and the Sandinista revolution, and seriously contributed to the mood of mounting distrust. On 28 December Fagoth was injured when a Honduran Air Force C-47 on which he was travelling crashed at Puerto Lempira.

Armed clashes along the Nicaraguan–Honduran border had stepped up by December 1981, yet, despite the difficulties, the Sandinista government continued the implementation of education and health programmes. The construction of a hospital at Bluefields was begun, and those in San Carlos, Bilwaskarma, Puerto Cabezas and the mines were renovated. Medical personnel increased threefold, and vaccinations were completed for 85 per cent of the coastal population. 480 new schools were built and 855 new teachers employed, while 12,000 participated in the literacy programme in the Miskito idiom.[5]

However, the roots of discontent and distrust had already been formed. Miskitos collaborating with the revolution began to be viewed as *orejas*, spies. Fears of 'communist indoctrination' were evoked, and with their confidence in the Sandinistas seriously undermined, Miskito aspirations towards autonomous rule only served to aggravate the already tense situation.

Red Christmas

By the end of December 1981 it was reported that Steadman Fagoth, in co-ordination with the Contra group, the Democratic Nicaraguan Force (FDN), and with CIA covert funding, had armed some 2,000 Miskito followers, and the government reported that between October 1981 and January 1982, 60 Sandinista soldiers and Miskito civilians had been killed in armed incursions in the Rio Coco region. The offensive was said to be part of a plan named 'Red Christmas' to provoke a Miskito uprising and capture a piece of Nicaraguan territory in order to appeal for direct United States military assistance and international recognition for the formation of an independent state on the Atlantic Coast.

Still highly esteemed as a leader among the Miskitos, Steadman Fagoth relentlessly pressed his message through radio transmissions that repressive measures were to be taken by the Sandinistas against the Miskito communities, and that aerial bombardment of their villages was imminent. The Miskitos should, he warned, flee to Honduras for safety. At the same time the Honduran Minister of Defence loudly accused the Nicaraguan military of crossing the Rio Coco in December and massacring 200 Miskito refugees. The Honduran College of Education investigating the allegation concluded that 'The news of the massacre was totally false and no Miskito has been assassinated by the Sandinista Popular Army'.[6] However, a pretext had already been established for the Honduran army to increase its presence in the area and to request United States military aid.

The Nicaraguan government responded to the crisis in a move which had disastrous and far-reaching repercussions for the government. Beginning on 13 January, 8,500 Miskitos from 39 communities were forcibly evacuated from the Rio Coco close to the Honduran border. Children, the infirm and elderly were carried by helicopter and trucks while the rest were escorted on foot to 5 resettlements, 40 miles from the border. As the move began, the Miskitos looked back to see their homes engulfed in flames as the Sandinistas burned the houses, churches, crops and fruit trees to prevent occupation of the region by the Contra forces. In Waspan, used as a staging post in the evacuation, Catholic missionaries recall the state of high tension as bells were rung to signify an imminent attack or evacuation. Many Miskitos, seeing no evidence of fighting, became convinced that the objective of the Sandinistas was to militarize the border zone and relocate the Miskitos to areas where they could be better controlled. The relocation had, however, been preconceived. According to a feasibility study carried out in November by the Nicaraguan Institute for the Atlantic Coast (INNICA), the resettlement scheme was designed to establish conditions for better social and economic integration of the Rio Coco communities into the revolutionary process, through the development of new agricultural projects and improved access to national markets. The declaration of a state of military emergency was considered by critics as a mere pretext for the move.

The Sandinista claim that they had uncovered a CIA plot to provoke a general uprising on Christmas Day, followed by the involvement of foreign troops in support of the secessionist movement, was also challenged by journalists James Evans and Jack Epstein who, after five months research, concluded that details of the CIA plans were fabricated in order to justify a preplanned relocation, and to pre-empt an indigenous insurrection.[7]

The Nicaraguan Conference of Catholic Bishops issued a statement in February 1982, criticizing the harshness of the move, while in the United States the Reagan administration seized on the episode to accuse the Sandinista government of major repression against the indigenous communities. Addressing the OAS, President Reagan claimed that Indians were being massacred; and Jeane Kirkpatrick charged, 'Some 250,000 Mestizo (*sic*) Indians are being so badly repressed that concentration camps are being built on the coast of Nicaragua to try to imprison them.' Secretary of State Alexander Haig produced a photograph, allegedly of Miskito corpses, which was later found to be a photograph of the Red Cross burning bodies in 1979 during the insurrection on the Pacific Coast.

Investigating claims by Steadman Fagoth of some 300 Miskito deaths and thousands of disappearances during the period of relocation from the Rio Coco, the Americas Watch Committee asked Fagoth for specific information to support his charges. The commission wrote:

> We uncovered no information which tended to confirm the Fagoth accounts ... In fact those who seemed to us most credible denied any widespread 'disappearances' and told us they had no specific information as to the alleged torture and killing of Miskitos during the relocations.

The most serious case encountered by the Committee, though not confirmed, was of 40–50 mine-workers in Leimus, who in December were allegedly shot, drowned or in one case buried alive by Sandinista soldiers.[8] Thus, Fagoth's claims were at the very least exaggerated, and at the most, pure fabrication for propaganda purposes.

The resettlement area, Tasba Pri or 'Free land', is comprised of five communities, occupying 53,543 hectares, on the road from Rosita to Puerto Cabezas, with a total population in 1984 of 9,500. New homes, health centres, churches and schools have been constructed and electricity and potable water have been provided. Agricultural projects are being developed and basic grains are being produced for local consumption.

However, officials at Tasba Pri say that the Miskitos have not forgotten the move, and still long to return to the Rio Coco. Lack of privacy and the high percentage of women and children has resulted in a breakdown in some family structures, and the Miskitos also complain that with the houses built close together there is no room to keep animals and fruit trees near their homes, as they are accustomed to doing.

Revolution and Counter-revolution: Mounting Conflict

The sudden uprooting of the Rio Coco communities and the harsh confrontation with the Miskito leadership had far-reaching and serious consequences for the Sandinista government. The first steps towards the transformation of the centuries-old structures of exploitation had barely begun before the very people expected to receive most benefit from the change had been alienated from the revolutionary process, and a growing movement in favour of autonomous rule was gathering momentum on the Atlantic Coast. Aware that early efforts to incorporate the Miskitos into the national scheme had often been counter-productive, Sandinista leaders also recognized the gravity of early errors in their approach to the indigenous people. Pressed in an interview, Interior Minister Tomas Borge acknowledged that the Miskitos had been incorrectly treated by the revolution, and that many had joined forces with the Contras.

> After the triumph, we sent a group of *companeros* into the region who didn't understand things the way they should have – they knew more about astronomy, some of them, than about anthropology. They made terrible, alienating mistakes in dealing with the Moskitos. At the same time, the main leader of the Moskitos, a former agent of Somoza's security police, began making some vicious broadcasts in the Mosquito language. It was claimed, among other things, that our government had a policy of exterminating all Mosquitos over the age of 30 – things such as that. Not surprisingly, with the coinciding of our blunt policies and that propaganda, many Mosquitos became confused. It remains a very painful situation.[9]

This painful situation was, of course, precipitated by Steadman Fagoth's declaration of 'open war against the Sandinistas', and later, with the backing of several Moravian pastors, his announced initiation of a 'Holy War' for the recognition of the Atlantic Coast as an autonomous region, with permanent representation in the United Nations. Envisioning himself as the new 'Rey Mosco' or Miskito king of the Atlantic Coast, Fagoth changed the name of MISURASATA to MISURA, and made an alliance with the CIA-backed Contra group, the Democratic Nicaraguan Force (FDN). Having been imprisoned in Honduras at the instigation of Fagoth, Brooklyn Rivera sought to attract his own following to Costa Rica, where he joined Edén Pastora's Democratic Revolutionary Alliance (ARDE). He pressed for regional autonomy, but not independence, and took the name of MISURASATA as the name of his organization.

The stated intention, however, of both MISURA and MISURASATA was to 'liberate a region of territory on the Atlantic Coast' and declare a 'provisional government', then calling for international recognition and US military assistance. In this context, a war of communiques and denunciations against the revolution began to develop, based on misinformation. On 9 December 1982, a Sandinista airforce helicopter crashed in northern Jinotega, killing 75 children, and it came to light that the government was in the process of another relocation of some 5,000 to 6,000 Miskitos from the region. Brooklyn Rivera, now in Costa Rica after his split with Steadman Fagoth, immediately called, in the name of MISURASATA, on the Inter-American Commission for Human Rights to open an investigation, accusing the Sandinistas of being 'responsible for this massive crime against our children'. He also accused the Sandinistas of 'having executed this macabre plan for propagandistic reasons in an attempt to divert the attention of the Nicaraguan people from their situation of desperation, confuse international public opinion and in this way continue justifying their policy of ethnocide against the Indians'.[10]

A further communique, issued by MISURASATA on 24 January 1983, alleged without any foundation that Comandante Daniel Ortega had said, 'if it is necessary to kill every last Miskito, we will do it without fear in order to implement our project'.[11] Again MISURASATA accused the FSLN of a policy of systematic extermination of the indigenous people through military operations during which the Miskitos were supposedly rounded up in large numbers under suspicion of collaborating with the 'guerrillas', later to be selectively executed before the community or transfered to regional prisons, tortured and sent to Managua to be arbitrarily condemned. Names, dates and locations were published to support a claim of 500 assassinations.

On 6 April 1983, a UPI report was issued from Mokoron in Honduras which ran,

> Nicaraguan Air Force planes bombed at least one Indian village during their attack against the rebels, forcing about one thousand Indians to escape in panic to Honduras, according to refugees and an official of the United Nations.[12]

The bombing had supposedly taken place in Santa Clara, one of five communities comprising Tasba Raya, a Miskito settlement area established in 1968, and populated by Miskitos brought from the Rio Coco region to work for the lumber companies. After the Red Christmas relocation, many Miskitos from Tasba Raya had fled to Honduras, and families had been divided as a result. According to Catholic

187

missionaries in Santa Clara, the villagers had known in advance the Contras were coming, and had their bags packed, ready to leave. It was said that while some were simply disposed to join their families in Honduras, open sympathies had also arisen towards the Contras. Reports that the departing Miskitos were bombed by the Sandinista air force were said to be untrue.[13]

The allegations by the MISURA leadership of bombings added still further to the tension on the Atlantic Coast, and the Miskitos, who have never recognized a territorial boundary between Nicaragua and Honduras, were inclined to leave, in expectation that conditions were better north of the Rio Coco. American staff of the evangelical organization, World Relief, who administer the Mokoron refugee camp in Honduras, said that when refugees first arrive they invariably complain of harassment by the Sandinistas and express objections to the formation of co-operatives, and to the political orientation of the revolution. Later, after having received instructions from the MISURA leadership, their stories change and they echo the MISURA claims of bombings, massacres and the machine-gunning by Sandinista soldiers of women, children and old people; they also say that they fled to the mountains to find refuge in areas controlled by the 'patriotic commandos of liberation'. Yet, according to the World Relief staff, the reports of massacres and bombings are never eye-witness accounts, there are never any wounded among the refugees, and the Miskitos invariably have had time to collect their belongings before leaving.[14]

By January 1983, many Miskitos from the Mokoron refugee camp had been resettled in small comunities nearby, where it was hoped they would eventually become self-sufficient. Steadman Fagoth opposed the relocation, and MISURA threatened those who attempted to leave Mokoron, evidently finding the squalid conditions of the camp fertile ground for recruitment.

The World Relief staff said that many Miskitos had begun to lose confidence in Steadman Fagoth. He had promised them a quick and easy victory, but it was becoming a hard fight, and many suspected that Fagoth was motivated more by personal ambition than by concern for the interests of the indigenous people. Some of his earlier followers had deserted from his ranks and as a result Fagoth had begun forcibly recruiting the Miskito refugees into MISURA's forces. The World Vision staff reported that armed groups of 10–20 were going from family to family taking away the youths over 15. Girls, they said, were also being taken, but 'not for fighting'. The World Vision staff said they knew of the existence of three MISURA camps at Strumlalaya, Twilbila and Rus Rus. Gregorio Winter, who returned from Mokoron to Nicaragua, after having been among 1,500 people from Slilma Lila on 22 April 1983, claimed that those who refused to collaborate were punished by MISURA with near drowning. Winter also claimed that the Honduran security forces, DNI, and the 5th Batallion of the Honduran army were openly collaborating with MISURA, and as the Miskitos were being instructed in what they should say to journalists, they were told 'Don't worry, because Papa Reagan is sending the dollars.' [15]

Manipulation of the Miskito Problem

The allegations made by MISURA and MISURATA of human rights violations by the Sandinista government were given impetus when a professor of geology at the University of California, Dr Bernard Nietschmann, testified before the Organization of American States Inter-American Commission on Human Rights concerning the situation of the Indians in Nicaragua. Dr Nietschmann made a 2-month visit to Miskito exiles in Costa Rica and Honduras; entering Nicaragua clandestinely, he visited Miskito villages in the interior of the country long since closed by the Sandinista government to outside observers. On his return, on 3 October 1983, he testified:

> It is with sadness that I report widespread, systematic and arbitrary human rights violations in Miskito Indian communities. These violations by the Sandinista government include arbitrary killings, arrests and interrogations; rapes; torture; continuing forced relocations of village populations; destruction of villages; restriction and prohibition of freedom to travel; prohibition of village food production; restriction and denial of access to basic and necessary food stores; the complete absence of any medicine, health care or educational services in many Indian villages; the denial of religious freedom; and the looting of households and the sacking of villages.[16]

The author, in an attempt independently to investigate the charges of Dr Nietschmann, found frequent reports of widespread and arbitrary arrests and interrogation, threats and some accounts of torture and arbitrary killing. Forced relocations have continued in areas where rebel activity has been high, but the looting and destruction of Indian villages were only reported in the context of the 1982 relocations. Restrictions on freedom of movement have been imposed in response to security considerations.

Complaints were made that the government was using spies to report deviant political thinking, and objections were made to the use of church property as barracks or temporary prisons. Food supplies were said to be insufficient. In general most complaints stemmed from the Red Christmas relocation and it was usually conceded that violations and abuses were far less frequent by 1983–4. The accusations by Nietschmann of restriction and denial of access to basic provisions, absence of medical and educational services and denial of religious freedom were without foundation.

The tendency to view any dissent as 'reactionary', and to condemn all critics as Contras, has created an atmosphere of fear and distrust, and there have been undeniable abuses. Even so, the evidence does not suggest, as Dr Nietschmann claims, that there is 'a government policy of widespread, systematic and arbitrary human rights violations', and far less a policy of 'ethnocide' as suggested by MISURA leaders.[17]

Dr Nietschmann characterizes the Indian struggle as not only a response to 'Sandinista military and political oppression', but also a response to the 'expropriation of their lands under the guise of agrarian reform'. Freedom for the Indian, he argues, is not democracy or socialism, but land, and their struggle is to 'recover and control their land'. To obtain arms and material support the Miskitos have, says Nietschmann, made 'alliances of convenience' with the CIA-backed Contra groups, the FDN and ARDE.[18]

It is perhaps in his zeal to defend the Indian struggle that Dr Nietschmann is blinded to the way in which the Contra groups, in close collaboration with the Reagan administration and the Central Intelligence Agency, have played on native ingenuousness and early British promises of indigenous self-rule to foment the fear that the Miskitos' lands are being usurped from them. And using the emotive facade of a just struggle for native rights, they have manipulated the issues of secession and regional autonomy to create an entirely false cause. Yet under this banner they have succeeded in dividing the indigenous people and have sent countless Miskitos to their deaths in the service of United States attempts to promote the destabilization of the Sandinista government.

Capuchin priest Francisco Solano, who has worked for 15 years with Miskito Indians, assesses the prospect of Indian self-determination as entirely unrealistic.[19] He argues:

> It is a pretention totally out of the context of the Coast and Zelaya province. This zone does not contain the resources that would permit it to maintain itself as an independent nation. Neither in terms of the means of production nor in terms of human resources. With what exists it is not possible to create a nation. In order to exist as a nation nominally independent it would simply have to be totally dependent upon North American imperialism. The present dependency upon the government in Managua would be replaced with a dependency upon the government in Washington. The Coast would go back to being what it was before, what it was always . . .

The Miskitos, like other peoples, have been manipulated by imperialist nations with the idea of constructing their own independent nation – in this case, as a means of weakening the national struggle for independence, directed by the Sandinista revolution.

The Miskitos: A Divided People

Following recommendations by the National Commission for Promotion and Protection of Human Rights and the Commission for Justice and Peace on the Atlantic Coast, the Sandinista government moved to improve relations with the Miskito communities and at the same time allow the possibility that those who had been taken to Honduras against their will would be able to return. On 1 December 1983 the government junta issued a decree granting amnesty to all Miskitos guilty of crimes against public order and security since 1 December 1981. The amnesty was followed three days later by a general offer of pardon to all those involved in the Contras who would surrender with their weapons.

Speaking during the ceremony in Managua on 1 December, during which 307 Miskito prisoners were set free, junta member Dr Rafael Cordova Rivas announced that the government had launched 61 projects to bring health, infrastructure and development to the Atlantic Coast region. Efforts to initiate the repatriation from Honduras of Miskito refugees were headed by the UN High Commission For Refugees (UNHCR), the International Committee for Migrations (ICM) and the International Red Cross. Attempts at repatriation have been hampered by the refusal of the Honduran government to permit the publication of the Nicaraguan government's offer in the Mokoron refugee camps.[20]

Less than three weeks after the announcement of the amnesty, on 20 December 1983, another Contra attack was made on Tasba Raya, and all the remaining inhabitants were marched to Honduras. With them were a 63-year-old Catholic Bishop, Otto Schlaefer, and Father Wendolic Shafer, both North Americans, who had been in the area on a pastoral visit. The Sandinista government mistakenly reported that Bishop Schlaefer had been killed,[21] and the US State Department announced that he was leading the Miskitos out of the country, under bombardment by the Sandinista air force. After three days, the Miskitos and Bishop Schlaefer arrived in Honduras. The Bishop was flown from the border in a US military helicopter to Tegucigalpa. According to the Bishop, he had decided to follow the group after two bridges on the road to Puerto Cabezas had been blown up by MISURA. He denied that the Sandinistas had attacked or bombed the procession, and said that whether the Indians had wanted to leave or not, when the armed MISURA came, there was little choice.[22]

The incident was again heavily exploited for propaganda purposes, both by Contra leaders in Honduras, and by the US government. Nicaraguan Archbishop Obando y Bravo described Bishop Schlaefer as 'a new Moses', and President Reagan, in a personal telephone call, congratulated the Bishop on his 'valiant attitude'.

In March and April 1984, attacks by MISURA became increasingly serious. The principal roads were lined with US-made mines, and on

29 March, 200 MISURA forces attacked the hydroelectric plant at Salto Grande Dam, which supplies eletricity to the Bonanza mines, causing damage valued at 10 million to 15 million cordobas. At the same time, an attack was launched by some 300–400 Contras in an attempt to capture the principal fishing community, Sandy Bay, a collection of scattered hamlets 40 miles from Puerto Cabezas. The following day the news was broadcast from Honduras that 2,500 people from Sandy Bay had fled 'indiscriminate bombing by the Sandinista air force'. Virgilio Taylor, a Miskito member of the FSLN, witnessed the MISURA, calling themselves 'Christ's gladiators', taking people from their houses, saying they had come to liberate the Miskitos because the Sandinistas did not believe in God.[23] Many had fled to the mountains, and by boat to sea when the MISURA attack began, later to return. There was no evidence that the villages had been bombed. A census taken a few days later revealed that of a population of 2,380, 980 Miskitos had been taken to Honduras. One week later, MISURA took 21 youths by force from the village of Mani-Watla, the following week 300 Contras attacked Tasba Pri, and in mid-April a further 1,900 Miskitos arrived at Mokoron, Honduras.

According to Orlando Wealan, who deserted from MISURA while on a mission to carry out an ambush, the principal objective of MISURA was to destroy the communities of Tasba Pri, and take the population to Honduras. 25-year-old Wealan, Co-ordinator of Education in Zelaya Norte, was among the inhabitants of Francia Sirpe abducted in December 1983. He said that on arrival in Honduras the youths were separated out for military training. He claimed to have spent two months imprisoned by MISURA, during which time he said he was tortured and interrogated. He was later given training with the Tropas Especiales Aereas (Special Aerial Troops, TEA), which, he said, were directed by two North Americans. He was sent back into Nicaragua on 26 March, in a group commanded by a former National Guardsman, 'Chang', and a member of the Honduran Tropas Especiales de Selva en Operaciones Nocturnas (Honduran Special Troops for Night-time Jungle Operations, TESON) who was named 'Papaya'. He escaped and surrendered at Tronguera, saying he was 'not prepared to be cannon fodder for the Contras'.

Wealan claimed that MISURA was supplied with arms by a US helicopter, and that food was dropped by parachute from Honduran air force helicopters. He also said that Steadman Fagoth had asked for an increase in monthly allowance from the CIA, and had been granted a raise from 150,000 Honduran lempiras a month to 250,000 lempiras.[24]

Sandinista Ministry of Interior delegate for Zelaya Norte, sub-comandante José Gonzales, estimated that by mid-April 1984, 3,000 to 5,000 members of the MISURA were operating in Zelaya, spearheaded by the Tropas Especiales del Atlantico (Special Troops for the Atlantic) under the direction of 150 North American advisers. Gonzalez claimed that the Honduran Security Forces' Direcion Nacional de Investigaciones (National Directorate of Investigations, DNI) and the Honduran armed forces collaborated closely with MISURA.[25]

United States military officials claim that military affairs on the Atlantic coast are 'run by Cubans', and expect the airport at Puerto Cabezas soon to be capable of landing Soviet MIG jet-fighters. It is claimed that the operations of MISURA from Honduras and ARDE from Costa Rica are a 'feint' designed to draw Sandinista forces away from the main thrust of the military offensive in the west of the country. They claim that Contra forces control most of the countryside outside the major towns, yet when ARDE forces for a short time took control of San Juan del Norte, near the Costa Rican border, saying they would establish a provisional government, they were driven back in a matter of days by Sandinista troops.[26]

Sandinista military officials describe the strategic objective of the United States as an effort to abduct the Miskito population, claiming the Miskitos are escaping from Sandinista repression and indiscriminate killing; thus justifying for propaganda purposes an escalation of US aggression and eventual US direct intervention in the Atlantic sector. Serious concern has also been expressed by the Sandinista government over US military exercises in Honduras which involve 'manoeuvres without previous warning' carried out close to Nicaragua's borders with Honduras and its Atlantic Coast.

Regional Development and Integration of the Indigenous People

Despite efforts by MISURA and MISURASATA to escalate the military conflict, the Sandinsta government has persisted in its attempts to promote the revolutionary transformation of the political, social and economic structures which for centuries have perpetuated the poverty and marginalization of the indigenous people. At the same time, they have attempted to incorporate these ethnic minorities into projects of regional and national development. Speaking in December 1981, Comandante William Ramirez emphasized that the war of liberation constituted an historic transformation which would permit the breaking down of class structures and the basis of racial discrimination and domination, and, through the creation of anti-imperialist awareness, would create confidence among the indigenous people in the possibility of directing their own destiny. Comandante Ramirez stressed that the challenge for the Nicaraguan revolution is to combat oppression and racial and ethnic discrimination in whatever form it may be manifest, and at its roots. In the wider context, he pointed out, racial discrimination forms part of a worldwide ideology based on capitalist socio-economic structures which justify the exploitation and extermination of ethnic minorities.

A series of measures addressing the problems of ethnic minorities were included by the FSLN in their 1969 'Historic Programme of the FSLN', which, in a section entitled 'Reincorporation of the Atlantic Coast' states:

> The Sandinista Popular Revolution will put into practice a special plan for the Atlantic Coast, which has been abandoned to total neglect, in order to incorporate this area into the nation's life.
>
> A. It will end the unjust exploitation the Atlantic Coast has suffered throughout history by the foreign monopolies, and especially US imperialism.
>
> B. It will prepare suitable lands in the zone for the development of agriculture and ranching.
>
> C. It will establish conditions that encourage the development of the fishing and forest industries.
>
> D. It will encourage the flourishing of this region's local cultural values, which flow from the specific aspects of its historic tradition.
>
> E. It will wipe out the odious discrimination to which the indigenous Miskitos, Sumos, Ramas and Blacks of this region are subjected.[27]

One of the first moves by the Sandinista government in 1979 was the nationalization of the mines in northern Zelaya and the elimination of concessions to the foreign companies who had been stripping the region of its natural resources. A programme of agrarian reform was initiated to lift the level of production and improve the living standards of the regional population, and credits were provided to small producers.

After the FSLN had taken control of the mining region of Rosita-Bonanza in May 1979, the mine-workers grasped the opportunity to form unions and press the Rosita Mining Company for better working conditions. A petition was drawn up, describing the ways in which the miners had been unjustly treated by the company, and demanding indemnity. However, the petition was not presented to the Sandinista government until it announced the nationalization of the mines in November 1979.

As a result of the severe economic crisis facing the country, the new government was unable to meet the miners' demands. The situation was worsened by a food shortage and price increases, resulting in a strike in Bonanza which was only solved by urgently sending food at subsidized prices. But by then, discontent towards the new administrators of the mines had increased considerably, and the miners had begun to resent state ownership as much as they had resented foreign ownership. Confusion and distrust arose as the state corporation responsible for the administration of the mines was also responsible for controlling the developments of any new type of workers' organization. Hopes expressed by the FSLN that the mineral wealth of the mines could be used to help finance the reconstruction of the country after the war were also resented by the miners who objected to producing for 'those of the Pacific'.[28]

Gold and silver mining, a major source of employment in the Zelaya region, has been seriously hampered by the shortage of spare parts and the lack of skilled personnel, particularly once the mining companies Neptune and Rosario had withdrawn and the Rosita mine closed as unproductive. Attempts were made in 1979 to improve the safety standards of the mines, and mine-workers were provided with safety glasses, helmets and boots. Mine-workers who had contracted tuberculosis or silicosis during the Somoza era were given medical treatment, and are now being paid indemnity by the Sandinista government. However, the production of gold and silver has declined considerably due to the poor condition of the mines and the poor quality of the ore.

Fishing, also a major source of employment and income on the Atlantic Coast, has always been a traditional occupation of the Miskito Indians. Before the revolution, Somoza had kept monopolistic control over shrimp and lobster fishing. By July 1979, Somoza's fishing companies, Booth and Promarblue, were decapitalized and the fishing tackle and boats partially destroyed. The shortage of refrigeration facilities and adequate means of transportation have also hampered the fishing industry. The Honduran Coast Guard and attacks by MISURA have in addition caused serious problems. In Sandy Bay, the principal fishing region of Zelaya Norte, eight fishing boats were attacked and three burned in 1983, with an estimated loss of one million dollars. Several fishermen were also kidnapped. In the case of Sandy Bay, government credits for $800,000 were provided to fishermen between September 1983 and April 1984, and production has increased as a result. The monthly income for each fishing boat is estimated at $50,000, and the state enterprise set up by the government to purchase and distribute seafood bought 7,274 lbs of lobster between September and December 1983.

The region of Bonanza has the largest forest reserve in Central America, the Bosawa Forest Reserve. Under a five-year reforestation project, 21,000 hectares are being planted with pine. However, much of this area cannot be worked as a result of the war, and in January 1984, 43 per cent of the wood-processing capacity of the region was destroyed by a Contra attack on Sukatpin.

In the agricultural sector levels of production have risen since the revolution. But they suffered in 1984 as a result of the abduction of many farming communities to Honduras, and the increasing mobilization of the population for military defence. Soils in the area are leeched and deficient for the cultivation of basic grains. As a result, the government

195

has encouraged the cultivation of annual and biannual crops, such as cacao, bananas and African palm.

The Miskitos, who have traditionally lived at a level of self-subsistence and a deficient diet, are now being encouraged to farm co-operatively, and are finding employment in a number of agricultural projects. In order to improve their diet and develop regional self-sufficiency in basic food production, 50,000 hectares of land have been sown with nine varieties of tropical grass to improve the cattle feed and the quality of meat for local consumption. The production of rice, beans and corn is also being stepped up.

A five-year project to plant 3,000 manzanas of cacao has begun in Tasba Pri and is expected to employ 1,500 permanent Miskito workers. During 1984, the first 300 manzanas were sown, and it is anticipated that within five years the majority of the crop will serve for export purposes. Two dairy projects have been established in Zelaya Norte to supply the region with milk, and the cattle herd is being increased with a view to exporting 50,000 head of cattle annually to the Caribbean market.

During 1983, the Miskitos were given title to 21,058 manzanas of land in four of the communities of Tasba Pri. The lands can either be sown collectively or individually, but prices are higher for crops produced collectively. It is expected that titles to a further 60,000 manzanas will be given during 1984, mostly to Miskito communities in the Pine Savanna, and to individual producers in the mining region. The giving of land titles, which correspond to the historical land claims of the Miskitos, is an attempt by the government to recognize the rights of possession of the indigenous peoples, and an attempt to counteract the fears of many Miskitos that their lands are being usurped.

On 13 February 1980, the Instituto Nicaraguense de la Costa Atlantica (Nicaraguan Institute for the Atlantic Coast, INNICA) was formed by the government to co-ordinate the state institutions involved in the implementation of development projects on the Atlantic Coast. Among the advances noted by INNICA were the reduction of illiteracy to 22 per cent, $10 million invested in improved housing, telephones and television installed for the first time, and a campaign carried out to eradicate malaria, dengue and polio. By 1984, no cases of polio had been reported for 2 years, and in Zelaya Norte the number of qualified doctors had been increased from 3 in 1978 to 30 in 1984. Medical attention is now provided free of cost to all inhabitants of the zone. Throughout the region, the number of teachers was increased from 898 in 1978 to more than 2,000 in 1983, and the number of schools from 374 to more than 1,000.

Health centres, schools and potable water have been provided for the first time in many Miskito communities, and newspapers and radio programmes are being produced for the first time in the Miskito language. Individuals are being assisted in the writing of books in

Miskito and Sumo, while traditional cultural activities and local artisanry are also being encouraged.

A road linking the Pacific with the Atlantic for the first time was opened in May 1982, and roads from Puerto Cabezas to the mining district have also been built. The first paved road was built at Puerto Cabezas. The landing strip at the Puerto Cabezas airport is being extended and airstrips at Bonanza, Siuna and Bluefields have been built. A deep-water port at El Bluff, close to Bluefields, is also under construction, and there are plans to improve the port facilities at Puerto Cabezas.

The socio-economic advances which have been made by the revolution have been seriously hampered by the military aggression from Honduras and Costa Rica, not only by attacks on strategic economic targets such as the destruction of bridges and infrastructure, but also by the diversion of the labour force and other resources into defence.

The development of the Atlantic Coast has been carried out with the consciousness that the Miskito, Sumo and Rama Indians are the most marginalized sector of society, and traditionally the most exploited. The regional government of Zelaya Norte in Puerto Cabezas has increasingly involved the Miskitos in decision-making and planning. 40 Miskitos have become members of the FSLN, representing 30 per cent of the Frente members in the region. Miskito leadership of CDS committees has also been emphasized, and the FSLN now looks more to the Miskitos for advice in the development of agricultural and social projects than was the case in the past.

In those areas where progress has been greatest, the Sandinistas can count on greater support from the indigenous people. However, many of the older generation of Miskitos still look to their ancestral lands on the Rio Coco, and they regard the past, when foreign companies brought imported goods and Dutch cheese could be bought in Waspan, as 'the golden years'. However, youths who have not left for Honduras are increasingly inclined to support the revolution.

Conclusion

The Sandinista government, in bringing revolutionary change to the Atlantic Coast, encountered conditions geo-politically different from those of the Pacific. The region, virtually untouched by the revolutionary war against the Somoza dictatorship, had nevertheless suffered under centuries of British and United States domination, and the ruthless exploitation of its natural resources by foreign companies left the indigenous minorities of the region marginalized and impoverished.

The problems of the indigenous people presented the Sandinista revolution with a unique challenge. Analysing the situation in terms of class structure and anti-imperialism, the Sandinistas were determined to bring revindication to the indigenous people and initiate their incorporation into the national project. However, the methods and structures being applied in the west of the country proved alien to indigenous society and were met with resistance.

Often remembering foreign enterprise not in terms of exploitation, but as the source of employment and of imported luxury goods, the Miskito Indians found revolutionary ideology scarcely comprehensible. In addition, the 'anti-communist' doctrine implanted during the Somoza years gave rise to distrust and misunderstanding concerning the nature of the revolutionary transformations promised by the Sandinistas.

The Sandinistas approached the Miskitos with an analytical and structural framework which failed to take into account the ethnic identity, ancestral traditions and mythology etched in their individual and collective consciousness. Having neither an understanding of the language, nor of the religious practices of the Miskitos, Sumos and Ramas, the Sandinistas often underestimated the role of the elders, and frequently did not recognize the work of the Moravian and Catholic Churches in providing health care and education. They also underestimated the authority and influence of the church leaders.

The Miskitos opposed the formation of revolutionary mass organizations such as the CDS, ATC, AMLAE and Juventud Sandinista, and disliked the political orientation of the literacy programme. Having always farmed the land individually, they resented the formation of co-operatives. And since they were accustomed to cutting trees on land which they considered theirs, they also resented the restrictions which were imposed for conservation purposes. They saw the Sandinistas as 'Españoles' who came to dominate, strip them of their autonomy and confiscate their land and its natural resources under the guise of agrarian reform. Based on the land titles given under the Zelaya regime, the Miskitos demanded 45,000 km^2 of land as their own territory, and MISURASATA leader Steadman Fagoth pressed for greater influence in the government junta and the Council of State.

When the Miskito leadership was imprisoned in response to the government's fear that an armed secessionist movement was taking root, the confidence and trust of the Miskito people in the revolution was thoroughly undermined, and armed resistance began to mount. After a series of attacks took place on the Rio Coco, and acting on alleged information that a plan, called 'Red Christmas', was being executed to seize territory and declare a provisional government with United States military and political backing, the Sandinista government forcibly evacuated 8,500 people from the border region, destroying their communities and relocating the Miskito and Sumo Indians in settlements further south. Some 10,000 Miskitos, traditionally recognizing no territorial boundary between Nicaragua and Honduras, fled north, where many joined Steadman Fagoth in armed opposition to the Sandinista government.

By 1984, the number of Nicaraguan Miskitos in Honduras had mounted to between 19,000 and 21,000, some of whom had been marched under force of arms from their communities by MISURA combatants. An open alliance was formed by the Miskito opposition with US-backed Contra groups attempting to overthrow the Sandinista government. Both the United States and MISURA argue that the Miskitos have fled to Honduras in order to escape Sandinista repression, and use the argument for propaganda purposes to justify the escalating conflict. As the war situation intensified, food shortages, restrictions on travel and certain abuses by the Sandinistas added to the mounting hostility of the Miskitos and their increasing alienation from the revolutionary process.

After almost six years of Sandinista government, the situation remains critical. Some headway has been made in understanding the Miskito culture. The Miskitos have been incorporated to a greater degree in the running of regional affairs. Resettlement communities and co-operatives have become more productive and credits and technical assistance have raised agricultural output and helped the local fishing industry. Progress has been made in the provision of basic services such as health care and education, relations have improved with some sectors of the Moravian and Catholic Churches in the region, and in some communities the confidence of the Miskitos, particularly the youth, is being re-established.

However, far from realizing the revolutionary plan to reverse the marginalization and historical exploitation of the Miskitos, the indigenous people have become the pawns once more of United States attempts to maintain political and military domination of the region, and under the guise of a struggle for autonomy and independence, encouraged by the United States, the Miskito people have become the victims once more of imperialist designs.

Editor's Note:
Since this essay was written, several important developments have occurred. During October 1984, talks were held in Nicaragua between the Miskito leader, Brooklyn Rivera, and top officials of the Sandinista government. After breaking with Edén Pastora's counter-revolutionary forces, Rivera was allowed to come to Nicaragua to speak with residents of the indigenous communities in the Atlantic Coast. At the time, he set forth his position that the Atlantic Coast should be given regional autonomy within the revolutionary state and the Nicaraguan nation.

In early December 1984, the Nicaraguan government established a national commission to hold public consultations with the peoples of the Atlantic Coast with a view to drafting legislation that would give autonomous rights to the peoples of this region. The commission has established two subcommissions – one for the northern area and one for the southern portion of the region. After carrying out extensive public consultations, the commission is expected to submit a draft statute to the National Assembly in December 1985. This commission is headed by Comandante Luis Carrión of the National Directorate of the FSLN, and includes representatives of all the ethnic communities in the region as well as sociologists with specialized knowledge of the area's cultures and social structures. The commission will consult with representatives from all sectors of the population in the area, including religious leaders, concerning the question of regional autonomy and related issues. According to Comandante Carrión, the commission does not want 'to come up with a law designed in a laboratory, but rather, a law that will reflect public sentiment, especially that of the ethnic minorities, in a direct and relevant way' (*Barricada Internacional*, 13 December 1984).

Since December 1984, meetings have been held between Rivera and Comandante Carrión in Bogota, Colombia, under the auspices of Colombia's President Belisario Betancur. Among other topics, the exchange of prisoners and the possibility of a ceasefire have been discussed, but no agreement has been reached as of this writing. Rivera, who claims he is now opposed to the Contras, has presented himself as a mediator between the Sandinistas and the Miskito people.

Notes

1. Declaration of Principles of the Popular Sandinista Revolution with respect to the Indigenous Communities of the Atlantic Coast. Frente Sandinista de Liberación Nacional and Government of National Reconstruction 12 August 1981.

2. 'Los Miskitos Y el Caso de Mons. Schlaefer', *Envio*, Instituto Historico Centroamericano, December 1983.

3. Philippe Bourgeois and Jorge Grundberg, *Informe de una Investigación Rural en la Costa Atlantica*, Managua, 1981.

4. Declaration of Principles . . ., *op. cit.*

5. 'Nicaragua Obispo, Misquitos y algo más'. *Pensamiento Propio*, nos. 10–11 (January 1984). Instituto de Investigaciones Economicas y Sociales.

6. *Diario de las Americas*, 9 January 1982.

7. J.H. Evans and Jack Epstein, 'Nicaragua's Miskito Move Based on False Allegations'. *National Catholic Reporter*, 24 December 1982.

8. *Americas Watch Report*, 1–10 March 1982.

9. Interview with *Playboy* Magazine, January 1983.

10. MISURASATA Communique, signed by Brooklyn Rivera, 18 December 1982 (Costa Rica).

11. MISURASATA Communique, 24 January 1982 (Costa Rica).

12. UPI Report by John Lantigua, 6 April 1983 (Mokoron, Honduras).

13. Information based on interviews with former residents of Santa Clara.

14. Interview with World Relief staff, July 1983, Tegucigalpa.

15. Interview with Gregorio Winter, April 1984, Puerto Cabezas.

16. 'A First-hand Account of the Violation of Miskito Indian Rights in Nicaragua', Dr Bernard Nietschmann, 6 October 1983: Declaration before the Inter-American Human Rights Commission of the OAS, 3 October 1983.

17. Information based on interviews carried out in Nicaragua, Honduras and Costa Rica with foreign missionaries and church-led human rights groups, the Red Cross and other relief organizations, Miskito villagers and community leaders, Miskito exiles, and Sandinista military and government officials, August 1982 to 19 April 1984.

18. An Awesasne Notes Interview, Autumn 1983.

19. 'Los Miskitos y el Caso . . .', *op. cit.*

20. Conversations with ACNUR (UNHCR) staff, April 1984.

21. Ministry of Defence Communique, 21 December 1983.

22. Interviews with Bishop Schlaefer, 4–5 April 1984.

23. Interview with Virgilio Taylor, 8 April 1984 (Puerto Cabezas).

24. Interview with Orlando Wealan, 10 April 1984 (Puerto Cabezas).

25. Interviews with Sub-comandante José Gonzales, 30 March to 8 April 1984 (Puerto Cabezas).

26. Interviews with US military officials who requested not to be identified, February to April 1984.

27. Programa Historico del FSLN, APUD, Manlio Tirado, *La Revolución Sandinista* (Mexico: Editorial Nuestro Tiempo, 1983), p. 183.

28. *La Misquita en la Revolución* (Managua: CIERA, 1981), pp. 200–8.

8   The United States and the Sandinista Revolution

Manlio Tirado*

Introduction

Since the Sandinistas took power on 19 July 1979, one of the most fundamental problems faced by revolutionary Nicaragua has been its relationship with the United States. For its part, the US government has been faced with the problem of how to deal with the revolutionary regime in Nicaragua.

Throughout this century, Nicaragua has been subject to the interests of Washington in a relationship imposed by the United States, first through direct military intervention and later by Somoza's National Guard – which was, in effect, a local army of occupation trained and equipped by the United States. Because Washington backed the Somoza dictatorship during its 45-year reign of tyranny, Nicaragua was an unconditional ally of the United States. As a result, the foreign policy of the homeland of Ruben Diario and Augusto Cesar Sandino was completely aligned with that of the White House.

One of the principal goals of the Nicaraguan revolution was to destroy this relationship. Thus, the Sandinista triumph altered radically the ties that had previously been established with the superpower to the north. Henceforth, the United States would not be considered a military, political or ideological ally. This does not mean, however, that the new government considered the United States as its enemy. Tomas Borge, Minister of the Interior and member of the national directorate of the FSLN, affirmed shortly after the triumph that 'we want to be friends, not serfs, of the United States'. For the Sandinistas, future United States–Nicaragua relations were to be founded on equality, mutual respect and peaceful coexistence.

Naturally, the change of regime in Nicaragua was not viewed in a positive light by the US government. However, because of a series of particular circumstances, the Sandinista government had to be accepted, albeit unwillingly. At the same time, plans were conceived to reverse the situation in Nicaragua.

* *Translated by R.L. Harris with the assistance of Mark Nechodom.*

Shortly after the revolutionary triumph, President Carter established the United States' position towards the revolution:

> It is a mistake that the American people take for granted ... that every time an evolutionary, but abrupt, change takes place in this hemisphere, it is in some way the result of large-scale and secret Cuban influence. We have a good relationship with the new government. We hope to better it. We are supplying some minimum humanitarian aid to the Nicaraguan people who have suffered so much. I believe that our position with regard to Nicaragua is appropriate. By no means do I attribute the change in Nicaragua to Cuba. I believe the Nicaraguan people are discerning enough to make their own decisions, and our efforts will be appropriately applied, without intervention, so that the voice of the Nicaraguan people can be heard in shaping their own affairs.[1]

Between July 1979 and the end of the Carter administration, relations between the United States and Nicaragua were, in general, good, in spite of misgivings, reservations and frictions on both sides.

The Carter administration was obviously not a sympathizer of the Sandinista cause, nor did it aim to strengthen the Sandinistas. Rather, the administration attempted to weaken them by strengthening the right-wing forces both within the new government and outside of it. Carter used economic aid as well as political and diplomatic pressure in an attempt to undermine the Sandinista regime. However, a military solution was only considered as a remote option.

During the same period, a powerful political bloc was forming in the United States: the 'New Right'. This concentration of ultra-conservative intellectuals and ideologists whose ideas, theories and programmes for action became guidelines for Carter's successor, Ronald Reagan, was rabidly antagonistic to the Carter administration's policy towards Nicaragua.

The world-view of the 'New Right' may be characterized as follows: the Carter administration in particular, but those of Nixon and Ford as well, have led the United States into political and economic disaster. US military power has become inferior to that of the Soviet Union. The Soviets, along with the Cubans, have extended their influence in the face of US passivity. Washington's most faithful allies have been betrayed in Vietnam, Iran and now Nicaragua as a result of human rights policies or the lack of a firm and competent leadership. Finally, the changes in the world are not fundamentally the result of internal conflicts, but the product of the east-west struggle for power; in the final analysis, the United States' hesitant and incoherent policies are giving increasing advantage to the Soviet Union and its allies. After so many defeats and misfortunes, the citizens of the United States are disheartened, humiliated and lacking self-confidence.

From this perspective, the Reagan administration's tasks were easily inferred: to surpass the Soviet Union in military power and to recover lost ground through a firm and inflexible policy which would use force when appropriate. The crusaders of the New Right recommended the decisive use of the economic, technological and military force of the United States without reservation. Thus, a second cold war and a world at the brink of armed conflict was created by the Reagan administration, as well as the millions of Americans who made Reagan's rise to the presidency possible.

The Reagan Administration and Nicaragua

In the eyes of the Reagan administration, the revolutionary triumph in Nicaragua symbolized a loss for the United States and a gain for the Soviet Union and Cuba. It also represented a regional threat because this revolution could spread throughout Central America and jeopardize the security of the United States. As a result, Reagan's electoral platform included a death sentence for the Sandinista revolution:

> We deplore the takeover of Nicaragua by the Sandinistas, as well as Marxist attempts to destabilize El Salvador, Guatemala and Honduras. We do not support U.S. aid to any Marxist government in this hemisphere and we are against the aid program of the Carter administration to the government of Nicaragua. However, we will support the efforts of the people of Nicaragua to establish an independent and free government.[2]

On 23 January 1981, three days after his inauguration as President of the United States, Reagan began the war against the Sandinistas. This war would be fought using economic, political, diplomatic and military means. As this offensive gradually increased, it acquired a predominantly military character.

The first manifestations of this war were economic and diplomatic. Between 23 January 1981 and 1 April 1982, Washington decided to stop all aid and loans to Nicaragua. Thus the remaining $15 million of the $75 million aid package approved by Congress during the Carter administration were withdrawn, and credits for the purchase of 60,000 tons of grain from US supplies were blocked. Moreover, the United States cancelled all future loans and credits to the Nicaraguan government. All of these measures were justified by the claim that the Sandinistas were providing military support to the guerrillas in El Salvador.

On the diplomatic front, official US delegations were sent to various governments in Europe and Latin America to accuse the Nicaraguans of supplying arms to the insurgents in El Salvador. The United States was trying to isolate the Sandinista regime, especially from those governments which, in one way or another, had declared solidarity with it. At the same time, the US Department of State published a White Paper on Nicaragua with the intention of demonstrating that the revolutionary regime in Nicaragua was an intermediary for the supply of Soviet and Cuban arms to the Salvadoran revolutionary groups which formed the Frente Farabundo Marti para la Liberación Nacional.

The campaign did not bear the fruits that Washington expected to harvest although it did, in some ways, damage the Nicaraguan image worldwide. In the end, Nicaragua was *not* isolated and several governments, along with the mass media (such as the *Washington Post* and the *Wall Street Journal*) questioned the evidence presented against the Sandinistas; it was neither sound nor conclusive. In this regard it is interesting to note what Piero Gleijeses, an Italian political scientist and former professor at the Foreign Service Institute of the State Department has to say about the White Paper:

> This report looked impressive at first, but soon careful observers began to find serious mistakes and incoherences. In its eagerness to provide devastating evidence, the administration manipulated and distorted facts, arriving at conclusions which were unjustified and, at times, contrary to the supporting documents. Suddenly placed on the defensive by unexpected inquiries, the answers given by the State Department were clumsy and not very persuasive. In the face of growing evidence to the contrary, the State Department refused to acknowledge serious errors in the presentation of the White Paper and did not offer any explanation for the report's inconsistencies, save for stating that its conclusions were based on a series of other documents which would be published later.[3]

Basically, the Reagan administration was trying to demonstrate that the Sandinistas had become a destabilizing factor and a regional threat because the exportation of revolution is a basic postulate of their foreign policy. The truth is that the Sandinistas have never based their foreign policy on the possibility of a revolutionary triumph abroad, as in the case of other revolutionaries. The possibility of a revolutionary victory in Central America was an element that they had taken into account, but it did not play a decisive role in the formulation of their foreign policy.

During the insurrection against Somoza and after the overthrow of his dictatorship, the Sandinistas received support from a wide assortment of foreign governments and international organizations of varying political and ideological hues. In contrast to other revolutions, their revolution was not isolated, rather it was supported internationally. The Sandinistas succeeded, in varying degrees, in obtaining the support of the governments of Mexico, Venezuela, Costa Rica, Panama, Ecuador, Cuba, Peru, Colombia, Bolivia and Brazil, as well as the governments of several Western European nations. The Sandinistas also received the support of the social democratic Socialist International and of the Movement of Non-aligned Nations. None of these governments and organizations would have continued to support the Sandinistas if they had been tempted to export the revolution.

It was obvious to the Sandinista government that any attempt to 'export revolution' would jeopardize the widespread international support of the Nicaraguan revolution. Moreover, the risks of such a political gamble were too high for the incipient government. The failure of such a venture would leave the Sandinistas isolated and vulnerable to the reactionary regimes surrounding it.

These were the essential elements which the Sandinistas took into account in the elaboration of their foreign policy, and they continue to act on these premises. On the other hand, the Sandinistas could not look upon the revolutionary effervescence in Central America, especially in El Salvador, with indifference. Nor could they adopt a neutral attitude. They have openly expressed their solidarity with the FMLN, but without any intention of playing a fundamental role in the course of El Salvador's revolution, a role which they could not and should not assume. The final fate of that revolution depends upon the Salvadorans themselves.

North American Aggression Against Nicaragua

While there were very short periods during 1981 in which it seemed that relations between Managua and Washington were improving, in the end they grew worse. Throughout that year, the Reagan administration set its military plans in motion. These included the formation of an anti-Sandinista military force from the remnants of the banished National Guard, and the upgrading of the Salvadoran and Honduran armies. At the same time, US armed forces held their first land and sea manoeuvres in Honduras and openly threatened to blockade and invade Nicaragua, thus creating a major crisis in the region.

When the Somoza dictatorship fell, the majority of Somoza's US-trained National Guard fled to Honduras. With the assistance of the Honduran government and military, they established 14 military camps along the 400-kilometre border with Nicaragua. During 1980 and part of 1981, ex-National Guardsmen began to cross into Nicaraguan territory where they engaged in robberies, assassinations and attacks against the Sandinista military outposts in the frontier region. In this period, the ex-guardsmen did not form any kind of army; they were poorly armed and their attacks were scattered and unco-ordinated.

In the final months of 1981, the Reagan administration, acting primarily through the Central Intelligence Agency, began to unite, train and arm these marauding bands. In the beginning, they were provided with $19 million in military support. When these funds were spent,

Washington granted an additional $24 million. By early 1984, another $21 million was scheduled for what had now become a counter-revolutionary army consisting of between 8,000 and 10,000 troops. The formerly disparate groups were consolidated by the CIA under a political and military collectivity known as the Fuerza Democratica Nicaraguense (Nicaraguan Democratic Force). The FDN – commonly known as the Contras – has been the main instrument used by the United States to wage its covert war against Nicaragua.

Between 1981 and 1982, the Reagan administration turned Honduras into a powerful military springboard for launching, at the appropriate moment, a large-scale attack on Nicaragua.[4] The Honduran army was restructured and trained; the number of enlisted men was increased from 14,000 troops in 1979 to 21,400 in 1982, an overall increase of 66.5 per cent. These troops were also provided with modern arms and equipment. By late 1982, the Honduran air force became the most important in Central America, having 20 Super Mystere B-2 combat bombers, 10 Sabre Jet F-86 jet fighter-bombers, 5 Dragonfly A-37A attack bombers, 22 Trojan T-28 training bombers, 3 RT-33A reconnaissance aircraft and 23 UH-1H and UH-19D transport helicopters.

By February 1984, and as a result of US military assistance, there were a total of nine military air bases in Honduras. US Senator James Sasser, a member of the Senate Sub-committee on Military Construction, is reported to have commented that Honduras was fast becoming 'the country with the most landing strips per capita in the world'. Senator Sasser travelled to Honduras in February 1984 and reported to the Senate that unauthorized and excessive military construction was being carried out in Honduras by the United States.[5]

Sasser's report included a list of the operating air bases and those under construction at that moment. In Palmerola a landing strip with night lighting was being enlarged which served as general headquarters for the Big Pine II manoeuvres as well as the Granadero I exercises. According to Sasser, in San Lorenzo, an 1,800 metre air strip was under construction to accommodate C-130 military transport aircraft. In El Aguacate, another air strip was being lengthened from 1,200 to 2,400 metres. In La Ceiba, an air strip was slated for improvement and is currently in military use. Two more were being built, one in Cucuyagua and another in Jamastrán, near the Nicaraguan border. In Trujillo, the existing air strip was enlarged for use by C-130 aircraft.

Also near Trujillo, at Puerto Castilla, the United States has established what it calls a Regional Center for Military Training for the purpose of training Salvadoran and Honduran troops. Actually, the plans are to turn this into a permanent US naval and air base.

The Honduran armed forces have benefited from the most rapid and comprehensive US military assistance effort in the history of Latin America. Annual US aid to Honduras increased from $3.5 million in 1980 to $96 million in 1984.[6] Participation by both the Honduran army and the Contras in recent US military manoeuvres inside Honduras has reinforced their fighting capacity because, at the completion of these exercises, the US forces always leave a huge arsenal behind for their use.

Since 1982, the United States has relied largely upon military means to achieve its goal of destabilizing and ultimately destroying the Sandinista regime. The harassment of Nicaragua has continued on the economic, diplomatic and political levels as well, but these other means have been subordinated to the military campaign. It is clear that the Reagan administration seeks an 'armed solution' to the Nicaraguan question. However, the administration's plans in this regard have run into both domestic and international opposition which have obliged it to feign interest in negotiating a peaceful resolution of the conflict between it and Nicaragua.

The US government has threatened to invade or take military action against Nicaragua on numerous occasions. Each time this has coincided with US and Honduran joint military exercises and an escalation of the Contras' attacks on targets within Nicaragua.

The first of these joint exercises, code-named Halcon Vista, took place between 7 and 9 October 1981 in an area very close to Nicaragua. The exercise was a simulated invasion of a region very similar to that in neighbouring Nicaraguan territory. The Sandinistas denounced these manoeuvres as a threat to Nicaragua's national security and to peace in the Central American region. The Nicaraguan armed forces were put on a maximum state of alert and hundreds of thousands of Nicaraguan civilians organized well-publicized marches and rallies to protest the exercises.

Instead of decreasing, tension grew after these exercises were over. In early November 1981, US Secretary of State Alexander Haig confirmed rumours to the effect that the US Pentagon was studying military options that could be used against Cuba, Nicaragua and Grenada. He also stated that the United States had contingency plans for a maritime blockade of Nicaragua as a prelude to a direct military intervention. However, these interventionist plans triggered vigorous opposition both within the United States and around the world. On 10 November 1981, President Reagan was forced publicly to appease his political opponents by stating: 'My government does not have any plan to place US combat soldiers in the Caribbean or in any other part of the globe' (*New York Times*, 11 November 1981). However, four days later, Secretary Haig contradicted the president by stating: 'The possibility of military action in Nicaragua cannot be discarded' (*New York Times*, 15 November 1981). Nevertheless, the lack of political support for this approach within the United States as well as in the United Nations, Latin America and Western Europe, forced the Reagan administration to back away from taking direct military action.

In March 1982, there were again signs that large-scale military action against Nicaragua was in preparation. Some 2,000 FDN troops concentrated in Honduras near the Nicaraguan border. Assisted by Honduran soldiers, the Contras began a campaign of almost daily attacks on Nicaraguan border posts and towns near the frontier with Honduras. Saboteurs dynamited the bridges on the Rio Negro and the Rio Ocotal in Northern Nicaragua. And during the first eleven days of March, there were four violations of Nicaraguan territory by US and Honduran reconnaisance planes as well as air and surface attacks on Nicaraguan shore patrols and fishing boats. Moreover, a US Navy destroyer, the USS *Caron*, was stationed off Nicaragua's Pacific Coast to perform electronic espionage. In the Panama Canal Zone, the headquarters of the US army's Southern Command, three companies of Somoza's former National Guardsmen undertook training in airborne assaults and the handling of explosives. These aggressive activities were denounced at the United Nations Security Council by Nicaragua, and an international diplomatic effort was mounted by the revolutionary government to head off what appeared to be an impending US invasion. Again, the United States backed away from an invasion due to the inappropriate political conditions prevailing at that time.

In late 1982, a retired colonel in the US Marine Corps with Vietnam combat experience, Col. John H. Buchanan, inspected both the armies of Honduras and Nicaragua for the Center for Development Policy, a non-profit research centre based in Washington. Buchanan's report revealed that Nicaragua's military build-up was clearly defensive in nature and he concluded that 'the Reagan administration is distorting the facts in order to justify covert operations aimed at overthrowing the Sandinistas'.[7] His report also indicated that Honduran military officials were expecting a US-backed war against Nicaragua, involving Honduras, to begin sometime in December 1982. Other sources confirmed the rumours he heard among Honduran military officials. On 22 October 1982, Mexico's Foreign Minister Jorge Castaneda said that: 'In Central America, tensions have increased and a conflict of incalculable proportions is in the making.'[8] The same day, Comandante Daniel Ortega denounced the United States' bellicose intentions, and claimed that 'there is sufficient information to indicate that December is the month fixed by the United States to move massively the counter-revolutionary forces in Honduras against the Sandinista Revolution'.[9] On 17 October, the *Washington Post*, referring to the Big Pine I manoeuvres, stated that the United States and Honduras were preparing military exercises on an unprecedented scale near the Nicaraguan border and that these exercises could provoke a war between Honduras and Nicaragua. Shortly thereafter, *Newsweek* published an extensive article on the Reagan administration's covert war against Nicaragua. The worldwide disapproval and the opposition to such a course of action within the United States forced the Reagan administration to postpone the Big Pine exercises until February 1983.

After US troops invaded Grenada in November 1983, the danger of direct US intervention in Nicaragua arose again. It was a month of great tension in Nicaragua. The government mobilized nearly the entire civilian population. The people were called upon to dig trenches and air-raid shelters as well as practise the defence of their neighbourhoods, villages and factories. In the end there was no invasion, and the tension declined.

While it was evident that the Reagan administration advocated a military solution to the conflict in Central America, other governments – particularly in Latin America – demanded a negotiated solution. Both positions were advanced in the international arena, leading to divergent diplomatic initiatives.

Regional Peace Efforts

As early as February 1982, Mexican President López Portillo had presented a peace plan for Central America in which he proposed that the United States cease its threats and military actions. He also called for the ex-National Guardsmen in Honduras to be disbanded and for non-aggression pacts to be signed between Nicaragua and the United States and between Nicaragua and its neighbours. Under these conditions, López Portillo argued that the Nicaraguan government could be expected to renounce both the acquisition of arms and aircraft, and the use of its scarce resources for the maintenance of a military establishment large enough to worry its neighbours.[10]

At the same time, Comandante Ortega put forward a peace plan similar to that of López Portillo. The main outlines of this proposal were as follows: (1) the signing of agreements of non-aggression and mutual security with Nicaragua's neighbours; (2) joint patrolling of the borders shared with Honduras and Costa Rica for the purpose of preventing irregular activities by groups disaffected with any of the three governments; and (3) discussions with the United States on all issues of mutual concern.[11]

Reagan declared, without enthusiasm, that he would study the López Portillo plan and that he was willing to negotiate with the Sandinista government. The Nicaraguan proposal did not receive any comment from the Reagan administration. Subsequent events demonstrated that the White House had its own plans which required the Sandinistas to come to negotiations on terms that the United States would define. Reagan has waved the banner of negotiations at appropriate moments in order to disguise his administration's true purpose: the unconditional surrender of the Sandinistas through the use of armed force.

Subsequently, the US government tried to take the offensive in the diplomatic arena. The United States rejected the repeated requests from the Sandinistas to start negotiations. Instead, it supported a peace plan proposed by the Honduran government. The Honduran Foreign Minister, Edgardo Paz Barnica, proposed at the Organization of American States (OAS), the establishment of a joint force, already proposed by Nicaragua, to control their common border.[12] He also proposed the reduction of the number of troops and armaments in Central America, as well as the number of 'foreign advisers, military or otherwise' in the region. Finally, he proposed that observance of the arrangements would require international supervision and vigilance. In principle, the plan was acceptable to the Sandinistas. However, it did not make any reference to the Contras engaged in attacking Nicaragua from their bases in Honduras. And it did not reflect a serious attitude on the part of the Honduran government since it was formulated to displace the proposals of the Mexican and Nicaraguan governments. Thus, the Sandinistas judged the Honduran proposal to be merely a diplomatic manoeuvre.

The Mexican and Venezuelan governments attempted to bring together Comandante Ortega and President Suazo Cordova of Honduras for discussions aimed at reducing the tension between the two countries. A meeting was set up in Caracas, Venezuela, but at the last minute President Suazo Cordova announced that he could not attend.

This failed effort coincided with the diplomatic manoeuvres of the United States. In late October, Washington organized the so-called Forum for Peace and Democracy in San José, Coasta Rica. This meeting was attended by the foreign ministers of Costa Rica, Colombia, Jamaica, El Salvador and Honduras as well as the prime minister of Belize and representatives from the governments of the Dominican Republic and Panama. Mexico and Venezuela were invited but did not want to attend. Guatemala and Nicaragua were not invited on the grounds that their governments had not been legitimated by democratic elections. Clearly, the intention was to form a bloc of countries which would support US policy in Central America and the Caribbean, and in particular isolate Nicaragua.

However, this diplomatic offensive failed. The forum was regarded by countries such as Venezuela and Mexico with misgivings by virtue of the fact that it was orchestrated by Washington. In addition, it had the defect of having excluded two of the five countries in the Central American region, and any political solution to the conflict in the region obviously required Nicaragua's participation.

The governments of Mexico, Colombia, Venezuela and Panama acted quickly to prevent Washington from consolidating this bloc. After several preliminary consultations, the foreign ministers of these countries met on 8 January 1983 at the Panamanian island of Contadora. They produced a declaration which expressed their deep concern over foreign involvement in the conflicts of the Central American region, and they criticized the inclusion of these conflicts

211

within the context of the global east-west struggle. As a result, they agreed on the necessity of eliminating the external factors responsible for aggravating the internal conflicts in the region.

They made an urgent appeal to all the countries in the Central American region to enter into negotiations aimed at reducing tension and establishing the basis for a permanent climate of peaceful coexistence and mutual respect. They also asserted that it was the obligation of all states to abstain from using force in their international relations. And they called upon the countries in the region to refrain from taking actions which might aggravate the situation and lead to a generalized conflict in the region. Finally, they called upon the entire Latin American community to join with them in a concerted effort to promote a peaceful resolution to the conflicts in Central America.

The formation of what immediately became known as the 'Contadora Group' succeeded in burying Washington's Forum for Peace and Democracy and initiated a genuine Latin American effort to solve a Latin American problem. Naturally, the United States did not welcome this initiative and ignored it for several months. However, as time passed, it could not maintain this position. Instead, it chose to give the impression that it supported this peace initiative, while in fact it began to do what it could to sabotage it.

During April 1983, the Contadora Group met again. However, this time the foreign ministers of all five of the Central American states also attended. It was at this moment that the Contadora effort began to pick up strength and hold out the real possibility of reaching a negotiated settlement to the conflicts of the region. In this meeting, a diagnosis of these conflicts was formulated. This diagnosis identified the following problems: the military build-up in the region, the black market in arms, the presence of foreign military advisers and other forms of foreign military assistance, actions aimed at destabilizing the domestic order of the states in the region, verbal threats of aggression, border incidents, the infringement of human rights and the grave social and economic problems underlying the crisis in the region.

As the Contadora effort to promote a negotiated solution to the conflict in the region progressed, the United States increased its military presence in Central America. The Pentagon announced new joint military manoeuvres in the area on a scale much greater than previous operations. There were also discussions in the US Congress as to what amount should be provided the Contras to destabilize the Nicaraguan government. In late 1983 and during the first months of 1984, the US-backed Contras greatly increased their attacks on Nicaragua, including the destruction of most of Nicaragua's oil storage facilities in the port city of Corinto and the subsequent mining of the country's main harbours.

In April 1984, the Reagan administration gave the go-ahead for a vigorous military offensive against Nicaragua by its surrogate forces.

Some 8,000 Contras infiltrated into the country, while most of the country's ports were attacked from the sea. At this point, Panama's President Jorge Illueca stated that the increased level of military activity in the region, the mining of Nicaragua's ports and the presence in the region of US troops were totally incompatible with the peace efforts of the Contadora Group. (Note: More recent developments are discussed in the Epilogue to this volume.)

Final Considerations

Since assuming power, the Reagan administration has made a concerted effort to overthrow the Sandinista government. It has undertaken an undeclared war against revolutionary Nicaragua, utilizing both direct and indirect means of aggression. It has backed the counter-revolutionary elements both within and outside of Nicaragua. Thanks to the backing they receive from Washington, the external counter-revolutionary elements are the only real threat to the new revolutionary social order. However, it is the United States which is the principal force opposing the revolutionary regime, and the only one capable of overthrowing it.

The Reagan administration's undeclared war against Nicaragua has so far failed in several fundamental respects, because it is based on false assumptions. For example, Washington believes that there is widespread popular discontent in Nicaragua and that the Contras and rightwing elements within the country can serve as the catalyst of a popular insurrection against the Sandinista regime. However, with the exception of several thousand Miskito Indians who abandoned Nicaragua and joined the FDN in Honduras, there has been no popular support for the Contras. The disaffected Miskitos have been used for anti-Sandinista propaganda purposes, but they constitute little real military or political threat to the Sandinistas. For a time, the Reagan administration also thought that the Contras could gain control of enough territory in northern Nicaragua to establish a provisional government there which could be recognized by the United States and its Central American allies. However, despite the intense efforts made by the Contras during the last two years, they have failed to hold any portion of Nicaraguan territory for more than a few days. Finally, the United States has failed in the diplomatic field as well, because it has continuously lost the initiative to Nicaragua and the Contadora Group. The actions of the United States have tended to discredit its pretence of seeking a peaceful solution to the conflict in Central America.

On the other hand, the United States has not failed completely. It has obtained favourable results from its efforts to destabilize Nicaragua's economy. The Contra attacks have caused serious damage to the infrastructure and productive processes of the country, particularly in

213

the agricultural areas near the frontier with Honduras. Production centres, warehouses, agricultural machinery, means of transport, bridges, roads, airports, health centres, schools, hydroelectric plants, fuel storage tanks, fishing boats, etc., have been destroyed or seriously damaged.

The counter-revolutionary forces have also brought painful suffering to the civilian population. According to recent official reports, close to 8,000 persons have been killed, both military and civilian. And close to 200,000 people who live in the border regions have been forced to abandon their homes and fields in order to go to areas where they will be safe from the Contra attacks. Moreover, the United States' undeclared war has forced the Sandinista government to divert a large amount of the country's material and human resources towards defence, to the detriment of the development of the economy and the implementation of important social programmes. This situation is further complicated by the repercussions of the world economic crisis, the fall in the prices of Nicaragua's main agro-exports and Washington's financial and economic blockade of Nicaragua. These conditions have caused critical shortages, serious supply problems and commercial speculation. These problems, although they are serious, are not yet grave. However, they could get much worse and create popular discontent and agitation.

The Reagan administration will continue to carry out hostilities against Nicaragua as long as Sandinismo is in power, because it views the Sandinistas as the source of all evil in Central America. It is a tumour that must be extirpated. This hostility weighs heavily over the entirety of Nicaraguan life and must always be taken into account by the revolutionary government in all its social, economic and political plans.

Washington has not yet played its last card – direct US military intervention. This is a possibility that cannot be discarded, even though it would be difficult to set in motion because the right pretext has not yet been found, nor has the proper climate occurred, and because all the other options open to the United States have not yet been exhausted, for example, using the Honduran army to attack Nicaragua.

On the other hand, negotiations between the United States of America and revolutionary Nicaragua cannot be discarded either. In Vietnam, the United States sought a military solution, but in the end it was forced to go to the conference table and accept a political solution.

In the short term, there does not appear to be any possibility of a compromise between the United States and Nicaragua. The prolongation of the present situation has both positive and negative consequences for the revolutionary process in Nicaragua. As time goes by, the Sandinista regime is consolidating its popular base of support and institutionalizing its revolutionary process. The continuing threat posed by US aggression has helped to maintain national unity and popular support for the revolutionary government. Moreover, the army and civilian militias are acquiring more combat experience and the country's structure of national defence is gaining greater strength. However, the prolongation of the war and US economic aggression will cost the country dearly in terms of its scarce economic resources and development plans, not to mention the continued loss of human lives and the destruction of homes, farms and invaluable infrastructure. In fact, the war threatens to cause an economic recession from which it would take many years for the country to recover.

Notes

1. Quoted from a speech delivered on 'The Voice of America' and reproduced in *La Prensa*, 22 August 1979 (Managua).

2. Quoted in 'La Administración de Reagan y los limites de la hegemonia norteamericana', *Cuadernos Semestrales*, no. 9 (first semester, 1981), p. 339, Centro de Investigación y Docencia Económica (CIDE), Mexico City.

3. Piero Gleijeses, 'La Politica del Presidente Reagan en Centro America', in *Centroamerica: mas alla de la crisis* (Mexico City: Ediciones SIAPM, 1983), p. 283.

4. On the militarization of Honduras see: Gregorio Selser, *Honduras: Republica Alquilada* (Mexico City: Ediciones Mex-Sur, 1983); and Philip Wheaton, *Inside Honduras* (Washington: EPICA, 1982).

5. See Gregorio Selser, 'Honduras ocupada: el informe al Senado Norteamericano del legislador James Sasser', *El Dia* 25 March 1984 (Mexico City).

6. See Allan Nairn, 'A Special Report on U.S. Military Strategy in Central America', *NACLA Report on the Americas* (May–June 1984), p. 40.

7. Reported in *Is there Militarization in Nicaragua?* (Managua: Centro de Comunicación Internacional, 1983), pp. 11–15.

8. Reprinted in *Excelsior*, 23 October 1982 (Mexico City).

9. Ibid.

10. *Excelsior*, 22 February 1982.

11. *Nicaragua: Bandera de la Paz* (Managua: Departmento de Propaganda y Educación Politica, FSLN, 1982), p. 41.

12. See Selser, *Honduras: Republica Alquilada*, p. 43.

9 National Liberation, Popular Democracy and the Transition to Socialism

Carlos M. Vilas and Richard L. Harris

The preceding essays reveal the nature and depth of the revolutionary transformations that are taking place in Nicaraguan society. Among the more important of these are: the restructuring of the relations and forms of property in the rural areas as a result of the agrarian reform; the creation of the Area of People's Property; the drastic reduction of the material bases of the landed and financial oligarchy, the increasing integration of industry and agriculture and the development of new agro-industrial projects; the unionization of both the rural and urban sectors of the working class and the increasing participation of the workers in the management of production; the creation of a popular army based on the principle of arming the people; the progressive institutionalization of a new popular democratic state; the democratization of the political process; the activation of civil society through the mobilization of popular participation in mass organizations and in a multiplicity of civic activities; the increasing participation of women in all aspects of social life and the progressive elimination of sexual discrimination; the introduction of popular forms of education and health care that have already significantly improved the level of education and health of the general population and particularly the popular classes; the active participation of Christians in the revolutionary process and the development of revolutionary popular forms of religious expression; and the reinsertion of Nicaragua into the international political economy as a non-aligned nation with diversified trading relations and an anti-imperialist foreign policy. Naturally, these transformations have encountered difficult obstacles, sharpened many of the contradictions in Nicaraguan society, and raised important questions about the character of the revolution, the direction it will take in the future and the major factors that appear to be shaping its course.

Like all previous revolutions in modern history, the Sandinista revolution has its specific traits and its own clear identity, which the essays in this volume have revealed. Nicaragua is not another Cuba, Chile or Vietnam. It is not copying the model of any other revolution, although it is clear that the lessons and errors of other revolutionary processes have been incorporated into the revolutionary thought and practice of the Sandinistas.

The pragmatic and eclectic nature of the revolutionary ideology and policies of the Sandinista leaders has been noted frequently by both foreign observers and by the Nicaraguans themselves. Nicaraguans refer to their revolution as the Sandinista revolution and in so doing call attention to its specific historical antecedents and authentically national character. The anti-imperialist struggle of General Augusto Cesar Sandino and his army of peasants, workers and artisans in the 1920s and 1930s has provided an important source of identity and historical experience for the contemporary revolutionary process.[1]

Nevertheless, the Sandinista revolution can be compared with the major social revolutions of our times. In its own specific way, and based upon the particularities of the country's history and social structures, this revolution has assumed the tasks that other exploited and oppressed peoples have undertaken previously in order to attain a better life: the struggle against imperialist domination; the creation of an independent nation-state; the elimination of hunger, ignorance, backwardness and the most flagrant injustices; the recognition of human dignity; and the conscious participation of the people in the elaboration of their own destiny as a national community.

The objective in the following pages is to offer a series of reflections on the progress of the Sandinista revolution during its first six years and its possible evolution in the future. What will be considered are various questions raised by the Sandinista revolution, and perhaps most Third World revolutions for national liberation. This will serve as a form of recapitulating the analysis provided in the previous essays, and allow us to discuss what appear to be the most apparent tendencies and prospects of the revolution. Our aim is to indicate where further analysis and subsequent studies might be fruitful, and to enrich the theoretical and political debate over the processes of revolutionary transition in backward and dependent societies.

The Creation of a National State Through Popular Revolution

A central aspect of the problematic confronted by the Sandinista revolution is the process of creating a modern nation-state by a block of social forces composed principally of the working masses. This represents an important difference with the general process by which states have been constituted in Latin America – a task fundamentally undertaken by the local bourgeoisie as part of their project of articulation with the international market, beginning in the first half of the last century.

The capitalist state existing in Nicaragua before July 1979 was

217

a product of North American military invasions and the political influence which the United States exerted on the country through the Somoza dictatorship, itself a direct product of these invasions. The effort to constitute a modern state, of the liberal bourgeois type, took place in Nicaragua later than in most parts of Latin America. It was not until the end of the last century that modernizing elements of the bourgeoisie gained political power and undertook capitalist reforms in the economy and the state as a result of the influence of the liberal reforms that had been introduced earlier in Guatemala, El Salvador, Honduras and Costa Rica.

However, the alliance of the conservative oligarchy with the United States (at the time interested in building a canal in Central America) put a rapid and violent end to the project of liberal reforms in Nicaragua. In 1909, President Zelaya was overthrown with North American support and the US Marines invaded the country on several occasions thereafter. In 1910, the imposition of the 'Dawson Accords' converted Nicaragua into a virtual protectorate of the United States; in 1912, North American troops occupied Nicaragua; in 1914, the conservative government signed with the United States the Bryan–Chamorro Treaty. This gave the United States the right to control the inter-oceanic potential of Nicaragua and delivered strategic domain to the United States over the area up to Panama; in 1917, the United States used gunboat diplomacy to put in the presidency the conservative caudillo Emiliano Chamorro, who as Foreign Minister had signed the treaty with US Secretary of State Bryan; and in 1921 and 1926, North American troops again invaded Nicaragua.[2]

Between 1927 and 1933, General Sandino's Army in Defence of National Sovereignty fought a genuine war of national liberation against the US occupation troops, which were finally forced to abandon the country. Nevertheless, the United States by that time had managed to create a local political and military apparatus to guarantee the continuation of its imperialist domination – the so-called National Guard with Anastasio Somoza at its head. Somoza used the National Guard as a trampoline to gain political power and install a dictatorial dynasty that remained in power until 1979. The Somoza dictatorship, with its neo-colonial state, provided the political context for an alliance between the dominant factions of the local bourgeoisie and North American imperialism.

The external domination that the United States exercised over Nicaragua through the Somocista state was more political and military in nature than directly economic. It was 'an imperialism of ambassadors and generals rather than of industrialists and bankers'.[3] During the Somoza dictatorship, Nicaragua was always a sure vote in the Organization of American States and the United Nations, and a reliable pawn in US strategy for domination of the Central American region – as opposed to an important location for economic investments. In this sense, it was subjected to one of the more primitive forms of imperialist domination.

The dominant local classes for a long time accepted without question their subordination to a dictatorial state which was itself subordinated. The subordination of the country's national sovereignty was the other side of the coin of their own subordination as dominant social forces by the Somoza dictatorship. Sandino's struggle, and later that of the FSLN, confronted this neo-colonial project with a combative and insurgent project of national sovereignty – as both the product and attribute of popular emancipation. The liquidation of the neo-colonial, Somocista state meant the end of the institutional linkage that tied Nicaragua to external domination. The slow, difficult and at times problematic creation of a new state by the triumphant popular forces has opened the way to the effective realization of the country's national sovereignty, but now as a dimension of a larger popular project – as part of a revolutionary process involving profound social transformations.

This task is obviously complex and plagued with difficulties. It implies taking responsibility for the effective spatial integration of the national territory; the creation of an effective administrative apparatus; the institutionalization of a new type of army based upon the principle of arming the people; the creation of an autonomous judiciary in a country without a genuine judicial tradition; the development of ideological and institutional mechanisms capable of integrating the entire population in a project that is for the first time really national. The obstacles, the limitations, the problems, arise at every turn. The development of this process has released tensions and contradictions, some of which have enormous potential for conflict, that were previously suppressed by the weight of the dictatorship and external domination. The creation of a centralized national state that aspires to exercising effective authority in all parts of its territory always generates regional jealousies, ethnic tensions and local resistance; the processing and resolution of which are complicated and for which the new state does not always have sufficient knowledge, resources and time.

This process of creating a modern and popular nation-state in Nicaragua is expressed in practice through a single political organization: the FSLN. This raises the question – which is always complex – of the relationship between the state and the party or political organization that leads the process of revolutionary transformation and constitutes the new state. The position of the FSLN on this question is as follows:

> the state is nothing more than an instrument of the people to make the revolution, an instrument of the motive forces of change, the workers and peasants, which provides a means for breaking the obstacles that the revolution encounters, and the manner in which we use the state to break these obstacles will determine the extent

219

to which we serve these motive forces ... Whoever does not understand that the state is nothing more than a means and not an end,
who believes that our people must be spectators while the state acts as
the source of all initiatives, wants consciously or unconsciously to
introduce our state within a reactionary mould.[4]

In accord with this perspective, the FSLN directs the state through the
members of its National Directorate who occupy positions in the
executive branch, and through FSLN members in the legislature as well
as the administrative apparatus. However, as the following quote
indicates, the FSLN does not attempt to replace the state:

The Sandinista Front has as its mission to assure and guarantee that
the state functions as an executive and administrative entity; therefore,
its mission is to confer on the state a political line, give it eyes by
which to orient itself, without tying its hands and feet because this
could cause the state to lose its executive character and complicate the
party's leadership mission.[5]

In practice, however, things have not been so simple, nor could they
ever be.

In the first place, the realization of national tasks by a political
organization makes partisan the external physiognomy of these tasks.
As a result, the opposition to the revolution has reduced the content, the
nature and national objectives of the new state, the creation of the new
political institutions, the activities of the state agencies and the
formulation and execution of public policies to a question of
partisanship; and on the basis of this reduction has adopted an
opposing position in the name of a 'nation' that stands above partisan
considerations. The opposition has denounced the Sandinista Popular
Army as an 'armed party'; and opposed the military service law on the
grounds that it recruits young people into the army for the purpose of
defending the interests of the ruling party, etc.

It is obvious that what is involved here is a confrontation between two
opposing conceptions of what constitutes the nation, reducible in the
last analysis to two different class positions: on the one side, the nation
as the property of the dominant classes and the neo-colonial state; on
the other, the nation as the property of the people institutionalized in
the revolutionary state. As mentioned previously, this political and
ideological confrontation has been a constant in the history of
Nicaragua throughout the 20th Century. The present conflict over this
question reveals the extent to which the Sandinista revolution has its
roots deep in the country's history.

Even though the present situation is one in which the tasks of nation-
building are being undertaken by a party – the FSLN – these tasks do
not lose their national character as a result of this circumstance. On the

contrary, it is precisely the national character of the tasks being carried out by this revolutionary organization that give the FSLN its national content and authority. The struggle of this revolutionary organization has rescued the title of the nation for the popular masses. Upon liquidating the Somoza dictatorship, it eliminated the link that subordinated the country to the United States. By questioning the old dominant classes and attacking the material bases of their domination, the FSLN has confronted the local allies of the previous foreign domination. The nation, as the property of the people, is an innovative, collective project that has been given expression by the FSLN, the revolutionary organization that made possible the political and military triumph of the popular majority over the Somoza dictatorship.

The shortage of resources of every kind has been very severe, and has meant that the few available must be shared between the state and the FSLN. The circulation of cadres between one and the other is frequent; the accumulation of state and party functions within the same ambit of activity continues to be a problem. The reinforcement of party authority with resources provided by the state administration, or the contrary, the strengthening of state authority by appealing to party authority, is a detectable practice, although not the rule. Basically, this can be interpreted as an effect of the unequal degree of development achieved by the structures of the FSLN and by the new state apparatus. It is not surprising that after two decades of existence, the level of organization of the FSLN is superior to that of a state that is only six years old – a state, moreover, whose administrative cadres continue to be, to a large degree, the same as those before the revolution.

Economic Accumulation and Transformation

In the six years since the triumph over the dictatorship, the Nicaraguan economy has reached levels of growth without comparison in Latin America – especially in the agricultural sector, in spite of the effects of the war of liberation, the inevitable dislocations involved in any process of profound transformations, the impact of the regional economic crisis and, more recently, the economic and military pressures directed against Nicaragua by the United States – credit restrictions, the attacks of the US-backed Contras against economic targets, etc. At first, this growth was sustained by increasing the country's external debt, which has continued to increase up to the present, but in recent years this growth has rested increasingly upon internal savings.

The growth of the economy has taken place along with important transformations in its structure and functioning. The economic policy of the revolution has promoted, in the first place, a relatively accelerated development of the productive forces – both material and human. Large investment projects (by Nicaraguan standards) in agro-industry, an

221

emphasis upon the integration of the different sectors of the economy, the promotion of projects which involve the local processing of raw materials and other inputs of national origin, the incorporation and adaptation of modern technology to the needs of the country, have been combined with the formation and training of technical, administrative and professional cadres in order to expand the productive forces upon which Nicaragua depends, improve their conditions of organization and elevate their efficient utilization and levels of productivity.

At the same time, new relations of production are being developed. The confiscation of the enterprises and other holdings of the Somocistas permitted the birth of the APP which, despite its limitations, provides the dynamic axis of the revolutionary government's project of economic transformation. The co-operative organization of small and medium agricultural production is being promoted. The most backward forms of rural production and the various forms of rent in labour and kind have been eliminated. In fact, a broad process of modernization is underway. Finally, the introduction of forms of worker participation in the administration of the state enterprises, the development of union organizations, the emphasis upon worker productivity, the slow but progressive development of new criteria of labour discipline are bringing about important transformations in the heart of the labour process.

The general framework for these transformations – the mode in which they are being carried out, their scope and limitations – is the schema of a mixed economy, which is one of the basic aspects of the Sandinista revolution. This schema is based upon the articulation of three major areas or sectors of production: the APP, the capitalist sector of large private producers, and the sector of small and medium production – individual, family and co-operative. Up to now, as various essays in this book have shown, the functioning of this model has shown that the fundamental effort at investment has been made by the state sector of the economy, while the large capitalist producers have received the fiscal, commercial and other incentives offered by the state without making any dynamic contribution to the economy, especially in the area of investments. And in the agro-export sector, the most strategic with regard to the development of accumulation, the deliberately poor performance of the large capitalist sector has been particularly notable.

This situation has given rise to sharp contradictions within the revolutionary process. The schema of a mixed economy and its political corollary, national unity, are based upon the confidence and hope that the FSLN deposited in the anti-Somoza sectors of the Nicaraguan bourgeoisie, who it was assumed would collaborate in the economic reconstruction of the country. However, there remain few doubts that, except in isolated cases, the collective conduct of this class has not corresponded to these expectations. Moreover, the strategy adopted by the FSLN has implied an increasing economic cost that directly or indirectly is transferred to the working class.

Up to now, the revolution has appealed to the political comprehension of the masses and made efforts to persuade the bourgeoisie to co-operate. However, it is possible to ask just how much more can a popular revolution that recognizes the working masses as its motive force appeal to their capacity to endure the economic consequences of their deteriorating real income, while at the same time similar sacrifices are not imposed upon the capitalists. It is evident, moreover, that the level of political and administrative development of the new state – the shortage of cadres, etc. – would make any substantial and rapid expansion of the APP very difficult, in the event this was the intention of revolutionary policy.

On the other hand, the negative impact of large capital's behaviour is evident upon the country's national defence at this moment. One of the fundamentals of the Sandinista strategy of national unity and mixed economy is that the revolution must dispute with the counter-revolution for the anti-Somocista elements of the bourgeoisie. Especially during the last few years, one gets the impression that the incentives which the state has provided to the private sector have less to do with encouraging them to invest in the economy than with guaranteeing their passive political adhesion to the regime and their rejection of the counter-revolution. But the question must be raised regarding the extent to which this financial generosity towards a class that has refused to assume its productive functions has affected the expansion of the economy, the social condition of the workers and the material basis upon which Nicaragua's defence against foreign military aggression is based.

Agro-exports continue to be considered the dynamic axis of accumulation. The economic strategy of the last six years has consisted in taking advantage of and strengthening the installed capacity of this sector of the economy and the comparative advantages that derive from Nicaragua's ecological conditions. Everything indicates that this strategy will continue in the future; the major investment projects are concentrated primarily in this sector. And it is through the agro-export sector that the Nicaraguan economy will hope to obtain the income to finance the general development and transformation of the economy as a whole.

The extensive industrialization of the economy does not figure in the agenda of the revolution in the short run, except in so far as agro-industry is concerned and the local processing of domestically produced inputs which will contribute to the inter-sectorial integration of the economy. However, important investments in the industrial sector are laying the basis for much more extensive industrial development in the future.

The Sandinistas and the left in general criticized the agro-export nature of the Somoza dictatorship and the type of capitalism that characterized the pre-revolutionary development of the country.[6] Nevertheless, in the definition of the economic policy of the revolution, the conviction has prevailed, despite initial internal debates, that the country's economic problematic is not the product so much of its dependence upon agro-exports per se as the type of social organization that has dominated production in this sector and in the economy as a whole, as well as the manner in which this sector is articulated with the international market. As a result, the revolution has placed a great deal of importance on elevating production in agro-exports, eliminating the most backward forms of production in this sector, reinserting the country's agro-exports in the international market and linking the country's industrial development to the expansion of this sector.

With this apparently conservative strategy, the Sandinista revolution has avoided the economic radicalism of other social revolutions in the Third World, the results of which have generally not been very encouraging. These results have not in themselves invalidated the more radical approach, but they have weighed heavily upon the decisions of those responsible for determining the economic policy of the Nica-raguan revolution. Moreover, a drastic reorientation of production towards the internal market and a concentration of investments in this direction would require alterations in the system of alliances upon which the leaders of the revolution have based their strategy of national reconstruction. And a rapid reduction of access to the international market in terms of imports would have a severe impact on the conditions of the popular classes – and not only on the higher-income groups – as a result of dislocations in the productive apparatus due to the country's extreme dependence on external inputs for the economy. At any rate, it is plausible to assume that a strategy of development based on a more radical reorientation of the economy would involve changes in the correlation of forces, in the profile of alliances and political as well as social costs that the revolutionary leadership has preferred not to face.

In the context of contemporary Nicaragua, reinsertion in the international market means, on the one hand, diversification of the country's agro-exports so that its foreign trade is freed from its traditional dependence on a small group of products – coffee, cotton, sugar and beef. The government's investment portfolio, for this reason, contains various important projects to develop the cultivation of the African palm, tobacco, sesame and other non-traditional export crops. This diversification will result in important modifications in the country's present growing regions, extension of the agricultural frontier into areas presently not under cultivation and the incorporation of vast unexploited zones into agricultural production.

On the other hand, reinsertion into the international market signifies diversification of the country's trading patterns and trading partners –

specifically the reduction of the traditional importance of the United States as the country's main source of trade, and increasing trade with Western Europe, the Third World and the socialist countries. The fact that Nicaragua now has trading relations and is receiving limited amounts of technical assistance from the socialist countries has been an object of severe criticism from the internal opposition and, of course, from the counter-revolution and the United States. However, even though the trading relations that Nicaragua now maintains with the socialist countries contrast strikingly with the pre-revolutionary period, the country still depends primarily for its trade upon the principal capitalist countries.

Within the revolutionary government and the FSLN, as well as among wide sectors of the Nicaraguan population, there is considerable sympathy and enthusiasm with regard to increasing economic co-operation with the socialist countries. International experience indicates that in general this produces much more positive results for developing countries than their traditional relations with the developed capitalist economies. However, a greater degree of integration of Nicaragua with the socialist economies requires certain minimal conditions upon which this integration could develop. Among these conditions, the most important is the establishment of a national system of planning and the development of the state's capacity to direct the national economy as a whole.

In every process of revolutionary transformation, one of the initial objectives of greatest importance consists of the state – as the institutional political expression of the strategic project of building a new society – acquiring the capacity to control and manage the economy. In a sense, the contradiction between state and market represents the opposition between the project of social, economic and political transformation and the tendencies towards reproduction of the pre-existing structures of the old society. The creation of the capacity to control and manage the economy implies a series of trials, tests, attempts and errors mixed with successes. In any event, it is a long and complicated process. Nicaragua is no exception in this regard. During the last six years, the government has been developing a system of annual programming which is indicative in character, and is only now establishing the basis for moving to a superior form of planning based on medium- and long-range plans.

Diverse factors of a political, economic and technical nature have affected the development of state planning in Nicaragua. One of the most important is the absence of a blueprint of the type of society that the revolution is attempting to construct. Important elements of such a design are contained in FSLN declarations that were elaborated during the struggle against Somoza, but they do not provide a blueprint. It was not until the end of 1981, and really during 1983, that the FSLN and the revolutionary government began to elaborate medium- and long-range development strategies, and the elaboration of possible models of social and economic organization.

The multi-class nature of the revolutionary block of forces, and the continuing commitment to a mixed economy schema, have also been important factors. The first, because the definition of a social, economic and political horizon for the process of revolutionary transformation implies an internal political debate within the revolutionary camp, and a relation of forces in which one of the components of the revolutionary block achieves an hegemonic position. This implies, therefore, the development of differences, tensions and even contradictions within the block. As for the mixed economy model, with the specific characteristics that it has assumed in the Sandinista revolution, an important and in fact majority role in the production system has been assigned to the private sector – large capitalists as well as small and medium private producers (individual, family and co-operative). As a result, planning is only imperative for the state sector of the economy. As in other cases of indicative planning within mixed economies, the fulfilment of goals depends upon the persuasive capacity of the state *vis-à-vis* private enterprise, the incentives that it offers the private sector and the efficacy of the public sector of the economy in carrying out its obligations.

Among the technical limitations upon the development of a national system of planning, Nicaragua suffers from a total lack of experience, the alarming absence of technical and professional cadres and the fact that the revolutionary state is still a state in formation. It is undeniably the case that the revolutionary government has made considerable progress down the road of economic planning, in some respects more than others. However, as the technical obstacles are overcome, the limitations of the mixed economy are made more evident, or at least, those having to do with the passive role adopted by private enterprise in this system.

In an economy such as Nicaragua, the adoption of a mixed economy schema under the conditions of continued insertion in the world market reduces considerably the capacity to plan the economy and to achieve greater economic and social rationality. In terms of the sector of small producers who produce for the internal market – especially peasant producers who are very important in Nicaragua – the state can plan prices, incomes and the general conditions of production, but it is not able to plan production itself, because this depends upon the decisions that are made by each of the thousands of small units of production that compose this sector. In relation to agro-exports generated in the APP, the state is able to plan production, but is not able to plan incomes, since these depend upon the international market over which the Nicaraguan economy has no control. In terms of the agro-exports that are produced by the private sector, planning is limited by two main factors: production depends upon the decisions of the bourgeoisie and prices as well as incomes are determined by the international market.

National Liberation and Social Revolution

Many foreign observers of the Sandinista revolution assume that it is a socialist revolution. The essays in this volume reveal that this is not so. It is not even possible to affirm that Nicaragua – like Cuba in the 1960s or Chile in the early 1970s – is undergoing a transition to socialism; if transition to socialism means the progressive socialization of both the forces and relations of production. This does not mean, however, that Nicaragua is undergoing a bourgeois democratic revolution. The Sandinista revolution has given birth to a popular, democratic and anti-imperialist regime, and has implanted forms of both popular and representative democracy in both the state sphere as well as civil society. Moreover, it is a social as well as a political revolution – and it neither serves nor represents the interests of the bourgeoisie. It clearly is a popular revolution that, while not intent upon eliminating the bourgeoisie, has severely undermined an important part of this class, and served the broad interests of the popular classes – the peasantry, the artisans, the workers, the semi-proletariat and fractions of the petty bourgeoisie. The incorporation of certain members of the bourgeoisie into the revolutionary government has taken place on an individual basis, not as representatives of their class, and always as subordinated elements to the revolutionary popular block of forces.

The Sandinista revolution can most accurately be characterized as a revolution of national liberation directed against imperialist domination as manifested in its contemporary neo-colonial and dependent capitalist form. As a result, the revolution seeks primarily to transform Nicaragua into a modern nation-state that is politically, economically and culturally independent of foreign domination.

This helps to explain the importance which the leaders of the revolution attach to national unity and to maintaining a multi-class alliance of political forces in support of a common project of national reconstruction. The contradictions between the classes that form the revolutionary block in this stage of reconstruction are considered less important than the advantages that the revolution obtains from unity. In other words, the revolutionary vanguard considers imperialist domination to be the principal contradiction in the present stage of the revolutionary transformation of Nicaraguan society. However, the effort to maintain national unity has implied increasing economic costs that in an important measure have been borne by the popular classes – the salaried workers in particular. As a result, the dialectic between national unity and class struggle appears to be the source of both tension and dynamism at this stage of the revolution.

Nothing that has been said above should be understood to mean that the Sandinista revolution is not interested in socialism or that the revolution will not lead Nicaragua towards a future transition to socialism. Nothing has happened in the last six years to indicate that a future transition to socialism will not be possible politically in the future. The basic documents of the Government of National Reconstruction indicate quite clearly that the tasks of national reconstruction cover a 'provisional period'.[7] As a result, it does not appear adventurous to suggest that the alliances which in this period support the revolution are also provisional. In fact, within this stage the project of national unity has undergone considerable change as the revolution has provoked the displacement of old allies and the incorporation of new ones.

Nevertheless, in the present historical moment, the priorities of the Nicaraguan revolution are national independence and popular democracy, not the transition to socialism. The possibility of a transition to socialism depends upon the achievement of these priorities and is, therefore, an option that remains open to the future development of the revolution. This option depends upon the dynamic unfolding of the revolution, which must at any rate first pass through the struggle to secure Nicaragua's national liberation and consolidate its new popular democracy.

Nicaragua should not be unfavourably compared with Cuba in this respect, since the rapid socialization of Cuban society took place under exceptional circumstances that have not been present in the case of Nicaragua. Six years is a relatively short period in the evolution of historical transformations that involve the replacement of one mode of production by another. The definition of the ultimate destination of social revolutions has generally taken much longer and involved considerable gestation. Thus, it is really too soon to pass judgement on the destiny of the Nicaraguan revolution.

As in other revolutions in the Third World, the transition to socialism in Nicaragua depends first upon a successful anti-imperialist struggle for national liberation. However, the many experiences where such struggles have not resulted in a genuine socialist project also indicate that such a transition is not spontaneous or inevitable. On the contrary, it is clear that national liberation struggles result in a transition to socialism only as a result of the conscious choice and organized efforts of the people led by a vanguard that assumes this project; in conditions that are in part given and in part created by the actions of this vanguard.

It depends upon the dynamics of Nicaraguan politics and the international context of the revolution, whether this choice and the required effort will be made to build a socialist society in Nicaragua. This is why the present effort to institutionalize both popular and representative forms of democracy, as well as Nicaragua's efforts to achieve a peaceful solution to the growing conflict in Central America are so important. The outcome in both cases will have a decisive effect upon the destiny of the Sandinista revolution.

In the present international context, marked by increasing US military intervention in Central America and aggression against Nicaragua, the prospects for a regional war appear to be growing. This has forced the Sandinista revolution to give priority to national defence and to maintaining production in the face of the continuous efforts of the United States government to blockade the economy and destabilize the revolutionary government. In this climate, the need to obtain international support for the survival of the revolution and for the defence of the country against the continuing attacks on its border areas, ports and economic infrastructure by the counter-revolutionary forces backed by the United States, have made it difficult for the revolutionary regime to adopt measures aimed at radically transforming Nicaraguan society.

The survival of the revolution in the face of US efforts to overthrow the Sandinista regime and turn the clock backwards in Nicaragua have demanded that the regime act with caution and reserve. In this kind of environment, the adoption of revolutionary measures and the definition of long-range revolutionary goals have been conditioned by the need to consolidate support for the regime and minimize internal conflict. The Sandinistas believe that a rapid move towards socialism at this time would cost Nicaragua much of the valuable support it receives from non-socialist countries, and give Washington grounds to justify its claims that Nicaragua is 'another Cuba'. The assistance which could be provided by the socialist countries could not compensate this loss nor come close to approximating the support received by Cuba over two decades ago.

We do not believe, however, that it is enough to ask whether a future transition to socialism is possible in the case of Nicaragua. It is clear that in the world today the concept of socialism is used to refer to a diversity of forms of social organization in countries as different as China and Czechoslovakia, the Soviet Union and Albania, Yugoslavia and the German Democratic Republic, Vietnam and Cuba – not to mention the multiple and many-faceted modes of transition to socialism in Africa and Asia. It is necessary, therefore, to ask what kind of socialism is likely to develop in Nicaragua.

The different forms of socialism that have emerged in the world are clearly the result of the type and degree of development of capitalism that existed at the moment of the revolutionary rupture. Various essays in this volume have indicated the heavy weight of small individual and family production in the Nicaraguan economy, and the unequal and incomplete character of the development of a capitalist class structure in Nicaragua. It is important, therefore, to ask what will be the destiny of these small producers if Nicaragua makes a transition to socialism. Will the country undergo a drastic and rapid process of collectivization, as has occurred in certain other cases? Or should we expect a type of socialism to develop, similar to that in certain countries of Europe and the Third World, where a large peasant economy continues to exist, although articulated and subordinated to a socialized state sector?

In such a case, what transformation would Nicaragua's APP have to undergo in order to assume effectively the role – proclaimed already in numerous documents and declarations – of the dynamic and strategic axis of structural transformation in the economy?

Even though the development of social revolutions in the 20th Century has provided a wealth of surprises and brusque changes in their orientation have been a frequent occurrence, the experience of the last six years in the case of the Nicaraguan revolution reveals the clear possibility that this revolution could take the road of a type of agrarian socialism, based upon small peasant producers, which incorporates elements of private enterprise and what in other contexts has been called the 'green revolution'. The country's medium-range investment projects are reinforcing this tendency, and the declarations of the leaders of the revolution appear to provide confirmation of it.[8]

In any case, the type of socialism that is constructed in Nicaragua will depend upon the composition of the block of popular forces that leads the process and the mode in which this block expresses itself as a political vanguard. Concretely, it will depend upon the political articulation between the peasantry, the small and medium producers in the urban areas and the working class; and the capacity of one of these to establish hegemony over the revolutionary block of forces. To the extent that it is possible to speculate about the future on the basis of present realities, everything seems to indicate that the perspective and interests of the peasantry will take primacy over those of the proletariat. Therefore, if there is a transition to socialism, it will be towards a socialism based on small property rather than a proletarian socialism, in the strict sense. A discussion of the possible achievements and the limitations of this type of socialism, of the material and international conditions affecting its viability over the long range, etc., obviously exceed the objectives of this essay and of this volume.

Popular Democracy in a Society under Siege*

The elections for president, vice-president and a constituent national legislature in November 1984 have helped to institutionalize the revolutionary state and democratize the revolutionary process at a time when Nicaragua is under attack by counter-revolutionary forces backed by the government of the United States, and when the revolution's long-range project of economic and social transformation has still not been clearly defined.

The calling of elections was in response to the commitment assumed voluntarily by the FSLN on 23 August 1980. This event has fulfilled the promise made by the Sandinistas on that occasion, and offers both to theoretical debate and the historical experience of social revolutions in the 20th Century what is possibly a unique situation.

* *This section revised by Richard Harris without the participation of Carlos Vilas.*

Traditionally, revolutionary parties and movements have denounced the institutions of representative democracy for being incapable of carrying through a social revolution, or even assuring popular parties a means of exercising effective governing power. Especially in the Third World, the complicity of this type of political system with the interests of the dominant classes and imperialist domination has been frequently denounced. The bloody demise of the Popular Unity Government of President Salvador Allende in Chile represents a tragic example of the failure of representative democracy in a situation where a popular government, with the broad support of the masses, was attempting to carry out social transformations demanded by the people.

Triumphant social revolutions have been more successful in constructing social and economic democracy than in permitting the direct participation of the people in the major political decisions of society. In general, these revolutions have created very centralized political systems, with a multiplicity of mediating institutions, where the most important functions of the state are not under the direct influence of the people.

Criticism of the limitations of traditional representative democracy has not always been accompanied by the creation of superior forms of participation. For this reason, the Sandinista revolution, by calling general and direct elections for the highest executive and legislative posts, has contributed something totally new to revolutionary experience – the articulation of revolutionary political legitimacy with the procedures of representative democracy. This will undoubtedly enrich the development of revolutionary theory, rejuvenate the debate over revolution and representative democracy and perhaps have important repercussions upon other societies where social revolutions are taking place.

The opposition to the revolution has lost considerable ground as a result of the calling of elections. For five years, they centred their criticisms and attacks on the revolutionary government around the issue of elections. They reduced the establishment of democracy to the exercise of suffrage and rejected the multiple forms of direct citizen participation that the revolution was creating and institutionalizing. When the FSLN in August 1980 made the commitment to call elections in 1985, the opposition denounced the government for the excessive delay and suggested that in fact the FSLN had no real intention of resorting to elections. However, when the FSLN and the revolutionary government made it clear that they would fulfil their promise and even move up the date of the elections to November 1984, the opposition repudiated the decision and began to threaten that they would not participate in the elections. It is difficult in view of these circumstances not to conclude that the issue of elections, as put forward by the opposition, has never been more than an excuse for opposing the revolution, instead of a real commitment on their part to democratic ideals and the exercise of representative democracy. Moreover, the historical background of the opposition parties and their social base of support offer few reasons to think otherwise.[9]

The Sandinistas sincerely want the bourgeoisie, or at least significant sectors of it, to participate in the revolutionary project. The FSLN continues to seek national unity in the form of a broad-based multi-class alliance committed to the development of the economy and the defence of the country's national independence. They have offered guarantees and incentives in return for the co-operation of the bourgeoisie. However, the conduct of this class since the revolutionary triumph raises serious doubts about whether they can be expected to participate in a revolutionary project that calls for their co-operation but restricts their political influence and gives priority to the interests of the popular classes (the peasantry and the workers).

The boycott of the recent elections by the ultra-rightist parties and COSEP has revealed the extent to which important sectors of the bourgeoisie – backed by the Reagan administration – are opposed to the Sandinista regime and its revolutionary project. It is now unmistakably clear that this internal opposition to the revolutionary process is directly linked to the external forces of armed counter-revolution and the interventionist project of the United States.

The right-wing bourgeoisie's boycott of the elections has contributed to their increasing political marginality and diminishing political influence within Nicaragua. In contrast, the large voter turn-out and the overwhelming majority of votes cast for the FSLN have given added legitimacy to the Sandinistas' political leadership. More than 75 per cent of the registered voters went to the polls, despite the ultra-right's appeal to the citizenry to boycott the elections. And 67 per cent of the voters gave their support to the Sandinistas. The remaining votes were divided between the other six parties on the ballot – three to the left of the FSLN and three to the right. Each of these parties are now represented in the new National Assembly. Only the abstaining ultra-right parties are without representation, due to their refusal to participate in the elections.

The elections and the institutionalization of representative demo-cracy in Nicaragua can be seen, at least in part, as a means of defending the revolutionary regime. The elections have discredited one of the main pretexts which the US government has used to justify its undeclared war, that is, that the Sandinista government is illegitimate and totalitarian. Moreover, the democratization of Nicaragua's revolu-tionary political system has helped to strengthen the international support which the Sandinista regime receives from social democratic governments and parties throughout Western Europe.

Through both direct aggression and indirect measures, the United States has created an extremely hostile international environment for revolutionary Nicaragua. In addition to US economic aggression aimed at destabilizing the economy, the Reagan administration has militarized two of Nicaragua's hostile neighbours – Honduras and El Salvador. And in the case of Honduras, it has turned this country into a forward base for direct US military intervention against Nicaragua. Moreover, as a result of US direction, financial support, training and equipment, the disparate counter-revolutionary groups (composed of Somoza's former National Guardsmen and reactionary Nicaraguan exiles) have been brought together into a co-ordinated armed force that has been able to inflict increasing damage and casualties inside Nicaragua. Thus, the Reagan administration has moved into place all the military elements for a full-scale invasion of Nicaragua. What is lacking is the right pretext and political climate for such an invasion.

If the Reagan administration does decide to invade Nicaragua, the Sandinistas know that it will be up to the Nicaraguan people to defend the country's national sovereignty. This is why they have mobilized the citizenry into civilian militia units at the neighbourhood and village level, and created a popular defence structure in which the entire population has been given the task of defending the country against an invasion.

Thus, the Nicaraguan revolution enters its seventh year since the triumph over the Somoza dictatorship with the Nicaraguan people confronting ever more difficult economic conditions and a war directed against them by the country with the greatest military power in history. In spite of these unfavourable conditions, however, this small country in the neo-colonial backyard of the United States continues to provide the world with an important example of a popular, democratic and anti-imperialist revolution. In the six years since the overthrow of the Somoza dictatorship, this revolution has irreversibly transformed Nicaraguan society and it holds out the prospect of even greater revolutionary transformations in the future.

Notes

1. The connection of the Nicaraguan revolution and the struggle of the FSLN with Nicaragua's previous history of anti-imperialist struggle was given particular importance by Carlos Fonseca, one of the founders and the leader of the FSLN until his death in combat in 1976. See, for example, his article: 'Sintesis de algunos problemas actuales', in Carlos Fonseca, *Bajo la bandera del Sandinismo: Textos Politicos* (Managua: Editorial Nueva Nicaragua, 1981), p. 315.

2. A complete summary of North American political and military interventions in Nicaragua can be found in Carlos Fonseca, ibid., pp. 235–6.

3. See Carlos M. Vilas, *Perfiles de la Revolución Sandinista* (Buenos Aires: Editorial Legasa, 1984), ch. 2.

4. Comandante de la Revolución Jaime Wheelock, 'El FSLN conduce al estado y jamás lo sustituye', in *Habla la Dirección de la Vanguardia* (Managua: Departamento de Propaganda y Educacion Politica del FSLN, 1981, pp. 54–5.

5. Ibid., p. 55.

6. See, for example, Orlando Núñez, *El Somocismo: Desarrollo y contradicciones del modelo agroexportador en Nicaragua (1950–1975)* (La Habana: Centro de Estudios sobre America, 1980).

7. See 'El Programa de la Junta de Gobierno de Reconstruccion Nacional de Nicaragua (9 de julio 1979)' in CEPAL, *Nicaragua: El Impacto de la mutación politica* (Santiago de Chile: Naciones Unidas, 1981).

8. See, for example, the speech of Comandante Jaime Wheelock in the Constituent Assembly of the Asociacion de Trabajadores del Campo 20 and 21 December 1979; also MIDINRA, *Tres Años de reforma agaria* (Managua, 1982), p. 18, and the statements by Comandante Wheelock in *Barricada*, on 20 April and 25 June 1982, and in *El Nuevo Diario*, 15 August 1983. According to these repeated declarations, the APP is not to represent, in the agricultural sector, more than 20 to 25 per cent of the arable land, the co-operative sector will account for 40 per cent and the rest will correspond to individual peasant farmers and capitalist enterprises.

9. See, for example, B. Diederich, *Somoza and the Legacy of U.S. Involvement in Central America* (New York: E.P. Dutton, 1981); and James Booth, *The End and the Beginning: The Nicaraguan Revolution* (Boulder: Westview Press, 1982).

10 Epilogue: A Revolution Under Siege

Richard L. Harris

US Aggression Against Nicaragua

During the last year, US aggression against Nicaragua has increased to an alarming degree. The US-backed counter-revolutionary forces based in Honduras and Costa Rica have greatly increased their attacks upon the civilian population and the economic infrastructure of the country. The participation of US troops, as well as air and naval units, in on-going military exercises in Honduras increasingly look like the preparations for an invasion of Nicaragua and less like actions intended merely to intimidate the Sandinistas. During April 1985, nearly 7,000 US military personnel – the largest contingent so far –were involved in joint military manoeuvres with Honduran forces near the border with Nicaragua. And another 43,000 US personnel were involved in related manoeuvres along the East Coast of the United States.[1] Moreover, Washington's false accusations about Soviet military assistance (e.g. the supposed delivery of MIG jet-fighters) to Nicaragua give the impression that Washington is trying to develop this pretext as the justification for a direct military intervention in the near future. Finally, the Reagan administration's recent decision to impose a total trade embargo and additional economic sanctions on Nicaragua are only the latest steps in its four-year campaign of economic aggression aimed at destabilizing the country's economy through cutting Nicaragua off from its traditional sources of essential imports, loans and credits.

The victims of the United States' so-called covert war against Nicaragua now include over 7,000 men, women and children who have been killed by the Contra attacks (see Table 10.1). Apart from soldiers and members of the civilian militia, this figure includes teachers, health workers, local government officials, members of the Sandinista mass organizations, technicians and international volunteers who were involved in carrying out social reforms and development projects aimed at improving the living conditions of the general population. Also included are innocent peasants, school-children, church workers and other civilians who have been in the path of the marauding bands of the

Contras. The number of children and adolescents that have been killed exceeds 3,000, and more than 6,000 children have been turned into war orphans. In a very real sense, the Contras are waging a war of terror against the civilian population. This has been the pattern ever since the first ex-National Guardsmen started attacking the frontier areas from their camps in Honduras, shortly after the revolutionary triumph. The terrorism that characterizes the Contras' tactics includes rapes, ambushes and massacres carried out against the inhabitants of small rural communities, co-operatives and private farms. In just over four years, these CIA-backed mercenary forces have attacked close to 100 civilian communities, and caused the displacement of over 150,000 persons from their homes and farms.

The Contras systematically kidnap civilians. This is not an original idea on their part. It is one of the tactics which the CIA has taught them to use, as revealed in the notorious manual on 'psychological warfare' prepared by the CIA for the training of the Contra units based in Honduras.[2] In practice, it seems the Contras are not as selective in their kidnapping as the CIA manual suggests. Not only do they abduct local civilian government officials, they also kidnap large numbers of peasants. According to the testimony of kidnap victims who have escaped, those who are not killed are either forced to work as 'beasts of burden' for the Contras or to join their ranks as recruits. Evidence of this and the many atrocities committed by the Contras has been collected by respected human rights organizations such as Americas Watch, the Washington Office on Latin America (WOLA) and the International Human Rights Law Group.

The Contras' attacks have destroyed or damaged an important part of the economic infrastructure of the country – bridges, port facilities, granaries, water and oil deposits, electrical power stations, telephone lines, saw mills, health centres, agricultural co-operatives, schools, dams, etc. Eighty state-owned enterprises and co-operatives have been destroyed and on average, ten farming co-operatives have been attacked every month. In the northern departments of Matagalpa and Jinotega, 700 peasants have been killed and more than 1,000 have been kidnapped and forced to replace casualties in the ranks of the counter-revolutionary forces. Material losses are estimated at over $5 million, including the destruction of a good portion of the 1985 coffee harvest.[3] Between January and March 1985, 17 private coffee farms were destroyed and some 50,000 people were displaced as a result of the Contras' attacks.

During the first months of 1985, the Contras made strikes in half of Nicaragua's 16 departments, and during January alone, the Nicaraguan army engaged the Contras in 71 battles.[4] The heaviest fighting has been in the northern departments of Matagalpa, Jinotega, Madrid and Zelaya. However, the possibility of the Contras seizing and holding enough territory to proclaim a provisional government seems quite

Table 10.1 Losses Incurred through December 1984

Total deaths	7,430
Children and adolescents killed	3,346
Private farm-owners killed	190
War orphans	6,339
Campesino and Indian population displaced	150,000
Health centers destroyed or damaged	41
Health workers killed (including 2 European doctors)	28
Health workers kidnapped or injured	41
Schools destroyed	14
Schools forced to close	359
Child-care centres destroyed	10
Teachers killed	170
Adult education collectives forced to close	840
Members of these collectives killed	247
Civilian communities attacked	97
State-owned co-operatives and enterprises attacked	80
Total economic losses	*US$ 1.1 billion*

Losses Inflicted During the Coffee Harvest (January–March 1985)

Private farms destroyed	17
Coffee-pickers killed	39
Material losses	US$ 1 million
Rural population displaced	50,000
Cost of resettling population	US$50 million

Source: *Barricada Internacional*, 4 April 1985, p. 6.

remote. In fact, US military experts say that the Contras need between $30 million and $50 million a year to pose a serious threat to the Sandinistas. This level of funding exceeds the $80 million channelled through the CIA between 1981 and 1984 and the $27 million which the US Congress has voted to give the Contras in 'non-lethal' aid during 1985. (Even during the temporary aid cut-off, the Contras had been receiving from private sources about $500,000 to $1 million a month.) Meanwhile the Nicaraguan army has undertaken a major offensive against the Contras. An estimated 60,000 troops have been deployed in the northern border regions. These troops are being used to inflict heavy casualties on the Contras and to force them to retreat back to their bases in Honduras.

The most numerous and important Contra group is the so-called Nicaraguan Democratic Force (FDN), which operates out of bases in Honduras and is estimated to have between 12,000 and 16,000 troops.[5] The core elements of the FDN are former members of Somoza's hated National Guard, who fled to Honduras when the revolutionary forces toppled Somoza's dictatorship. Washington refuses to acknowledge that Somoza's former murderers and torturers are among those whom Reagan refers to as 'freedom fighters' and 'the moral equivalent to the Founding Fathers of the United States'. Since 1983, the CIA has exercised direct tactical control of the FDN's operations inside Nicaragua.[6] The second largest group, the Democratic Revolutionary Alliance (ARDE), was formed in 1981, and is based in Costa Rica. ARDE contains about 2,000 combatants and claims to have another 8,000 non-combatants.[7] Its military commander is Eden Pastora Gomez, a former Sandinista comandante. He is on poor terms with Adolfo Robelo Callejas, the political director of ARDE, who was one of the bourgeois members of the original five-person junta formed after the revolutionary triumph in July 1979. Pastora has received very little aid from the CIA, and has refused to co-operate with the FDN leaders whom he views as tainted by their former association with the Somoza dictatorship. The remaining counter-revolutionary forces are composed of Miskito and Rama Indians. One group, MISURA, is led by the Miskito leader, Steadman Fagoth Müller, who has between 2,000 and 3,000 armed followers. MISURA has received support from the CIA and is allied with the FDN. The other group, MISURASATA, is headed by Brooklyn Rivera, who is at present negotiating with the Sandinistas. This Miskito group, which has no more than 600 combatants, was formerly allied with ARDE but has recently suspended military actions. Rivera claims that both the FDN and ARDE have plans to assassinate him.[8]

Even with renewed financial assistance from the US government, it is highly unlikely that these counter-revolutionary forces can topple the revolutionary government in Managua. They have succeeded in disrupting the economy and terrorizing the population, but it is clear that only a direct military intervention on the part of the United States can overthrow the Sandinistas. The feasibility of a US invasion appears to depend in part upon how quickly US forces and the Contras, perhaps in combination with Honduran and Salvadoran troops, could dominate the military situation in Nicaragua. If the country could be brought under control in a few weeks, the Reagan administration could achieve its goal before the US Congress and public opinion could react.[9] However, most US military experts appear to agree that a more prolonged conflict would be necessary. Most invasion scenarios envisage an invasion force of at least 60,000 US troops, air strikes on Nicaragua's major cities and ports and a prolonged war against the Sandinistas in the more remote areas of the country. The political costs of a military undertaking of this nature would appear to be too high to justify such a course of action under present circumstances.

An easy, backdoor means of overthrowing the revolutionary regime in Nicaragua does not exist for the United States. In order to overthrow the Sandinistas and reverse the revolutionary process in Nicaragua, the Reagan administration will have to send US troops to Nicaragua and be willing to pay for this with the lives of thousands of US soldiers. It has been estimated that US casualties would be between 4,000 and 5,000 dead and 9,000 to 18,000 wounded. Probably tends of thousands of Nicaraguans would die defending their villages, factories and neighbourhoods. Since the Reagan administration does not appear to be willing at the present time to pay this price, it has chosen to increase pressure on the revolutionary regime and the Nicaraguan people through the application of a variety of measures designed to destabilize the economy and brutalize the population. These measures include the present US trade embargo and the possibility of breaking diplomatic relations and perhaps imposing a naval quarantine on the country.

Elections and the Institutionalization of Democracy

In view of this extremely hostile climate, the decision of the FSLN to institutionalize a system of representative democracy in Nicaragua is an extraordinary occurrence. The national elections held in November 1984 represent an important achievement in the democratization of the revolutionary process. The results of these elections have demonstrated quite clearly that the Sandinistas are supported by the vast majority of the Nicaraguan people. Thus, the elections have reinforced the legitimacy of the revolutionary process as well as the leadership of the FSLN, both within Nicaragua and internationally.

Since the FSLN received 67 per cent of the votes cast, its presidential and vice-presidential candidates, Daniel Ortega and Sergio Ramirez, were elected to office, and the FSLN was guaranteed a substantial majority of the seats in the new National Assembly. The rest of the votes were distributed in the following manner: 14 per cent for the Democratic Conservative Party (PCD); 9.6 per cent for the Independent Liberal Party (PLI); 5.6 per cent for the Popular Social Christian Party (PPSC); 1.5 per cent for the Nicaraguan Communist Party (PCN); 1.3 per cent for the Nicaraguan Socialist Party (PSN); and 1 per cent for the Marxist-Leninist Popular Action Movement (MAP-ML).[10] All of these parties gained representation in the new National Asembly in direct proportion to the percentage of votes they received in the elections. Moreover, the presidential candidates of these parties were also given seats in the assembly. Thus, the electoral system has guaranteed that the legislature reflects the plurality of political positions in the country, with the exception of the ultra-right-wing parties who followed Washington's bidding and boycotted the elections. The National Assembly now contains 61 representatives of the FSLN, 14 of the PCD, 9 of the PLI, 6 of the PPSC, 2 of the PCN, 2 of the PSN and 2 of the MAP-ML.

The character of the election campaign was not what many had originally expected. In contrast with the other parties, the FSLN made very few promises. It largely confined itself to making appeals to the people to defend the country's national sovereignty and to consolidate the gains of the revolution. Its principal promise was to continue the struggle for a just society based upon popular participation. The results of the voting were a clear rejection of the positions taken by the other parties. The PCD and the PLI blamed the Sandinistas for the war and demogogically proposed the abolition of obligatory military service as well as government controls over the distribution of basic commodities. There was even less support for the parties to the left of the FSLN (PCN, PSN and MAP-ML), who called for a 'revolution within the revolution' and promised to give Nicaragua's small working class a hegemonic role in the revolutionary state.[11]

The elections were regarded by the Sandinistas as important to the defence of the country's national sovereignty and its revolutionary process. The elections were also an important manifestation of the Nicaraguan people's right to self-determination. In effect, the elections have eliminated one of the pretexts which the United States has used to justify its aggression against the revolutionary regime, namely, the supposed illegitimacy and totalitarian nature of the Sandinista government.

Of Nicaragua's 1.5 million registered voters, 75 per cent participated in the elections. This high level of participation in the electoral process repudiated the arguments of the counter-revolutionary opponents of the regime who claimed that proper conditions for fair elections did not exist. The large voter turn-out and the large number of votes received by the FSLN, in what all international observers agreed was a corruption-free election, was a clear refutation of the abstentionist position taken by the ultra-right parties grouped together in the so-called Nicaraguan Democratic Co-ordinating Coalition (CDN). This coalition is made up of the Social Christian Party (PSC), the Social Democratic Party (PSD), the Constitutional Liberal Party (PLC) and the Nicaraguan Conservative Party (PCN); as well as two right-wing trade union federations and the Superior Council of Private enterprise (COSEP).

Under the titular leadership of Arturo Cruz, former Nicaraguan ambassador to the United States and one of the original members of the five-person revolutionary junta set up after the fall of Somoza, the CDN coalition did everything it could to discredit the Sandinistas and convince the voters that they should abstain from voting in the elections. Cruz, who has lived in the United States since he was forced to resign his post as ambassador, was sent by Washington to be the last-minute presidential candidate of the CDN and to demand that the elections be postponed and the Sandinistas enter into negotiations with the Contras as a condition for the CDN's participation in the elections. The Sandinistas refused to accept these conditions, and the parties in the CDN refused to participate in the elections. However, their refusal to enter the elections and the fact that they now have no representation in the new National Assembly has only served further to marginalize these reactionary elements from the political process in Nicaragua.

The by-laws and general statute of Nicaragua's new National Assembly were approved on 20 March 1985, after six long sessions of heated debate between the seven parties represented in this body. The general statute defines the assembly as the legislative body of the government and empowers it to draft a new constitution for the country. A special commission of the legislature, composed of representatives of all seven parties, must present a draft constitution to the assembly by February 1986. The commission is required to hold national hearings in order to obtain the opinion of the different sectors of Nicaraguan society concerning the drafting of the constitution. In drafting each article of the constitution, the commission will seek to achieve consensus among its members in order to reflect the actual range of views in the country.[12]

The National Assembly is empowered to decree amnesties, ratify international treaties and interpellate ministers. The president has the power to decree laws relating to fiscal and administrative matters and enter into international and economic agreements. The president may also declare a state of emergency if the situation warrants, during which time the executive branch would assume legislative powers, except for the drafting of the constitution. The general statute stipulates that legislative bills may be introduced by any member of the assembly, the president, the Supreme Court and the Supreme Electoral Council. It also provides for the composition of the assembly executive committee, which presently consists of representatives from the FSLN, the Democratic Conservative Party, the Socialist and Popular Social Christian parties.[13]

The general statute of the assembly has met with criticism from five of the six opposition parties. Only the Democratic Conservative Party (PCD) joined with the FSLN in giving overall support to this basic law which establishes the legislature's character, functions, etc. For example, the Marxist-Leninist Popular Action Movement (MAP-ML) has voiced disapproval of the formal prerogatives that the law gives to the right-wing parties (the PCD, the PLI and the PPSC), and argues that this reflects the 'FSLN's attempts at reconciliation with the bourgeoisie'.[14] The reference here is to the provision in the general statute which recognizes what are called 'parliamentary factions' (i.e. parties with four or more seats) and gives these factions an administrative budget, office space, etc. The Nicaraguan Communist Party (PCN) has also voiced the same criticisms, and views with concern the alliance between the FSLN and the PCD. Moreover, all the smaller parties have objected to the provision which requires only 60 per cent of the membership to be present for a quorum (this requires only the FSLN representatives to be present), and the same percentage for over-riding an executive veto and approving the constitution.[15]

In general, it appears that the parties to the right of the FSLN favour a 'Western democratic' constitution in which the mass organizations would be separated from the state and there would be few restrictions on private enterprise.[16] They want new elections within two years, municipal autonomy for Nicaragua's local governments and an executive branch with less powers than at present. In other words, they want a constitution that provides the traditional institutional framework of a bourgeois parliamentary democracy. The parties to the left of the FSLN, on the other hand, want to put an end to the country's mixed economy and replace its present governmental structures based upon political pluralism with a more revolutionary state based upon 'workers' control'. In contrast to both the left- and the right-wing parties, the FSLN seeks to institutionalize the embryonic system of 'people's power' through increasing the involvement of the mass organizations in the formulation and implementation of state policies, while at the same time institutionalizing parliamentary representative structures.

Nicaragua's Economic Crisis

Although the elections represent a major advance in the political realm, Washington's undeclared war on Nicaragua has greatly aggravated the economic problems faced by the revolutionary regime. The damages caused to the economy by the war are estimated to exceed more than $1 billion,[17] and the losses during 1984 were the equivalent of 30 per cent of the nation's exports. The Contra attacks have caused a fall in the production of basic grains as well as the cultivation and harvesting of the country's agro-export crops. Furthermore, more than one-quarter of the national budget was spent on defence in 1984, and the amount destined for defence in 1985 will amount to 40 per cent of the total budget.[18] The financial burden of defence has forced the government to raise taxes and limit funds for education and other social programmes. The government has also been forced to discontinue its previous policy of providing subsidies for a variety of basic consumer goods and allow the prices of these goods to be determined by the market. This has resulted in stiff price increases and an annual inflation rate of over 200 per cent.

By February 1985, the economic situation had deteriorated to such an extent that President Ortega, speaking for the National Directorate of the FSLN, was forced to tell the Nicaraguan people that 'no one should expect that we will be able to overcome the destabilization of our economy in the short-run ... We are living through decisive moments for the future of our country and these moments demand a spirit of struggle and sacrifice.'[19]

In this same public message, President Ortega announced a series of emergency economic measures, including a reduction in state spending, a freeze on government hiring, the devaluation of the currency, the elimination of subsidies on basic goods, a readjustment of wages and salaries, new incentives for the producers of certain products (especially agro-exports) and a revision of all programmes within the various ministries with a view to eliminating those not considered to be essential. In other words, the critical economic situation has required the government to change the course of its economic policies. The present course involves directing an increasing proportion of the country's scarce resources to the war effort, and eliminating or reducing many of the programmes aimed at improving the material conditions of the general population.

The country's foreign debt has climbed to $4.35 billion (65 per cent more than the GDP and equivalent to more than Nicaragua could earn from its exports in the next ten years). In 1985, the interest payments on this debt will amount to $872 million.[20] Since Nicaragua's annual export earnings total no more than $450 million, it is highly unlikely that the government will be able to make good on these payments.

The Reagan administration's decision to impose a trade embargo on Nicaragua is designed further to aggravate the country's already precarious economic situation. This measure has frequently been mentioned by US officials as a measure which will transform widespread grumbling among the population into active resistance to the revolutionary government. However, in spite of Nicaragua's economic crisis, the US trade embargo will not have the desired effect. Although the United States has been Nicaragua's main trading partner throughout this century, the revolutionary government has diversified the country's trade over the last six years. In 1980, Nicaragua sold 33 per cent of its exports to and bought 27 per cent of imports from the United States, but now these percentages have dropped to 5 per cent and 16 per cent respectively.[21] New customers in Japan, Canada and Western Europe are likely to buy the meat, bananas, coffee and seafood which Nicaragua has exported to the United States in recent years.[22] And US spare parts, chemicals and other imports are less and less necessary as new machinery and equipment are imported from the socialist countries, Europe, Mexico and Brazil. Furthermore, the population's discontent with the worsening economic situation – rising prices, shortages, etc. – is not likely to turn into active opposition to the regime, since most people know that the United States is largely responsible for the hardships they are now enduring.

The Objectives of US Policy

The government of the United States has aggravated Nicaragua's economic problems. The Contra attacks and the measures taken by Washington to prevent Nicaragua from obtaining loans, credits and essential imports have complicated an already critical economic situation. The Reagan administration has left little doubt that it seeks the overthrow of the Sandinista regime and a reversal of the revolutionary process. At a televised news conference on 21 February 1985, President Reagan stated boldly that the objective of US policy was to 'remove' the 'present structure' of government in Nicaragua. When pressed to say whether he meant that the United States was seeking the overthrow of the Sandinista government, he replied: 'Not if the present government would turn around and say "uncle" to the Nicaraguan rebels ...'[23]

For the Reagan administration, the existence of a revolutionary, anti-imperialist state in the neo-colonial backyard of the United States is intolerable, since it places in doubt both the willingness and the capacity of the US government to maintain not only its hegemony in the Western hemisphere but its global predominance.[24] Thus, global considerations compel Washington to substitute the popularly elected government in Nicaragua with one that will follow Washington's dictates. The same considerations led the United states to depose the popularly elected governments of Jacobo Arbenz in Guatemala (1954), Juan Bosch in the Dominican Republic (1965) and Salvador Allende in Chile (1973). However, in the case of Nicaragua, there is considerable domestic opposition to US efforts to overthrow the Sandinista government. Following the mining of Nicaragua's ports in early 1984, the outraged US Congress voted to suspend further financial assistance to the Contras. 'Non-lethal' aid to the Contras has recently been approved by the US Congress (June 1985), in spite of the opposition of a large number of Representatives.

The Reagan administration claims that it is interested in negotiating with Nicaragua's revolutionary government in order to arrive at a peaceful resolution of the conflict between the two countries, but the actions of the United States government appear to contradict these claims. Washington also repeatedly states that it supports the Contadora Group's efforts to find a political solution to the conflict in Central America. Yet the actions taken by the US government in the region appear to run counter to the efforts being made by the Contadora Group.

The draft peace treaty produced out of the meetings between the Contadora Group and the five Central American governments has so far been agreed to by only Nicaragua. US objections to the original draft have kept Costa Rica, Honduras and El Salvador from agreeing to it. At the April 1985 meeting in Panama, the representatives of the Contadora Group and the Central American states addressed most of the objections raised by the United States and its Central American allies. However, shortly before the meeting, President Reagan released a 'peace proposal' that clearly appeared to block the Contadora process. Reagan's proposal called for an immediate 60-day cease-fire between the Sandinista government and the Contras, during which the local hierarchy of the Catholic Church (closely associated with the US and the counter-revolution) would mediate negotiations between the two sides and preparations would be made for holding new elections in which the Contras would participate.[25] According to this proposal, if no agreement was reached by the end of the 60-day period, the US government would resume military aid to the Contras. The Nicaragua government immediately rejected the proposal as an ultimatum and described it as 'a pistol pointed at our head'. Managua reiterated its position favouring direct dialogue with the US government, and called on the Reagan administration to return to the bilateral talks in Manzanillo, Mexico, which were unilaterally suspended by the United States in June 1984.[26]

The Reagan proposal resembled in many respects a declaration signed on 2 March by some 40 counter-revolutionary leaders meeting in San José, Costa Rica. This document called for an immediate cease-fire, negotiations between the Contras and the Nicaraguan government, the disarming of the population and the dissolution of the National Assembly. It gave a deadline to the revolutionary government of 20 April to accept these conditions or face a continuation of the war without any further prospects for negotiation. Among those present at the meeting were Arturo Cruz of the CDN, Alfonso Robelo of ARDE and Adolfo Calero of the FDN. On 6 April, these three leaders came to the United States to solicit support for their position. Shortly thereafter, Reagan announced his peace proposal.[27]

In an 11 April letter to the heads of state of the Contadora Group, President Ortega described Reagan's peace plan as 'a dictatorial interference in the internal affairs of a sovereign nation' and an open admission that the US government is waging war against Nicaragua. He also accused the United States of blocking and discrediting the search for a peaceful solution to the problems of the Central American region.[28] During the April Contadora meeting, a permanent verification and control commission was established to monitor the military situation in each Central American country, including the number of troops, armaments and foreign advisers. The Contadora peace plan proposes an immediate end to the arms race by requiring each country to halt acquisitions of military equipment, close down all foreign military bases and remove all foreign military advisers. No agreement has been reached so far between the Central American states concerning these provisions of the proposed peace treaty. However, the tentative agreement on the setting up of a permanent verification and control mechanism is an encouraging sign, given all the setbacks which the Contadora process has experienced and Reagan's recent 'peace proposal'.

Having three times invaded and occupied Nicaragua in this century, and having recently invaded Grenada, the United States has shown that it will use direct military intervention to achieve its objectives in the Central American and Caribbean region. Moreover, it appears that the Reagan administration, after the 'success' of the Grenada invasion and Reagan's re-election, is now less constrained than before by the prospect of strong public reaction within the United States to future military action directed against Nicaragua. The opponents of Reagan's Nicaragua policy in the US Congress have so far helped to prevent such a course of action, but Nicaragua's military preparedness and the readiness of the civilian population to defend the country against an invasion have been the primary factors that have deterred a direct military intervention by the United States. Comandante Humberto Ortega, Nicaragua's Minister of Defence, stated this clearly at the celebration of the founding of the country's civilian militias when he said that the Reagan administration has not launched an invasion 'fundamentally because our people have weapons in their hands, and know how to use them'.[29]

If the United States does decide to invade Nicaragua, it will find the population armed and capable of defending their homeland. The Sandinistas have organized and armed the citizenry into popular militia units at the neighbourhood and village level. As many as 250,000 people – men and women – can be mobilized on this basis in a matter of hours.[30] Their basic function is to defend their own communities, which makes them a fundamental element in the government's strategy of defending the country against an invasion. They have undergone basic military training, are led by seasoned regular army personnel and are armed with AKA assault rifles, rocket-launchers, mortars and grenades. They are an essential complement to the regular army (composed of about 48,000 troops) which is considerably smaller than the combined forces of Honduras (15,500), El Salvador (39,000) and the Contras (16,000 to 18,000).[31]

Thus, Nicaragua's revolutionary leaders have placed the major responsibility for defending the country upon the citizenry. In fact, the nature of the country's popular structure of national defence is such that only a massive invasion, involving a sizeable number of US ground troops, could hope to overwhelm it. And even an invasion of this nature would probably only succeed in gaining control over the urban areas, leaving the rural areas to become the staging grounds for a prolonged guerrilla-style popular resistance against the occupation forces.

Conclusion

After throwing off the yoke of over half a century of US domination and the tyrannical dictatorship which the United States kept in power for 40 years, the Nicaraguan people are determined never again to submit to Washington's dictates. The Reagan administration's undeclared war against Nicaragua has failed to undermine this determination or overthrow the country's popularly elected revolutionary government. After years of trying to rally opposition to the Sandinistas and millions of dollars of financial support and military assistance, Reagan's 'freedom fighters' have failed to weaken popular support for the Sandinistas or gain control over any important part of Nicaraguan territory. However, the war of destruction and terror carried out by these surrogate forces of US imperialism has succeeded in disrupting the country's economic recovery and brutalizing the population. Thus, the Contras have little support among the Nicaraguan people and the United States is rightly blamed for the country's present economic crisis as well as the atrocities committed by its brutal henchmen.

Nicaragua and the Contadora Group countries are committed to finding a peaceful solution to the conflicts in Central America that threaten to engulf the entire region in a regional war. Nicaragua is the only country which has agreed to accept, without conditions, the draft peace plan elaborated by the Contadora Group. However, a peaceful solution to the conflicts in Central America clearly requires the support of the United States, and the actions of the Reagan administration indicate that Washington does not want a political solution which permits the revolutionary government of Nicaragua to remain in power. As a result, a peaceful solution to the problems of the region is blocked by the United States.

What the US government fears is that revolutionary Nicaragua will succeed in demonstrating to the rest of Latin America and the world in general that it is possible for a small, underdeveloped country to follow an independent course of political and economic development – even if it is located in the neo-colonial backyard of the United States. This not only threatens US hegemony within the western hemisphere, it threatens the global interests of the United States and its credibility as the predominant force in the international system. Washington has responded to Nicaragua's assertion of national independence with a vengeance. It has cut off trade, loans and credits to Nicaragua and has backed the counter-revolutionary forces that are waging war on the Nicaraguan people from their bases in Honduras and Costa Rica. The course of the revolutionary process in Nicaragua has been adversely affected by these actions, but it has not been reversed or subverted. Only a direct military intervention by the United States appears capable of stopping the revolutionary process in Nicaragua. The destiny of the Nicaraguan revolution, therefore, depends upon the capacity of the revolutionary government and the Nicaraguan people to deter a US military intervention. This requires that the revolutionary regime continue its support for the Contadora process, strengthen its international backing, extend the democratization of the revolutionary process and maintain at a high state of readiness the country's popular-based structure of national defence.

Notes

1. '7,000 Going to War Games in Honduras', *San Francisco Chronicle*, 12 April 1985, p. 23.

2. 'CIA: Reagan Orders it to Probe Manual', *Los Angeles Times*, 19 October 1984, p. 8.

3. 'New Life for Displaced Families', *Barricada Internacional*, 28 March 1985, p. 7.

4. *Barricada Internacional*, 28 February 1985.

5. 'Nicaragua: Will US Squeeze Lead to War?', *US News and World Report*, 1 April 1985, p. 30.

6. Allan Nairn, 'Endgame', *NACLA Report on the Americas*, vol. 18, no. 3 (May–June 1984), p. 48.

7. *US News and World Report*, 1 April 1985, p. 30.

8. *Barricada Internacional*, 28 February 1985.

9. Nairn, 'Endgame', p. 50.

10. 'First Free Elections', *Barricada Internacional*, Archives no. 17, 20 December 1984, p. 2.

11. William Robinson and Ken Norsworthy, 'Elections and US Intervention in Nicaragua', *Latin American Perspectives* (Spring 1985), pp. 83–102.

12. *Barricada Internacional*, 28 March 1985, p. 4.

13. Ibid.

14. Ibid.

15. *Barricada Internacional*, 4 April 1985, p. 9.

16. Ken Norsworthy and William Robinson, 'Strengthening National Unity, Deepening Popular Power', *Line of March* (21 January 1985), pp. 8–9.

17. *Barricada Internacional*, 14 February 1985, p. 6.

18. Ibid.

19. Ibid.

20. Ibid.

21. *Barricada Internacional*, 4 April 1985, p. 6.

22. 'Nicaragua to Boost Exports to Europe', *San Francisco Chronicle*, 2 May 1985, p. 15.

23. 'President Asserts Goal is to Remove Sandinista Regime', *New York Times*, 22 February 1985, p. 1.

24. See W. Bollinger, 'Central America, National Security and the 1984 US Elections', Occasional Papers series no. 6 (Los Angeles: Interamerican Research Center, 1984).

25. 'President Asks Pope's Advice on Latin Policy', *San Francisco Chronicle*, 6 April 1985, p. 1.

26. *Barricada Internacional*, 18 April 1985, p. 1.
27. Ibid.
28. Ibid.
29. *Barricada Internacional*, 7 March 1985, p. 12.
30. *Barricada Internacional*, 28 February 1985, p. 4.
31. Nicaragua Information Center (Calif.), 'The Militarization of Nicaragua: Fact or Fiction?', *Bulletin*, 19 February 1985), pp. 1–2.

Index

Abbreviations used in this Index:

AMNLAE	Luisa Amanda Espinosa Association of Nicaraguan Women (Asociación de Mujeres Nicaraguense Luisa Amanda Espinosa)
AMPRONAC	Association of Nicaraguan Women Confronting the National Problem (Asociación de Mujeres Ante la Problemática Nacional)
APP	Area of People's Property (Area de Propiedad Popular)
ARDE	Democratic Revolutionary Alliance (Alianza Revolucionario Democrática)
AREs	Assemblies of Economic Reactivation (Asambleas de Reactivación Económica)
ATC	Rural Workers Association (Asociación de Trabajadores del Campo)
CASs	Sandinista Agricultural Co-operatives (Cooperativa Agraria Sandinista)
CAUS	Confederation of Trade Union Action & Unity (Central de Acción y Unidad Sindical)
CDN	Nicaraguan Democratic Co-ordinating Council (Coordinadora Democrática Nicaraguense)
CDSs	Sandinista Defence Committees (Comites de Defensa Sandinista)
CEBs	Ecclesiastical Base Communities (Comunidades Eclesiales de Base)
CGT-I	Independent General Confederation of Labour (Confederación General de Trabajo – Independiente)
CIA	Central Intelligence Agency
CNI	Inter-union National Commission (Comisión Nacional Intersindical)
COIP	People's Industrial Corporation (Corporación de Industrias del Pueblo)
COSEP	Superior Council of Private Enterprise (Consejo Superior de la Empresa Privada)
CSN	Co-ordinating Labour Council of Nicaragua (Coordinadora Sindical de Nicaragua)
CST	Sandinista Trade Union Confederation (Central Sandinista de Trabajadores)
CTN	Workers Confederation of Nicaragua (Central de Trabajadores de Nicaragua)
CUS	Council for Union Unification (Consejo de Unificación Sindical)
DPs	Delegates of the Word (Delegados de la Palabra)
EAP	economically active population
FDN	Nicaraguan Democratic Force (Fuerza Democrática Nicaraguense)
FSLN	Sandinista Front for National Liberation (Frente Sandinista de Liberación Nacional)
INNICA	Nicaraguan Institute for the Atlantic Coast (Instituto Nicaraguense de la Costa Atlantica)
INRA	Nicaraguan Institute of Agrarian Reform (Instituto Nicaraguense de Reforma Agraria)

250

MAP-ML Marxist-Leninist Popular Action Movement (Movimiento de Acción Popular Marxist-Leninist)
MIDINRA Ministry of Agricultural Development and Agrarian Reform (Ministerio de Desarrollo Agropecuario y Reforma Agraria)
MISURA organisation of Atlantic Coast Peoples led by Steadman Fagoth Muller
MISURASATA entries prior to p.187 refer to the organization of Atlantic Coast peoples led by Steadman Fagoth Muller, from p.187 onward to the organization led by Brooklyn Rivera
MPS Sandinista Popular Militias (Milicias Populares Sandinistas)
MPU United People's Movement (Movimiento Pueblo Unido)
N./Nn. Nicaragua/Nicaraguan
PC de N Nicaraguan Communist Party (Partido Comunista de Nicaragua)
PCN Nicaraguan Conservative Party
PLC Constitutional Liberal Party
PLI Independent Liberal Party
PPSC Popular Social Christian Party (Partido Popular Socialcristiano)
PSC Social Christian Party (Partido Socialcristiano)
PSD Social Democratic Party
PSN Nicaraguan Socialist Party (Partido Socialista de Nicaragua)
UNAG National Union of Farmers and Cattle-raisers/Ranchers
UPANIC Union of Agricultural Producers of Nicaragua (Unión de Productores Agropecuarios de Nicaragua)